DREAMING

DREAMING

*Remembering * Interpreting * Benefiting*

DEREK & JULIA PARKER

New York · London · Toronto · Sydney · Tokyo · Singapore

In memory of

James Mitchell

Editor   *James Hughes*
Art Editor   *Denise Brown*
Assistant Designer   *Tina Hill*
Picture Research   *Brigitte Arora*
Production   *Philip Collyer*

 A Fireside Book
Published by Simon & Schuster
New York

Copyright © 1985 by Mitchell Beazley Publishers
Text Copyright © 1985 by Julia and Derek Parker
Illustrations Copyright © 1985 by Mitchell Beazley Publishers
All rights reserved including the right of
reproduction in whole or in part or in any form.

Fireside and colophon are registered
trademarks of Simon & Schuster,Inc.
A Former Prentice Hall Press Publication
Library of Congress Cataloging Card Number
89-42534
ISBN 0-671-76630-9

Edited and designed by Mitchell Beazley Publishers Ltd
Part of Reed International Books
Michelin House
81 Fulham Road
London
SW3 6RB

Typeset by Litho Link Ltd, Welshpool, Powys, Wales
Origination by South Sea International, Hong Kong
Produced by Mandarin Offset
Printed in Hong Kong

10 9 8 7 6 5 4

Contents

Introduction

Everybody dreams. A normal night's sleep always includes not one but several periods of dreaming. This has been experimentally established beyond any doubt. A few people entirely forget every dream they have, and claim they don't dream at all; some have almost complete recall of their dreams; most of us remember a few elements of our dreams, and occasionally recall in great detail a dream which seems, for some reason, to be specially impressive, specially important. And almost everyone has the feeling that some dreams, at least, have something interesting to say to us.

Dreams needs not be prophetic – though some seem to be; they need not warn us of a coming illness – though some have; they need not be connected with any pressing problems we may have in waking life – though often that proves to be true. Nevertheless, we almost all have a nagging feeling that our dreams must *mean* something – if only we knew what. A belief in the significance of dreams has survived far beyond the age when they were thought to be messages from the gods. The work of Freud, Jung and others has made dream analysis an important feature of psychotherapy, and in our understanding of the unconscious mind. There is no doubt that life can be enriched if we recall and examine our dreams, and learn eventually to work out what they might mean to us as individuals.

The Victorians had their dream books, which said quite straightforwardly that to dream of a black cat indicated good luck, or that to dream of a violet meant love. At the other extreme, psychologists and psychiatrists, ever since Freud and Jung, have used dreams as a help in analysing their patients. But no one now accepts that one person's dreams can mean the same as another's, while only a few of us feel we need analysis. There are many books on the subject, but they tend either to be modern dream books, or treatises by psychiatrists.

In the last 35 years much experimental work has taken place in dream laboratories. Here the occurrence, frequency and content of the sleeping subject's dreams are scientifically studied and correlated. Their duration and quality are compared against physical and physiological bodily processes that occur in sleep and dreaming. Experiments in this area are also suggesting new lines in the interpretation of their significance.

This book takes up the psychologists' theories and the facts discovered by dream researchers, and offers you the opportunity to test them in your own life. This means that you may learn to be the interpreter of your own dreams. If you are a normally healthy and rational person, subject to the usual pleasures and concerns of life, and if it is true that your dreams can open the door to areas of your inner life of whose presence you may be unaware, or can offer comments on your waking problems or worries, it seems silly not to take advantage of them.

If you are interested in, or just beginning to study your dreams, you are about to embark on one of the most fascinating trails that can be experienced. Once involved, you will not only learn a great deal about yourself and your psychological motivation, but discover how your unconscious, that important area of your personality which lies beneath the surface of your conscious mind, can comment on your problems. A series of dreams, for instance, can reveal to you your true, innermost attitude to those problems – perhaps an attitude of which you may not be fully aware. This is often of considerable importance at times of decision-making, and can be crucial. Those who are already aware of the importance of their dreams but are often confused about their meaning will find that the *Dream Directory*, which forms the second half of this book, will offer hints and lay down pointers to help interpretation.

A whole new, often very beautiful world will be opened up for you by the experience of the symbols that your unconscious, sleeping self sets before you – symbols more complex, ingenious and arresting than any you could conceive in your waking hours. Dream pictures and events, sometimes entirely remote from daily experience, are often of great beauty, and the more you come to terms with them, the more you will recognize this. In many respects you need never be bored again! The more imaginative and sensitive you are, the greater the dream experience is. All this rich imagery comes from *your* mind – nobody dreams your dreams but you; it is you who creates within your mind situations as exciting as those from *War and Peace*, as absurd as those from *Alice in Wonderland*, or as romantic as those from *Gone With the Wind*.

However, the world of dreams is also an extremely practical one, because it is very informative, and while we can romance about our dreams, the amount of sheer practical help we can get from them is also enormous. Life these days is more complex than it has ever been; any discipline that helps make it easier and less complicated is worth considering. Many methods achieve this for most of us. But here is one which, after all, costs us nothing and is waiting to be tapped. With a little attention to your dreams, many of the complications of 20th century living can be put into a sensible perspective. Surely it is worth using this apparently magical but very practical source to comment on, and help with, our lives.

The Dream Workshop

The Mystery of Dreaming

From the earliest times humans have been fascinated by their dreams, by the relationship between the shadowy people and events which crowd into our sleeping hours, and the people and events of our waking life. At one time, dreams were thought to be of divine origin. Even today, they contain an element of mystery that separates them from our ordinary existence. So it's not surprising that a belief in the significance of dreams has survived to this day, and even though we may no longer believe in their divine origin, dreams continue to be important to us.

It takes little effort to realize that dreams affect our waking lives. Watch your dog as he wakes from a dream: having barked and twitched for several minutes, he will, on waking, often behave as though he has just come in from an energetic walk, wagging his tail cheerfully – or, on the other hand, put his tail between his legs and look thoroughly cowed, as though expecting to be reprimanded for bad behaviour. Similarly, we ourselves can wake up in the morning cheered by a happy dream or depressed by a bad dream; there is some evidence to suggest that when we feel irrationally depressed, the depression may be the result of a forgotten dream.

A 15,000-year-old dreamer and his vision. A cave painting from Lascaux, France, probably depicts a shaman, bird staff at his side, attacking his prey with psychic weapons. Note that the shaman has an erection characteristic of dreaming sleep (see p. 41).

What *is* a dream? That is the mystery. The question is hard to answer, since it involves the basis of mental activity, just as it is hard to define gravity, or what people mean by the soul. At one level, we dream when, in a certain phase of sleep, our brain creates a series of images, usually in the form of events which appear to us on the private screen of our mind; we are conscious of these images just as though they were real to us – it is only very rarely that we know that they are only dreams.

It is important, here, to dispose of the "lucid dream" – the dream in which we *are* conscious that we are dreaming: we jump happily off a mountain top in the knowledge that it is "only a dream"; we can even shape our dreams as though we are writing a screenplay for a film in which we are starring. In this book we disregard the lucid dream, for by its nature, because we can control it, because we know we are dreaming it, it seems extremely unlikely to be of real use to the dreamer. The whole point of the psychological interpretation of a dream is that, in it, we are not ourselves (or in another sense most completely ourselves!) – our guard is down, we are uninhibited and free of the constraints of waking life. Intervening in a lucid dream, we may destroy its usefulness, we may be devaluing our dream as a means of revealing ourselves to ourselves.

The images in a normal dream sometimes relate to each other in a fantastic, surrealist, unreal way. On the other hand, they sometimes tell a straightforward story of an easily understood kind, or they can simply exist as disconnected snatches, scenes which seem entirely unrelated to each other or to our waking life.

The general view held by those, from Freud onwards, who have studied dreams, is that while some of them have no meaning other than as distorted memories of incidents we have experienced while awake, many are probably messages from the unconscious, from the depths of our personality, depths with which we are not consciously in touch. They may indeed be the chief source of readily available information about what we are really like, under the surface veneer of education, environment, social consciousness, for dreams are notoriously unaffected by social considerations.

Dreams in antiquity

The earliest records of the life of man show that dreams have always been regarded as important. The ancient Egyptians believed that they were messages from the gods, and produced, 1,300 years before Christ, the earliest dream book giving over 200 interpretations of those messages. Interestingly, the Egyptian interpreters put forward the theory of opposites: that to dream of death was an omen of long life, for instance. Freud, the great originator of modern dream theory, also advanced the theory that dream symbols often relied on a system of contrary symbols.

In Ancient Egypt dreams had their own god, Bes (*above*), and the earliest interpretation book (*right*), written by priests of Horus 4,000 years ago, one of the oldest existing documents.

Ancient dreamers include Jacob (*opposite*), founder of the 12 tribes of Israel, who dreamt he saw angels ascending and descending a ladder; and Assurbanipal (*above right*) of the nearby Assyrian nation. The Greek god of sleep Hypnos (*above*), was the brother of Death and the son of Night. Many ancient peoples considered dreams to be divine messages.

The Assyrians, too, had their dream books: the library of the Assyrian king Assurbanipal (*c.*669–626BC) is believed to have contained books of dream interpretations dating from 2000BC; and his own personal dream book is said to have been one of the chief sources used by the Greek Artemidorus, who wrote the most famous dream book of the ancient world.

The Old Testament is full of dreams, probably the oldest dreams familiar to most people – those of Daniel and Jacob, Nebuchadnezzar and Solomon. Despite religious differences, there were few disparities between the Jewish interpretations of the dreams sent to man by their God, and those dispatched by the multifarious gods of other religions. The prophet Mohammed believed dreams to be extremely important, starting each day by asking his disciples what they had dreamed, and telling them his own.

The Greeks, with their passion for the rationalization of knowledge, made use of Egyptian, Assyrian, Jewish, Babylonian and Persian dream theories. Their interpretation of dream symbols was widely different: for instance, while the Greeks thought that a dream of a snake signified sickness and enmity, the Assyrians believed that dreaming of seizing a snake meant that you would receive the special protection of an angel. The Jews thought that a dream of being bitten by a snake meant that the dreamer's income would be doubled, while to an Egyptian a snake, appearing in a dream, signified the settling of a dispute. These beliefs are echoed, even today, in the so-called "dream books" which suggest that if you dream of, say, a black bird, it is an omen of evil.

The Greeks also believed dreams to be divine messages. Homer records dream messages from Zeus, sent to man through a gate of horn (forged messages were also received, issuing from a gate of ivory). Herodotus reports some famous dreams, including that which persuaded Xerxes to set off on what proved a disastrous expedition into Greece. And Delphi, spiritual centre of ancient Greece, was famous for ambiguous interpretations.

Many sacred places in Greece were used for the "incubation" of dreams: visitors would take drugs and herbal potions to induce sleep, and regard their dreams as important prophecies, with special reference to their ailments and afflictions. Aesculapius, the god of medicine, was the tutelary deity of over 300 incubation temples from the first millennium BC onwards, and the temple at Epidaurus in Greece was in use for many hundreds of years. Here is yet another anticipation of the future: twentieth century psychiatrists encourage patients to remember their dreams not for reasons of prophetic revelation or physical cure, certainly, but rather for reasons of self-revelation and self-help. The whole purpose of this book is to enable you to remember your dreams, record them, and interpret them, in the belief that they can be helpful in the waking life.

The idea of dreams as a revelation of man's true nature – the modern view – also originated with the Greeks. Plato, in *The Republic*, claimed that man's true nature showed itself in dreams.

The snake, a potent symbol in myth and dream, has assumed a number of different meanings and interpretations, good and bad. The ancient Egyptian Apop (*right*) was a demon of darkness, as was the Persian Azi-dahak (*below*), the "throttler". But to the Greeks and Romans snakes symbolized healing (*below right*).

Snakes bring healing dreams to a patient in a temple of incubation (*below*), sacred in Classical times to the physician god, Aesculapius. Thousands of such temples existed in ancient times.

Plato, Greek philosopher of the 5th century BC, held the modern view that dreams show a person's true nature.

Plato wrote:

> *When the gentler part of the soul slumbers and the control of reason is withdrawn; then the wild beast in us, full-fed with meat or drink, becomes rampant and shakes off sleep to go in quest of what will gratify its own instincts. As you know, it will cast away all shame and prudence at such moments and stick at nothing. In fantasy it will not shrink from intercourse with a mother or anyone else, man, god, brute, or from forbidden food or any deed of blood. In a word, it will go to any length of shamelessness and folly.*

Aristotle, on the other hand, tried to explain dreams as the products of purely physiological functions: when one slept, the food in the body evaporated, and liquids passed to the head where dreams were mirrored on the surface of the fluids, like images on water. Nevertheless, he believed that dreams could usefully predict the onset of diseases unobserved by the waking body. In the *Parva Naturalia* he states that "since the beginning of all things are small, obviously the beginnings of disease and other distempers, which are about to visit the body, must be small. Clearly, these must be more evident in sleep than in the waking state." Hippocrates took the same view. Both Plato and Aristotle, then, advanced theories which our twentieth century psychiatrists have confirmed. With such notions, especially those of Plato, we are almost at one bound in the world of Freud, and surprisingly little original work on dreams was done in the centuries between.

The first substantial published work on dreams, the *Oneirocritica*, a five-volume work of the Greek Artemidorus (2nd century AD), argued that a dream was individual to the dreamer. The book, which had an enormous influence (it was published in English for the first time in 1644, and went into 24 editions during the next century) is in many ways extremely modern. Perhaps most importantly, it underlined the principle of association – the fact that a dream image generally evokes some associated image in the conscious mind (though Artemidorus relied on the association in the mind of the dream interpreter, rather than that of the dreamer, which seems irrational).

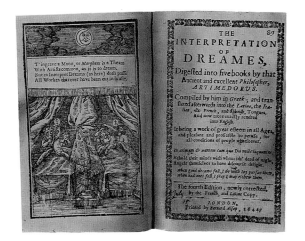

The most influential dream book of all, Artemidorus' *The Interpretation of Dreams*, was written in the 2nd century AD; re-issued in 1644 in England, it had a phenomenal success. Despite some absurdities, it represents an early attempt at dream analysis.

Artemidorus wrote, potently, that dreams "are infused into men for their advantage and instruction". He happened to believe that they were messages from the gods; but the attitude was again a modern one. He condemned arbitrary and over-literal interpretation, studied recurring dreams, and like Jung two millennia later, believed in the idea of the "great dream", the seminally important dream, which he believed most difficult to interpret.

In interpreting a dream, Artemidorus suggested that there were six important things to be considered: one was simply the dreamer's name, but the others were his occupation, the conditions under which the dream had occurred, and whether it was natural, lawful and customary. He was conscious of many of the tricks dreams can play – including the use of puns – and some of his interpretations seem to anticipate the kind of approach used by modern psychiatrists: a dream of the mouth, for instance, he interprets as probably representing a house, and the teeth the inhabitants; so the loss of a tooth therefore symbolized the death of a member of the household.

Christianity revived the view, never really discarded, that dreams were sent by the gods to communicate their commands to their subjects (in this case, of course, the communicator was the Christian God). The Bible is full of such dreams, and so are the writings of St Clement, St John Chrysostom, St Augustine and many other early Church fathers. St Jerome, almost single-handedly, reversed this trend: troubled with "difficult" dreams which appeared to run counter to current Christian morality, he asserted that they came from the devil, and condemned them; from then on, the Church took the view that dreams were not from God, and must be ignored. Martin Luther suggested that dreams could help us by showing us our sins.

Christianity and dreams: The Dream of the Virgin (*left*), was divinely inspired, but Hieronymus Bosch's monsters (*above*) were thought to come from the Devil.

Mohammed's dream (*opposite*) of the Night Journey on Elboraq (a half human mare) took him to the centre of the world, the depths of hell, and the seven celestial spheres.

Dream interpretation and cultural diversity

In India, the ancient Hindu scriptures called the Puranas reported that dreams were messages from the gods; to the Buddhists, emerging in India somewhat later, in the 5th century BC, they were "signs traversing the paths of thought" which rose mistily before the dreamer like mirrored reflections. In the Hindu *Brihadarmyaka-Upanishad* (*c*.1000BC) it was made clear that dreams occurred in a never-never land between the real and the promised world, but that the "real" world was in fact less real than the dream one, in which the lack of physical sensations freed man from inhibitions, so that his true character emerged.

In the Islamic world, al Mas'adi, an Arab writer, asserted that sleep was a "preoccupation of the soul", though dreams could be suggested by the physical condition of the dreamer. Al Mas'adi also took the Freudian view that in dreams the most secret desires could rise to the surface, uninhibited by moral attitudes:

> *If the sleeper sees things which meet his desires, that is because the soul*
> *. . . can, when it is purified in sleep from the defilements of the body,*
> *float at its ease over everything that it desires to possess.*

Nevertheless, to the Prophet Mohammed, dreams remained "a conversation between man and his God", and as with the Christian priests, Islamic mullahs and religious men insisted that they were the only reliable interpreters – and they also underlined a view which was positively discriminatory: unimportant people did not need to dream, so the slave's dream was obviously a message for his master, that of the wife must be for her husband, that of the child for its parents.

Chinese scholars believed that dreams occurred when the spiritual soul, the *hun*, was temporarily separated from the body, and could converse with spirits, the souls of the dead, or the gods. In the 14th century AD all visitors to an important city had to spend their first night there in the temple of the city god, so that they could receive any messages, a practice which shares some features with the "incubation" temples of the classical period.

In the West, the earliest dream books appeared soon after the publication of the Gutenberg Bible in the 15th century, teaching among other things how to encourage predictive dreams (eat a salted herring before going to sleep and you would dream of a future partner). A dream book based on the writings of Artemidorus, also circulated widely, as we have seen, giving firm meanings for almost every conceivable dream symbol.

The Romans, much given to divination of all kinds, had allowed soothsayers to run riot in the interpretation of "significant" premonitory dreams. Galen (c.130–201 AD) made some attempt to show that a dream might indicate an unsuspected illness, but Cicero accepted the idea of predictive dreams; Synesius of Cyrene, a Platonist (4th century AD) also believed that in dreams we "conjecture the action of the future". It was this attitude which engendered an atmosphere in which dream books flourished, interpreting a particular symbol in a particular way, whoever the dreamer might be. For over 1,500 years these presented the simplest notion of dreams as arbitrary symbols.

The approach to dreams made by relatively primitive 20th-century peoples bears some resemblance to the traditional attitude of Western cultures until comparatively recently. They all regard their dreams as important, and many of them believe that the dreams relate the adventures of the soul when it leaves the body during sleep (as did the ancient Egyptians and Chinese). Natives of Greenland and New Guinea alike hold this view. Some African tribes – and in parts of Africa dream life is held as being almost as important as waking life – believe that dream battles can take place; waking with sore arm muscles, a man will assume that he has been wielding his club during the night! The Zulu people regard dreams as messages not from gods but from ancestors (they perform much the same function, however). Some Indians will try to paint the face of a sleeping enemy, in order that the soul, adventuring in dream, will fail to recognize its body, and so be forever lost.

Mapping the dream world: an Australian *churinga* (*above*) illustrates an episode from the *Dreamtime* and emphasizes the basic importance of dreams to many so-called "primitive" peoples. A shaman's drum (*below*) from Lappland, makes reality of a dream event – a cosmic journey through the centre of the three worlds.

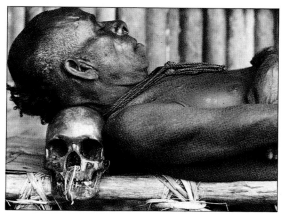

Matter and spirit worlds coexist in dreams, according to many cultures where dreaming is a perfected art. In addition to the Lapp shaman's drum (*above*), a Cuna Indian *mola* (*above right*) from Colombia bears designs from dreams. With his head pillowed on an ancestor's skull (*right*) an Asmat (New Guinea) tribesman feels close to his ancestor in dreams.

The American Indians have always regarded dreams as of the utmost importance, especially in the education of the young; after initiation, a boy with a rich dream life, who could relate it in vivid detail, was regarded as particularly wise and valuable to the tribe. Potent dreamers such as Black Elk of the Sioux people, have recorded their lives and the part that dreams played in them. The Iroquois saw dreams as the language of the soul, more important and valuable than the language of man's waking state, and, in a theory somewhat analogous to that of Freud, they believed that dreams could be indications, often in a highly developed code, of the dreamer's deepest and most secret wishes.

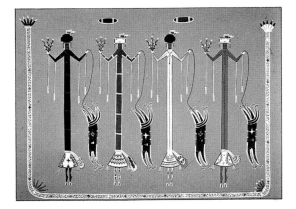

Navajo sandpainting of the Nightway Chant records the visions and dreams of the nation's original dreamer, Bitahini. The painting depicts supernatural beings with healing herbs.

The value of dreams to the most primitive society is fascinatingly seen in the Senoi, a people living in the jungles of the Central Highlands of Malaysia, and studied by the anthropologist Kilton Stewart in the 1930s. The Senoi believed that people should call on the characters and forces of their dreams to help them cope with everyday living: dreams were analysed each morning, and adults advised children on their conduct in dream life. Dreamers were encouraged to cultivate their dreams, and live them to the full, trying to bring each dream to a satisfactory and rewarding conclusion. It is interesting that the Senoi, who seem as a culture to be the most advanced dreamers in the world, are particularly concerned with developing their abilities in lucid, or "conscious" dreaming.

Interestingly, anthropologists studying the dreams of various societies have found several common strains which seem to reflect Jung's concept of a collective unconscious serving all mankind. In Ireland, Switzerland, China, Greece, the Ukraine, Nigeria, Tanganyika, Borneo and Sumatra, dreams of raw meat are all interpreted as presaging misfortune; Artemidorus interprets fire in the sky as foretelling war – and so do the Africans. And the Africans, like Artemidorus, also believe that losing a tooth in a dream means one will lose a member of the family.

To return to Europe in modern historical times, the 18th century Enlightenment began to put a stop to the consideration of dreams simply as predictive symbols. As Carl Gustav Jung (1875–1961), one of the most notable dream interpreters of our time, put it conclusively: "No dream symbol can be separated from the individual who dreams it, and there is no definite or straightforward interpretation of any dream." In other words, your dream belongs to *you*, and even if someone else dreamed the identical dream, its meaning would be different for them.

After many centuries of often irrational treatment of dreams, the 19th century saw a move to examine their real meaning and importance. One of the pioneers was the French psychologist, Alfred Maury, who designed various experiments on the connection between external stimuli and dreams: for instance, he discovered that a person whose lips and nose were tickled with a feather while he was asleep dreamed that tar was being applied to his face,

Henry Havelock Ellis
(1859–1939), author and
investigator into the psychology of sex.

Henri Bergson, author of
Memory and Matter (1896)
and *Creative Evolution*
(1907).

and the skin pulled off. When someone sharpened a pair of scissors near the sleeping Maury, the psychologist dreamed that he heard the pealing of bells, then the ringing of an alarm. An example of the effect of external stimuli which most people will recognize was a dream of the psychologist Havelock Ellis (1859–1939):

> *I dreamed that I was in an hotel, mounting many flights of stairs, until I entered a room where the chambermaid was making the bed; the white bedclothes were scattered over everything, and looked to me like snow; then I became conscious that I was very cold, and it appeared to me that I really was surrounded by snow, for the chambermaid remarked that I was very courageous to come up so high in the hotel, very few people venturing to do so on account of the great cold at this height. I awoke to find that it was a cold night, and that I was entangled in the sheets, and partly uncovered.*

In a paper on sleep and dreams published in 1861, Maury suggested various questions which should be asked about them. Were dreams associated with external stimuli? If you tickled the toes of a sleeping man, would his subconscious immediately respond by inventing some event in his dreams to explain the feeling? Did a man dream more vividly the sounder he slept? Was it possible to measure just how long it took a dream to dream? Did dreams relate to unconscious longings or emotions affecting the dreamer? Did dreams become different as one grew older? Was it possible to discover the "real meaning" of dreams? Indeed, how important were they?

Maury was responsible for the view, still widely believed, that the events in dreams are somehow telescoped together so that even an eventful dream covers a very short period of time. Dream laboratory research has shown that in fact a dream goes on for as long a period as the dreamer would take to imagine it in a daydream, so that an eventful dream really does have a comparatively long duration. Maury's theory was based on his famous guillotine dream, in which a series of events led up to his execution by guillotine. He awoke to find that the bedstead had fallen on his neck, and assumed that all the events must have been compressed in the period between this happening and his waking up. Today it is thought that the experience may not have been a dream but a fantasy.

The French philosopher Henri Bergson (1859–1941) took a more severely rational line even than Maury: dreams were, he argued, simply forgotten memories dredged up from remote corners of the mind as the result of physical stimuli.

Freud,
the great pioneer

It was in 1900 that the psychologist Sigmund Freud (1856–1939) published *The Interpretation of Dreams*, in which he insisted that they were far from haphazard meanderings, perhaps prompted by outside stimuli, but were on the contrary extremely important manifestations of our inner lives – in fact, disguised fulfilments of the dreamer's sometimes most secret wishes, often rejected by his waking mind. Certainly there was a sort of scaffolding of confused and perhaps meaningless images (which he called the *manifest content* of the dream), but this supported "dream-thoughts", the *latent content*, which were entirely logical, and could be interpreted under psychoanalysis. Dreams, according to Freud, combined two functions: they enabled forbidden wishes to be expressed in concealed form and, by conceding the true nature of these wishes, allowed the sleeper or the dreamer to continue undisturbed. The dream, he argued, was the guardian of sleep.

The question you have to ask yourself about a dream, Freud insisted, is "Why did I dream it?" If it were as simple as that, of course, there would be no mystery to unravel. But the truth seemed to be, Freud claimed, that we all have a censor who presides over the inmost chambers of our mind, and often refuses to allow us to think about, or even to know, some of our deepest

A dreamlike portrait of the great pioneer of modern dream analysis, Sigmund Freud (1856–1939). Freud's proposal that dreams are "coded" messages from the unconscious is the starting point for much modern dream analysis, even though many of his other assumptions are no longer widely accepted.

emotions or inclinations. This censor, he said, refused to allow such intimate thoughts to reach our conscious minds until they were so disguised as to conceal their real meaning. Often, "untrue" thoughts were allowed through, while "true" thoughts remained unconscious.

But it was certainly worth trying to discover the truth beneath the cloak, for while we were asleep, Freud argued, our conscious mind was so relaxed that it would allow us to dream dreams which could reveal more about our real nature than any conscious thought. The difficulty, of course, in interpreting our own dreams is that we are our own censor, and the more we try to find the true meaning of our dreams, the more the censor's office tries to prevent it – by making us forget important parts of our dreams, by making them apparently more and more meaningless, more and more ridiculous.

Freud insisted that under analysis every part of a dream could be revealed as in some sense true. Talking to a patient on his couch, he would fix first on some very striking episode of a dream, and then begin to question the dreamer about it, asking him or her to comment on that episode almost irrationally, in other words without trying desperately to make it mean something. He believed that the true significance of the dream would be revealed as the patient gradually attached more and more possible meanings to every part of it.

There are innumerable examples of how this theory works in Freud's own notebooks and those of more recent analysts: in a simple example, a young man dreams of being hungry, and eating with enormous enjoyment a mushroom omelette; but almost as soon as he has finished it, he begins to feel nauseous, his mother appears, reprimands him for eating something which he knows will disagree with him, and forces him to take a dose of salts to "get rid of the sickness". Analysis reveals that the man knows a girl whom he fancies, who is fond of mushroom omelettes. His choosing to eat this same dish, for which he is very hungry, reveals his sexual longing for the girl; but the fact that he begins to feel ill after eating it equally suggests that he is repressing those longings, and that that repression is connected with his relationship with his mother, who wants to keep him "pure" (the salts) or to purge him of that sexual experience which is "bad for him".

Time transfixed, by René Magritte. To Freudians, the engine may have an obvious phallic significance, but Magritte's picture contains many dream symbols, not all of which need be sexual.

Reading such analyses of other people's dreams, and attempting to apply the system to their own, some people still assert that these are simple variations on themes from their everyday life. They dream of a gunfight, they say, because they happened to watch an old cowboy movie on TV before going to bed. But they must then ask themselves why their unconscious chose to focus on the theme of a gunfight rather than on, say, a love scene or a comedy scene in the same film; or indeed why their dream should hinge on the film at all, rather than on a hundred and one other incidents of their daily life. To dismiss dreams on that basis is, to say the least, unscientific!

As with Freud's other writings, his work on dreams attracted criticism; but its value was undeniable, and is underlined by the fact that almost every work on dreams since its publication has made use of it, and to some extent been inspired by it. It is safe to say that one aspect of it with which almost every worker in the field now disagrees is Freud's insistence that certain "symbols" always mean the same thing. For instance, he claims that a snake, in a dream, is always a phallic symbol, standing for the penis. His concentration on sexual symbolism in dreams can easily be criticized: such statements as "all complicated machinery and apparatus in dreams stand for the genitals", or "there is no doubt that all weapons and tools are used as symbols for the male organ" seem now far too cut and dried. Which is not, of course, to say that a gun or almost anything else cannot represent the penis in a dream. Freud gives an amusing example of a woman who dreamed that she went into a bathroom to discover a nude man who clasped his shirt to his neck, exclaiming "Excuse me, but I've not got my necktie on!" No doubt, in that dream, the tie represented the penis. But it is a long stride from that to the statement that *all* neckties in dreams are phallic symbols. There is also criticism of Freud's methods of attempting to discover the true meaning of his patients' dreams: all very well, said his critics, to start the patient off on a trail of unrelated associations with the events and symbols of his dreams – but how did he know when to stop?

Jung and the archetypes

The second major psychologist whose work on dreams remains of the greatest importance is Carl Gustav Jung, who when he was 79 claimed that for many years he had "carefully analysed about two thousand dreams a year", and had acquired a certain amount of experience in the matter.

Jung, though an admirer and sometime follower of Freud, differed from him in some respects:

> *I was never able to agree with Freud that the dream is a "façade" behind which its meaning lies hidden – a meaning already known but maliciously, so to speak, withheld from consciousness. To me dreams are a part of nature, which harbours no intention to deceive but expresses something as best it can, just as a plant grows or an animal seeks its food as best it can.*

Carl Gustav Jung (1875–1961), originally Freud's disciple, came to disagree with him on several key issues. Jung used dreams to develop his theories of the collective unconscious and the archetypes.

Taking a more mystical view of dreams than Freud, Jung seems to have been led towards the root of his theory by a dream he himself had in 1909, in which he found himself in an unfamiliar house which he nevertheless knew he owned. He explored two floors of it before finding a door which revealed a staircase leading down to a beautiful and obviously very ancient cellar; yet another staircase led down again, this time to a cave where bones and scattered pottery lay, two human skulls among them. To Jung this meant that below, or within, the ordinary level of human consciousness (the house in which we all live) lies another layer, that of our "unconscious"; and below that again, a deeper level representing "the world of primitive man within myself". That deepest level of consciousness is common to all men and women, of whatever race or creed or cultural background – the concept of "the collective unconscious" which played such a part in his psychological theory.

Jung was much more tentative in his approach to dream interpretation than Freud, conscious of the difficulties, and even emphasizing them: "I have no theory about dreams," he wrote, perhaps a little disingenuously;

> *I do not know how dreams arise. I am altogether in doubt as to whether my way of handling dreams even deserves the name "method." I share all my readers' prejudices against dream interpretation as being the quintessence of uncertainty and arbitrariness. But, on the other hand, I know that if we meditate on a dream sufficiently long and thoroughly – if we take it about with us and turn it over and over – something almost always comes of it. This something is not of a kind that means we can boast of its scientific nature or rationalize it, but it is a practical and important hint which shows the patient in what direction the unconscious is leading him.*

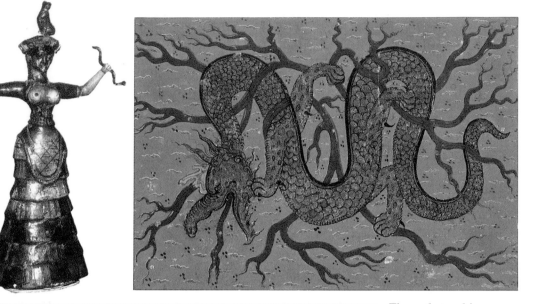

The archetypal images of myth and dream reflect, according to Jung, "psychic structures common to all men". The Minoan snake-goddess (*above left*), *c.*16th century BC, represents the *anima* or female principle as well as the *snake* or *dragon* (*above*). The *well* (*left*) or *cave* is another common symbol, here seen in a Kangra (India) painting of the 17th century AD. The *mandala* (*below*) or *circle* has important associations of wholeness, the self and completeness. Despite the universality of such symbols, Jung stressed that "the interpretation of dreams and symbols largely depends upon the individual circumstances of the dreamer and the condition of his mind."

The Little Paradise-Garden, *c.*1410, a medieval painting containing many symbols frequently found in dream imagery and identified with the Jungian archetypes.

"Great dreams", the "biggest", most "meaningful" of our dreams, Jung proposed, come from the deepest level of the *collective unconscious*. In an attempt to define what he meant by this now much-used phrase, Jung wrote (*Modern Man in Search of a Soul*):

> *If it were permissible to personify the unconscious, we might call it a collective human being combining the characteristics of both sexes, transcending youth and age, birth and death, and, from having at his command a human experience of one or two million years, almost immortal. If such a being existed, he would be exalted above all temporal change; the present would mean neither more nor less to him than any year in the one hundredth century before Christ; he would be a dreamer of age-old dreams, and, owing to his immeasurable experience, he would be an incomparable prognosticator. He would have lived countless times over the life of the individual, of the family, tribe and people, and he would possess the living sense of the rhythm of growth, flowering and decay.*
>
> *Unfortunately – or let us say fortunately – this being dreams. At least it seems to us as if the collective unconscious, which appears to us in dreams, had no consciousness of its own contents . . . The collective unconscious, moreover, seems not to be a person, but something like an unceasing stream or perhaps an ocean of images and figures which drift into consciousness in our dreams or in abnormal states of mind.*

"Great dreams" are usually dreamed when one is in one's early youth, at the time of puberty, when one faces the crises of middle age, or not long before death. They are the most difficult of all dreams to interpret, for they are full of symbols which come not from the dreamer's outward, or even perhaps psychic life, but from a great fund of general, universal ideas – common experience of which all mankind partakes. These dreams can be dreams of great heroes, of mythical enemies – snakes, dragons, monsters – of hidden treasure, caves and wells, walled gardens. It is not out of the way to claim that the dreamer is moving in the recognizable world of fairy tale, for fairy tales themselves, and such ancient tales as the legends of the Ring and the Holy Grail seem to have originated in the same vast area of universal human experience. "Little dreams", on the other hand, use symbols from everyday experience, and are concerned with everyday matters.

Image and archetype: a Hopi *kachina* mask (*above*) disguises the wearer's personality. The shadowy self (*left*) of Peter Birkhauser's painting is black because he comes from the nocturnal world of the unconscious.

Dreams and reality

In a sense, Jung's attitude to dreams is a romantic one: he and the other members of the "Zurich school" of analysts, including Silberer, Maeder, Adler and Stekel, sometimes seem to be asking us to regard our dreams as actual messages – but from whom? Perhaps we ourselves are dreams: "One does not dream, one is dreamed", he writes; "we undergo the dream, we are the objects." He seems to be as confused, or perhaps as imaginative and creative, as the 3rd-century Chinese philosopher Chuang-Tzu, who one night

> dreamed I was a butterfly, fluttering hither and thither, content with my lot. Suddenly I awoke and I was Chuang-Tzu again. Who am I in reality? A butterfly dreaming that I am Chuang-Tzu, or Chuang-Tzu imagining he was a butterfly?

It is a familiar predicament: the French philosopher René Descartes wondered whether *anything* was more real than a dream – doubting that he was actually sitting by his fire in a dressing-gown, for after all he had sometimes dreamed that he was there when in fact he was naked in bed. Pedro Calderon de la Barca shared the same confusion: "For I see now that I am asleep," he remarked, "that I dream when I am awake!" Bertrand Russell, in the 20th century, took that same problem seriously: "I do not believe that I am now dreaming," he once remarked," but I cannot prove that I am not."

One of Jung's most fascinating theories is of the *persona* and the *shadow*. The *persona* is the character we assume in our daily life, "us" as we are known to our friends. The *shadow* is the "us" we repress, and emerges when we try to kid ourselves that our *persona* represents all that is to be known about us. A self-regarding businessman for instance might dream of himself as a king, attacked by a revolutionary anarchist. The king represents the *persona* – the businessman is a monarch to his underlings, and would like his friends and family to regard him royally; the anarchist is the *shadow*, who knows that he is far from royal, but human like the rest of us, and badly in need of seeing himself more clearly.

That very example, incidentally, reminds us that Jung believed that one thing dreams strive to do is to give the dreamer a more acute sense of balance. A dream will often take the opposite attitude to the one we take when we are awake, just as some people, for the sake of argument, will adopt attitudes opposite to those they really hold. It seemed to Jung that if a man's conscious attitude to life in general was a well-balanced one, dreams might comment on his attitudes and opinions, but the comments would be unlikely to be so outrageous as to be worrying. However, if the dreamer was in his conscious life very much prone to taking extreme attitudes, his dreams would be more likely to "tease" him by placing him in situations where he would be forced to reject or correct his views. (The self-consciously heterosexual man is perhaps more likely to have a homosexually oriented dream than the man who recognizes homosexuality as a part of the pattern of life; the man who believes with great force in a property-owning democracy might find himself plagued by dreams in which the world's beggars successfully claim his worldy portion from him.)

Incidentally, Jung found that dreams which might be very unwelcome to the dreamer often had a very practical aspect. On one occasion, for instance, a young patient of his, recently engaged to a beautiful young girl of good family and impeccable reputation, was extremely distressed by dreams which continually suggested that she was less virtuous than he supposed. Jung suggested that he should do a little quiet investigation – and this revealed that the dreams were right. The engagement ended, and so did the patient's neurosis.

Rather than encouraging patients to talk about their dreams in great detail, one of Jung's interpretative techniques was to invite them to enlarge on the events of the dreams – to "take them further", to invent conclusions for them; this, he believed, could lead to a revelation of their meanings. Jung believed that dreams not only indicated, but also to some extent corrected, the state of balance between an individual's conscious and unconscious attitudes. Even obscure dreams, he claimed, would yield an answer to the question, "What conscious attitude does the dream compensate?" Jung's final view was that an inbuilt, almost biological, tendency towards psychological health existed in the individual human organism, and that dreams seemed to reflect the way this tendency worked for the improvement of mental health and the attainment of maturity.

He looked, too, at "prophetic" dreams, seeing them not as genuinely prophetic but as evidence that even when we are asleep we are capable of projecting our thoughts forward into the future, sometimes with great freedom and occasionally hitting on the truth.

Warnings and predictions in dreams may reflect an unconscious awareness of a situation, based on observations actually made but no longer recalled to the conscious mind. When, for instance, the Duke of Portland dreamt that a processional coach for which he had responsibility might not fit through one of the triumphal arches on the route (see p. 58), he may have been unconsciously aware that the coach looked too high, and this anxiety emerged in the form of a warning dream – which proved correct.

However, some dreams which seem to prophesy the future are perhaps not quite so easily dismissed. What would Jung have made of the dream of the English astronomer Edmund Halley, for instance? Halley, according to the biographer John Aubrey:

> Had a strong impulse to take a voyage to St Helena, to make observations of the southern constellations, being then about 24 years old. Before he undertook this voyage, he dreamt that he was at sea, sailing towards the place, and saw the prospect of it from the ship in his dream, which he declared to the Royal Society to be the perfect representation of that island, even as he had it really when he approached to it.

There are many other prophetic dreams on record, and well authenticated. Abraham Lincoln dreamed, a few days before his assassination, a dream in which he clearly saw his own coffin lying in the White House, surrounded by weeping people. Bishop Joseph Lanyi, tutor to the Archduke Franz Ferdinand, not only dreamed of his pupil's assassination at Sarajevo in 1914, but held a Mass for him on the morning of the day of his death.

But such clear dreams are perhaps the exception. No one needs to be told that dreams are confusing: Havelock Ellis believed indeed that it was only in the moment after waking that one's mind arranged into semi-logical sequence the mass of random images in a single dream. Some people will still argue that their dreams are so random, so haphazard, so obviously "meaningless" that it would be absurd in the extreme to suggest that they reveal anything serious about their personality or motivations. Jung started one of his earliest essays on the subject (*The Analysis of Dreams*, 1909) by warning readers not to be deceived into thinking that a dream was "the confusion of haphazard and meaningless associations".

We find our dreams confusing because they do not obey the same laws as real life: personality seems to lose its meaning – we can be both ourselves and some other person at the same time, or our employer can also be our father; we may find ourselves enjoying situations we would loathe in real life, or being enormously disturbed by some event which we would treat lightly, were we awake. Among the most disturbing of dreams are those in which our normal preferences are jumbled and contradicted.

This is all part of what Freud called "dream displacement", in which some person, thing, emotion or activity "becomes" some other person, thing, emotion or activity: your boss may then represent your father, or your father, your boss; a necktie can indeed represent a penis; winning a race may represent successful promotion in your career. Such "displacement" may be partial – your boss representing your father in the context of a perfectly ordinary setting; or it may be more total, so that the whole context of the dream actually "means" something else – as the house and its cellars, in Jung's dream, represented his own psyche. Anyone who wants to understand their own dreams, to discover what the dreams are saying, must learn his or her way about this strange world in which almost nothing is what it seems. The Greek philosopher Aristotle suggested, over two thousand years ago, that the best interpreter of his dreams was the man who could understand "similarities" – who could comprehend metaphor.

The help dreams offer us is sometimes easier to grasp than Freud or Jung might suggest. Graham Greene, the novelist, for instance, has made great use of dreams not only in the plots of some of his novels, but in the actual writing of them. In *Ways of Escape* (1981), he recalls:

> *Dreams, perhaps because I was psychoanalysed as a boy, have always had great importance when I write. The genesis of my novel* It's a Battlefield *was a dream, and* The Honorary Consul *began too with a dream. Sometimes identification with a character goes so far that one may dream his dream and not one's own. That happened to me when I was writing* A Burnt-out Case. *The symbols, the memories, the associations of the dream belonged so clearly to my character, Querry, that the next morning I could put the dream without change into the novel, where it bridged a gap in the narrative which for days I had been unable to cross. . . .*

"I prefer my dreams to realities because there you always meet a much nicer type of girl," said some anonymous dreamer. It is a happy thought, but there is a danger involved. Jung pointed out that it is too easy, especially if one knows relatively little about dream interpretation, to become over-confident that "the unconscious knows best". (In which case, as he points out, there seems little virtue in being conscious!). "The unconscious functions satisfactorily only when the conscious mind fulfils its task to the full", he writes: "a dream may perhaps supply what is then lacking, or it may help us forward where our best efforts have failed."

What is Sleep?

The need for sleep – the need for us to cut ourselves off from normal activity for as much as one-third of every day – is clearly very strong indeed. By now, animal life would have rid itself of sleep by natural selection were this not so, for however light the sleep, during it animals are particularly vulnerable to attack by enemies. But sleep tenaciously keeps its hold on almost every moving thing. A sleep pattern is common to them all.

Normal sleep in all human beings follows the same pattern. It does not relate to climate, nor to place – the long, dark hours of the Arctic do not produce a different sleep pattern to the shorter periods of darkness experienced elsewhere, and people who have spent many weeks underground and utterly out of touch with the rest of the human race have fallen into a recognizable sleep pattern little different from any other.

Neither body nor mind is truly comatose during our sleeping hours. Parts of our body are certainly relaxed – anyone who has tried to lift a sleeping person knows just how much so. Yet we still, from time to time, change our position as we lie asleep. Certain muscles remain contracted and the muscles of the eye and eyelids keep the eyes closed. By and large, however, muscular activity is limited to about 30 seconds in any hour spent asleep. During a normal night's rest we may move, briefly, between 20 and 40 times: the movement half-awakens us, though we hardly ever become conscious during these periods of activity.

During our sleeping hours our reaction to outside stimuli also alters. In our waking hours, the various sense organs of the body continually send messages to the brain, which analyses them, and on the basis of previous experience decides what action, mental and physical, to take. We touch something wet, slimy and unpleasant, our brain is made aware of the fact, and probably instructs us to remove our hand from the mess. But if you placed the hand of a sleeping person in contact with a similarly repulsive object, it would not necessarily be removed at once. There is obviously some interruption or

Special areas of the brain are associated with human activities, functions and skills, translating exterior sensory stimuli into an organized picture of the world. In dreams, however, the same stimuli produce a very different picture. The left hemisphere of the brain, shown here, is more concerned with "rational" than with "intuitive" skills.

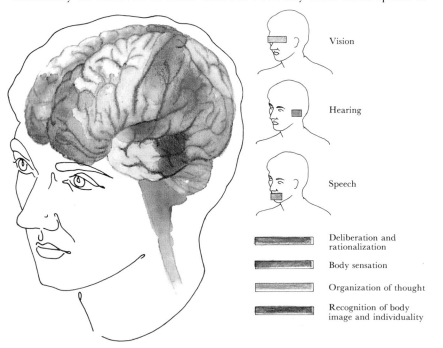

Vision

Hearing

Speech

Deliberation and rationalization

Body sensation

Organization of thought

Recognition of body image and individuality

alteration to the route by which the sense of touch conveys the sense of what is touched to the brain – though that sense does in fact get through to the brain, and some kind of message may make its way into our dreams.

The sleep cycle seems to be regulated by what is called the circadian rhythm, the biological processes occurring regularly at about 24-hour intervals. The word derives from the Latin phrase *circa dies*, which means *approximately one day*. This rhythm announces itself in various ways, but perhaps most obviously in our body temperature, which rises and falls regularly by about two degrees during the course of each day. It is when it is at its lowest, normally between 1 and 5 am., that most of us feel (and are) least capable of complex thought and action; and it is the regularity of this body temperature clock that makes us feel the effects of jet lag, when it is upset by a sudden time change. It can take between three and ten days for the body to adjust itself to a changed rhythm of activity and sleep; and it is not only the body temperature that adjusts itself, but the heart rate, the blood pressure and blood cell count, the metabolism, the kidney function, and a number of other unconscious physiological activities.

Within the rhythm that persuades our body to sleep, another set of rhythms is at work regulating its behaviour during sleep itself. From sleep laboratories all over the world material has been collected to provide a reliable picture of what happens to us during an average night's sleep. Electroencephalograph (EEG) machines that record electric activity in the brain – literally, brain waves – have shown the different levels of brain activity occurring while we are unconscious. The pattern that emerges is common to all normal sleep, and divides itself into regular and recurring stages, from a pattern closely resembling the waking state (Stage One) to one similar to coma (Stage Four).

This cyclic wave of sleep, from lighter to heavier and back again, is gone through several times a night. Each stage within the cycle can be recognized by the movements of the pen on the EEG print-out, and each complete cycle endures for approximately 90 minutes.

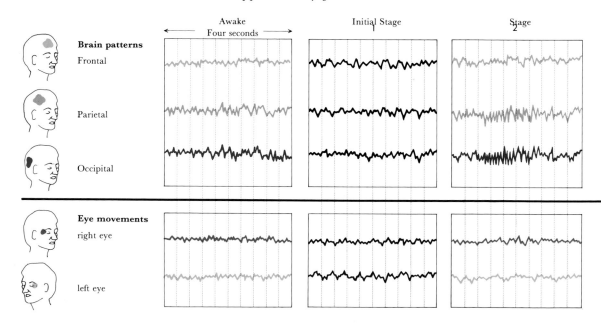

Electrical activity from three areas of the brain, collated with the subject's eye movements, show patterns characteristic of each stage of sleep. The "alpha rhythm" pattern of the first column shows the subject awake but resting with eyes shut.

A different pattern appears as sleep begins (initial Stage 1), but with little eye movement. Stage 2 is marked by "sleep spindles", short bursts of waves. The subject descends to Stage 4 sleep quite quickly in the first 90-minute cycle, and experiences

Stage One sleep is the lightest, corresponding quite closely to EEG recordings of the brain when we are awake. It occurs first as we drift off to sleep, our muscles relax, and our heart rate slows. In the course of a night's sleep, we will return several times to the Stage One level, emerging from the deeper stages of sleep for increasingly long periods.

Stage Two marks the onset of deeper sleep, beginning quite soon after we have fallen asleep and are quickly descending to the really deep sleep of Stage Four. Sleepwalking and sleeptalking are often associated with this stage. Then the EEG's distinctive recording of Stage Two's electrical activity gives way to the next stage.

Stage Three sleep is characterized by stronger electrical impulses from the brain: during our waking hours only about 60 microvolts are generated, whereas in Stage Three sleep a power of 300 microvolts has been recorded. Now it will take a considerable effort to awaken us, we are breathing slowly and regularly, our heart rate has slowed, our temperature fallen.

Stage Four is the deepest level of sleep, characterized by the appearanced of large, slow waves on the EEG. We spend a considerable time at this stage during the first of the night's sleep cycles, before swinging back to Stage One – which in this and subsequent sleep cycles is accompanied by rapid eye movement and often vivid dreams.

During a normal night we will at first spend a large proportion of the time in Stage Four sleep, which appears to be extremely important to us – we need more of it, the more physically or mentally exhausted we are. Normally, a sleeper may spend 30 minutes or more of his first 90-minute period in Stage Four sleep. Then as we drift back towards Stage Two sleep, we enter a paradoxical period during which the slightest whisper of a familiar name can wake us, yet quite a loud explosion will leave us slumbering peacefully. And

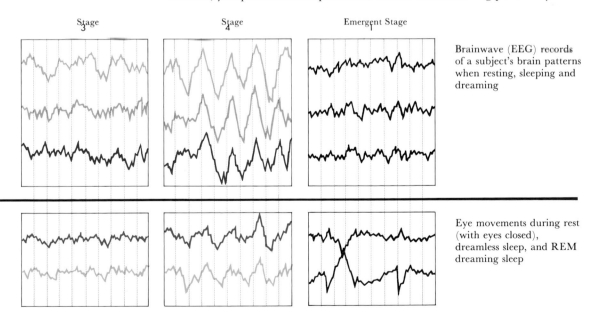

Stage 3   Stage 4   Emergent Stage 1

Brainwave (EEG) records of a subject's brain patterns when resting, sleeping and dreaming

Eye movements during rest (with eyes closed), dreamless sleep, and REM dreaming sleep

large, slow waves somewhat similar to brain activity during coma. Nightmares sometimes occur at this stage, but it is usually associated with dreamless sleep (the eye movements recorded here are misleading). The brain wave patterns then return to Stage 1; but whereas the initial Stage 1 is accompanied by almost no eye movement, emergent Stage 1 reveals the rapid eye movement (REM) that research has shown to be closely connected with dreaming.

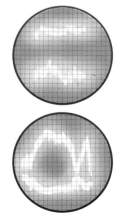

Eye movements in sleep vary, with the oscilloscope showing hardly any movement in deep sleep (*top*); but in the sleep stage associated with vivid dreams (*above*), rapid eye movement (REM) is marked.

The contrasting patterns of deep and REM stage sleep, polygraphically recorded. Note how, in the REM stage, eye movement coincides with changes in breathing, blood pressure and pulse rate, indicating that the subject is excited.

now comes the most fascinating aspect of our sleeping pattern: we re-enter Stage One sleep – but with a difference. Whereas the first Stage One period of entry into sleep is accompanied by vague and disconnected images, emergence back into Stage One at the end of the first 90-minute cycle marks the point at which we really begin to dream.

This emergent Stage One sleep is characterized by rapid eye movement (or REM), in which both eyes move quickly and alertly in unison, as though the sleeper were watching something from beneath his trembling eyelids. Laboratory subjects who were awakened from this and subsequent periods of REM sleep were nearly all able to report vividly detailed dreams. Some eye movement has been observed during other (non-REM) stages of sleep, and dreams of a nonvisual and less coherent sort have been reported by sleepers awakened during these periods, but the connection between REM sleep and visually detailed, usually vivid dreams has now been established scientifically and beyond any question.

The first period of REM sleep will probably last only a short while and you are extremely unlikely to remember your dreams from this time, unless you remain awake for at least ten minutes immediately after it. (Loss of recall is probably effected by the descent to deeper sleep levels.) But there is a great deal of activity during that time: the brain temperature rises, the heart rate and blood pressure fluctuate, we breathe more irregularly, with a higher rate of oxygen consumption in the brain. The body is surprisingly still, with no turning over in bed, but the signals registered by the EEG machine are often similar to those of intense waking concentration. After perhaps ten minutes, the sleeper sinks back down the scale of sleep once more, but this time will either not reach Stage Four sleep or spend far less time in this state. Climbing up to Stage One again, the sleeper then experiences a longer cycle of REM sleep with dreams, perhaps lasting for 20 minutes. Then comes the next descent to NREM (non-REM) levels and so the 90-minute cycles continue until morning, the last period of REM sleep producing probably the most vivid and impressive, and certainly the most easily remembered, dreams.

Deep sleep

REM stage sleep

	EEG		Blood pressure
	Eye movement		Pulse
	Respiration		Muscle activity

With each cycle, however, NREM sleep periods decrease, and REM sleep periods become longer. It has been estimated that we spend approximately 12 percent of an 8-hour sleep period in Stage Four sleep, and 25 percent in Stage One sleep.

It may seem that the mechanics of sleep are very easy to observe. But the division of our sleeping time into four or five 90-minute stages contains many variations: within each stage there are graduations, differences between individuals, and fluctuations within one person's sleep pattern from night to night and from stage to stage. The EEG is a helpful tool, but it does not enable the scientist to compare one "brain wave" with another similar one, and to discern differences of quality between them, yet such differences occur. Computer analysis is beginning to suggest certain facts, based on examination of the sleeping patterns of healthy people and those under the influence of drugs, or suffering from mental disorder.

Close observation of many thousands of people in sleep laboratories all over the world has revealed a great deal about sleep patterns and their effects: what we can consider as good or bad sleep, for instance. At the University of Chicago, Lawrence J. Monroe examined "good" and "poor" sleepers, and found that on the whole the poor sleepers tended greatly to exaggerate their hours of sleeplessness and the time they took to fall asleep. But there were also significant differences in pulse rate and body temperature between the two groups of sleepers. The poor sleepers tended to be more physically restless than good ones and spent much more time in Stage Two sleep than the others, being much easier to wake. They also spent considerably less time in REM sleep, and seemed to recall very little. Psychological rather than physiological factors may be important here.

Insomniacs who tell their doctors that they never sleep are usually wrong. At the Downstate Medical Center in Brooklyn, New York, some years ago, people who claimed to lie awake all night were found to sleep like babes in the laboratory – but still claimed, in the morning, to have been awake. However, the insomniacs should not be condemned, for a study of their EEG records shows that even during their deepest sleep they seem on the point of waking, and they will certainly not awake feeling as refreshed as someone whose sleep-pattern is more normal.

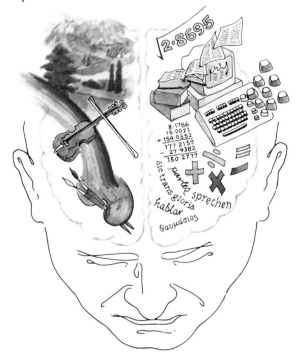

Different mental functions are controlled by the left and right hemispheres of the brain. EEG records suggest that the left hemisphere, which governs the right side of the body and is the dominant hemisphere, controls so-called rational activities such as language, numbers and analytic thought. The right hemisphere tends to be more concerned with formal properties and visual or spatial organization; it is therefore the "artistic" side. Cultural emphasis on functions controlled by the left hemisphere may help to account for the dominance of this area of the brain, sometimes to the detriment of "right-hemisphere" activities.

The quality of sleep is a fascinating subject of research, but one which has so far led to few really conclusive theories. Experiments with mental patients began at Yale University in the early 1960s, and have continued there and elsewhere; at St Elizabeth's Mental Hospital, Washington DC, work has been done with schizophrenic patients, but the results are often equivocal. Some schizophrenics, for instance, have a perfectly normal cycle of REM sleep, while others display "brain-wave" rhythms very different from the norm. This is obviously a field in which work will continue for many years.

One slightly comic but occasionally dangerous, and even tragic, habit into which there has also been some research is sleep-walking – happily a comparatively rare event. It takes various forms, but usually involves the physical acting out of some dream event. An English lady was awakened from sleep to discover that her sleep-walking butler had laid dinner for 14 people on her bed; an American housewife put on a bathrobe, packed her dogs in her car, and drove over 20 miles before awakening at the wheel.

Research shows that sleep-walking does not take place during REM sleep, when bodily movement is usually very small, but during the NREM period of Stage Two sleep, and scientists have discerned a distinctly different response from the sleep-walker's brain to sensory information transmitted to it during deep sleep, but so far no medical cure has been suggested.

The growth in the drug industry, and the increased willingness of some doctors to prescribe barbiturates and sleeping pills indiscriminately to their patients, have resulted in considerable interference with the normal sleep pattern, and perhaps in some permanent damage; little is known about the effect some barbiturates may have on the brain. Amphetamines, the pep pills prescribed to liven up the system and kill the immediate need for sleep, have an equally radical effect on the sleep pattern, and may be even more dangerous if taken in excessive quantities.

The popularity of barbiturates is easy to understand, and it is difficult to persuade a user that a pill which can produce something as soothing and apparently beneficial as "dreamless sleep" can be bad for him. But apart from the obvious problems of dependence and accidental overdose, sleeping pills certainly do not produce what we could call "normal" sleep: sleepers under the influence of barbiturates (or alcohol) have considerably less REM sleep, at least until they have adjusted to the drug, and the absence of REM sleep – and consequently of dreams – has been shown to have a physiological effect, and perhaps a biochemical one. Scientific experiments have confirmed that the abnormal behaviour of drug and alcohol addicts may be connected with the suppression of normal REM sleep. (This may be triggered by body chemicals, with which drugs or alcohol interfere.) Some work has been done to attempt to produce a drug which will encourage and increase the amount of REM sleep, but results are so far inconclusive.

A less than normal amount of REM sleep is recorded for senile and mentally handicapped people, and a far *greater* than normal quantity is experienced by premature babies (up to 80 percent) in the period before the expected time of birth, who presumably have a lot of "catching up" to do. This suggests that REM sleep may play a part in the more evolved functions of the brain, such as thinking, remembering and learning. Experimental subjects who were required to wear distorting glasses, and therefore literally had to learn a new way of seeing the world, also enjoyed an unusually large proportion of REM sleep – further evidence supporting a connection between this kind of sleep and the functions of learning and remembering.

NREM sleep, on the other hand, which is not characterized by vivid dreams but is usually associated with a condition where dreams are less prominent, may well be concerned with keeping the whole bodily organism rather than just the brain in good repair. Experiments have shown that after prolonged physical exercise athletes enjoyed a greater than usual proportion of Stage Three and Stage Four sleep. These deeper sleep levels have also been

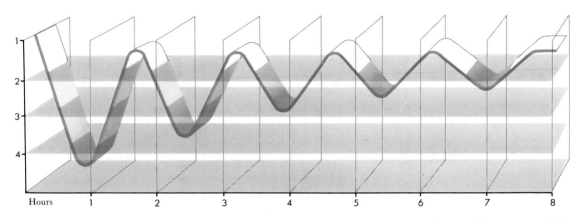

| Hours | 1 | 2 | 3 | 4 | 5 | 6 | 7 | 8 |

The pattern of sleep during an 8-hour period rises and falls through a number of stages. After the first 90-minute cycle, when the sleeper descends rapidly to Stage 4 sleep, each cycle includes an increasing period of Stage 1 sleep associated with the REM dreaming state. A majority of sleep laboratory subjects, awakened at this time, reported vivid and detailed dreams. During non-REM stages dreams may be reported, but they differ in quantity and quality from REM dreams.

observed to correlate with the body's production of growth hormone, which is essential not only for the growth but also for the maintenance and repair, through protein synthesis, of the total organism. It is certainly true that more time is spent in NREM sleep by people in a state of growth – children and adolescents – than by fully grown adults, and also that NREM sleep deprivation has an immensely worse effect on the sufferer than REM sleep deprivation. All this suggests that REM and NREM sleep have different biological functions, physical and mental.

However, there is still much to do before we know just what sleep *is*: just how it affects our body, the precise effects of sleep deprivation. Much valuable work is being done in examining the chemical changes within the body during sleep, though there are connections which are still obscure: why, for instance, should people suffering from liver disease feel particularly sleepy? Why should fulfilled love-making be followed, almost invariably, by satisfactory sleep? – the physical exercise involved is apparently not responsible! What provokes the overpowering sleepiness which comes with early pregnancy? What effect do the sex hormones (and thus the birth-control pill) have on sleep patterns? Is there (as seems possible) a connection between fertility and the nature of our sleeping habits? Work continues on these and other questions; some are solved, there are suggested answers to others, while yet others still elude the scientists.

One thing is clear: if we are to lead a healthy life, we must all sleep, preferably for a set period in each 24 hours. For the average man and woman, unanswered questions about the nature of sleep are hypothetical. Yet they may prove to be of vital importance to our health and well-being; and certainly, as Aldous Huxley said, "That we are not much sicker and much madder than we are is due exclusively to that most blessed and blessing of all natural graces – sleep."

What is a Dream?

In the last three decades scientists have made enormous strides in discovering and understanding the mechanisms both of sleep and of dreaming. The 90-minute sleep cycles recurring throughout the whole period of sleep, the stages of sleep as indicated by EEG recordings, the discovery of the existence of REM sleep and its connection with vivid dreaming, the balance between REM and NREM sleep, the universal nature of dreaming – all these are scientific breakthroughs of great importance.

Subjectively, however, the nature of sleep is mysterious, and dreams are an even greater mystery. They exist, we all have them, but you cannot see someone else's dream. It is as though suddenly our lines to reality are cut, and we enter a world where there is neither time nor space: we can be young again, we can live in the past or the future or some world where there is neither; we can step through a door in London and emerge in India or Australia, or a place we have never known.

Many dreams seem to take us into the land of fairytale, where a stone can become a cake, a mother a wicked witch, or our bitterest enemy may turn out to be our saviour. Indeed, the connections between fairytales and dreams have been traced by many researchers; both provide insight into the workings of the unconscious mind with its language of symbol and transformation, both ignore ordinary logic, and both have a mysterious "subjective reality".

In comparison to our waking lives, our dreams may appear random, strange and inexplicable, but even in sleep we can sometimes recognize their strangeness. "It's only a dream", we tell ourselves, even while the pig pushes us over the precipice. Some dreamers can even manipulate events in such so-called "lucid dreams". Recent research has devised a way of getting lucid dreamers who are aware that they are dreaming to signal certain events in the dream so that the moment is indicated on the EEG trace.

Much interesting work has recently been done in the area of lucid dreams. Some researchers claim that a lucid dream can actually provide the dreamer with a better understanding of the real situation, because he or she can question characters in the dream about attitudes and motivations. It is also possible to "re-run" a bad dream and give it a happy ending, or even to make a beautiful dream occur that will elevate your mood on waking.

However, lucid dream research is still in an early stage, and this kind of dreaming obviously has important differences from the ordinary type. It is our aim in this book to show how the dreams we all have, every night, can be looked at in a different and more useful way, and for this we have to consider ordinary dreams rather than special or induced dreams, however interesting.

But the question remains: what are dreams, and why do we have them? Experts continue to argue and differ, as we have shown in an earlier chapter. But there are certain elements of agreement, and within the past 30 years there has certainly been progress in finding out what happens to us *physically* while we dream.

Experts still argue about the amount of sleeping time we spend in dreams, but it is certainly a considerable amount. Often we forget all our dreams, sometimes we remember a few of them. Some people may claim that they never dream; but of course the scientific evidence all goes to show that what in fact happens is that people who "never" dream actually forget their dreams as they wake. Forgetting some of our dreams is only natural; we forget many of the events in our lives, after all, if only because we do not have the time to recall them all. In dreams, as in our waking life, we are selective in our recall,

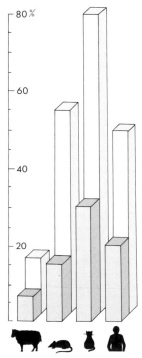

All mammals seem to need the type of REM sleep associated with dreams in humans. Young animals (*mauve*) always seem to spend more time in this state than adults.

Typical lucid dreams, in which the dreamer is aware at the time that "this is only a dream", have been experimentally induced in sleep laboratories, and may include out-of-the-body experiences (*right*). Lucid dreams seem only to occur in REM sleep, when most of the body, apart from the eyes, is inhibited from movement. The eye movement record of a lucid dreamer (*below*) shows a pre-arranged signal to the researcher. Muscle inhibition typical of REM sleep stops ordinary movement, but eye signals get through.

REM sleep eye movement

Eye signals

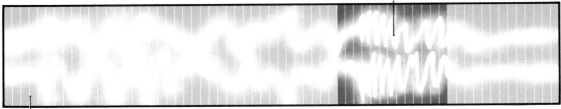

Seconds

tending to remember important or vivid dreams, and to forget those that are trivial, apparently meaningless or painful. It is interesting that laboratory subjects often report less eventful dreams than those dreaming "naturally", which suggests that vividness is a factor in recall in the sleeping as in the waking state.

It is now possible to tell with great accuracy when certain types of dreaming begin. Thirty years ago, Dr Nathaniel Kleitman of Chicago noticed that when they were asleep people from time to time moved their eyeballs, disturbing the closed eyelids above them. If they were awakened during this "rapid eye movement", or REM period of sleep, they invariably proved to have been dreaming. It is widely accepted that the movement of the eyes together and in unison indicates that we are actually "looking around" in our dreams, and often REM-dreaming sleepers, on being awakened, have agreed that they were watching, say, a horse race when their eyeball movements were particularly excited and frenzied.

On the other hand, rapid eye movements occur in congenitally blind people whose dreams are only dreams of touch and smell, so this is evidently not the whole story. Indeed, as we have seen (p. 32) there are other physical phenomena which coincide with REM: the electrical activity of the brain never stops, and there is a surge of neurological activity when REM sleep begins. The blood pressure can rise sharply, the pulse rate become erratic, breathing uneven, and all the symptoms of what in a waking state would seem to be great excitement – perhaps amounting to panic – can be clearly displayed.

Yet these physical signs do not always seem to be specially related to similarly exciting dreams. Indeed, bodily movement is almost nonexistent in REM sleep. It has been pointed out by experimenters that when we are in REM sleep we are physically immobile, but that when the subject is physically restless while asleep, dreaming is rarely reported. So there seems to be positive inhibition against movement during dreams, a sort of safety-

Entering sleep, a normal person experiences dream fragments and isolated images, known as "hypnagogic" or sleep-bringing dreams, at the beginning of the first 90-minute sleep cycle. This initial Stage One sleep is not accompanied by rapid eye movement (REM).

Deep and usually dreamless sleep stages are attained early in the first 90-minute sleep cycle. Within half an hour, the sleeper's EEG pattern indicates a coma-like stage of sleep from which dreams are rarely reported.

catch, perhaps, in order to prevent our throwing ourselves out of bed and perhaps injuring ourselves. Sleepwalkers do not walk during REM sleep, nor do people who talk in their sleep do so in the middle of a REM dream: parts of the muscular system seem to be immobilized by the very process of dreaming, these scientists suggest. Somnabulism is very much a product of the mysterious dreams that come to us in NREM sleep.

Rapid eye movement is still imperfectly understood. There is some evidence to suggest that it just might be connected with the Alpha rhythms of the brain, which are associated – amongst other things – with meditation and relaxation. It has been found that people in an "Alpha state" while meditating can enhance that state by rolling their eyeballs upward under their closed lids, and that we may unconsciously use eye movements to regulate, in some way, the rhythms of our centre of intelligence. Work is still proceeding on the connection between eye movements and the most fundamental rhythms of the brain, but recent researches suggest that there may be important differences between the rapid eye movements of dreaming sleep and those associated with Alpha waves.

One thing seems clear, however: rapid eye movement is associated most obviously with what have been called "adventurous dreams" – dreams in which we are very active, in one way or another. It has also been shown that the NREM dreams we experience during periods of sleep when our eyeballs show no movement at all, tend to be verbal, ruminative or intellectual dreams. Experimenters asked sleepers awakened at such NREM periods whether "anything was passing through their mind", and most admitted to having been "thinking about something", or possibly receiving some important message even though they had been asleep. Wakened from REM sleep, they tended to reply that they had been doing or watching something. It seems to be during NREM sleep that we are capable of "learning" things in our sleep, or when solutions to problems come to us. There are well attested cases of scientists solving problems while asleep. John von Neumann, the mathematician who laid the foundation of modern computer studies, often

Vivid dreams often accompany the return back to Stage One sleep at the end of each sleep cycle. The Stage One EEG pattern is now associated with rapid eye movement (REM), suggesting that the dreamer is closely watching something of interest.

Dreams recalled from deeper stages of the sleep cycle, where rapid eye movement does not occur, tend to be of a verbal, reflective, "thoughtful" kind, as opposed to the visual, vivid quality of most REM sleep dreams.

The imagery of revelation can be manifested in dreams. Kekulé's famous dream of a snake with its tail in its mouth enabled him to establish the molecular structure of benzine, which he suddenly saw must have a circular form. Such dreams, whose apparent importance may evaporate in the waking state, have been associated by some researchers with the non-REM area of sleep.

wrote theorems in his sleep! It may well be that when we ask our dreams for help in solving problems of one sort or another, it is during NREM sleep that the answers are indicated in dream symbolism.

How important is dreaming to healthy living? It was once generally thought that if a person was deprived of the opportunity to dream, he would go mad. William C. Dement, who began to study dream deprivation in the 1950s, was of this opinion. His experiments showed just how determined man is to dream. Dr Dement woke his subjects the moment they entered REM sleep. By the end of a fortnight of this, the subjects were so in need of their dreams, or so it appeared, that even when stood on their feet and shaken, subjected to loud noises, or dragged back into wakefulness, they would return within seconds to the unconscious state, which eventually became virtually impossible to interrupt. And when the subjects were allowed to sleep normally, their periods of REM sleep were at first very much longer than usual, as though they were making up dreaming time.

However, the theory prevalent in the 1960s that there is a definite "need to dream" has come under fire recently. Certainly there is pressure to enter REM sleep, but in experiments where certain drugs have been used to suppress REM sleep (and with it, of course, REM dreams), the subjects have shown no serious adverse effects. Some researchers claim that REM deprivation can even improve some abnormal psychological conditions, such as depression.

Other experiments have shown that people who are deprived of REM sleep and dreams may become anxious and uneasy, and when they are allowed to dream again also dream much more than usual, to make up for lost time. Certain personality changes have been observed during dream deprivation; some men, for instance, begin to behave irresponsibly and to demonstrate a sexual libido higher than common.

On the other hand, it is difficult to disassociate dream deprivation from sleep deprivation, for despite the most recent advances in the techniques of observing and recording dreams, it is still possible for someone under the closest observation to have a dream without the most elaborate scientific equipment registering the fact. A subject driven to desperation by the need to dream can break all the physical rules previously observed in order to snatch a dream under the noses of the watchers and their experimental gear. Nevertheless, the effects of sleep deprivation are infinitely more serious than those of dream deprivation.

Whatever we are dreaming, our mind fixes tenaciously upon it; it is notoriously difficult to rouse someone from REM sleep – we are at such times perhaps as far from the known world as we can get. A noise registering 80 decibels has been needed to awaken someone from dreaming sleep. On the other hand, some quiet sounds can slide under our guard and get through to our dreaming mind – certain names, for instance.

Some very interesting work has been done in this area of dream research, relating what goes on around our sleeping body to what happens inside our dreaming mind. Our body still apparently conveys accurate messages from our senses to our brain, though it sometimes distorts them: wet the foot of a sleeper and he may perhaps tread in a puddle in his dream, tap him on the head and he may dream that he is being assaulted. Perhaps more interestingly, we seem to hear quite acutely in our sleep, though again the mind can make mistakes, or play jokes, with the sounds.

Doctors have recorded the fact that patients recovering from major surgery have been able to repeat to them conversations they "heard" while lying, heavily anaesthetized, on the operating table. But the mind of a sleeper does not always work as rationally as that. In one experiment at Edinburgh University, sleeping students were read a list of names which included those of boyfriends and girlfriends, and it was found that at the sound of the name of their friends the skin of the palms of their hands registered distinct psychogalvanic responses. And occasionally the names themselves "got

The frequency of REM sleep (*right*) during 13 sleep periods of 6 hours, shows how the same subject's REM periods (horizontal bars) can vary greatly from night to night. The overall picture of eye movement (*bottom*), combining all 13 periods, demonstrates that REM stages of sleep, together with the likelihood of memorable dreams, can be predicted by researchers.

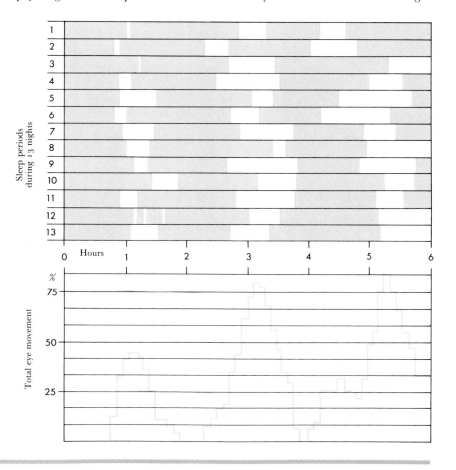

through" to the students' dreams, though often distortedly. One man heard the name of a previous girlfriend, Jenny; but his dreaming mind distorted it so that he dreamed he was opening a safe with a *jemmy*. Interestingly, he noticed that the jemmy was the only coloured thing in that particular dream – it was "a sort of red". The girl, Jenny, was a redhead!

Similarly, when the name Sheila was spoken, another sleeper dreamed that he had left a book behind at the university, a book of poems by the German poet *Schiller*. A girl heard the name Robert, and dreamed of a *rabbit*, which appeared in a film, and looked "distorted".

Why our dreaming minds should apparently make such different judgments, create such different visions, and should take attitudes foreign to those we adopt in our waking lives, remains a mystery. One interesting theory relates to the left and right halves of the brain.

The American psychologist Robert Ornstein seems to have been the first to suggest that the two halves of the brain have different functions (see p. 33) and it has since been conclusively demonstrated that the left side deals with our learning functions, and controls our speech; it is usually the more dominant of the two hemispheres. The right side apparently has a connection with our imagination, with our artistic instincts. The relationship between them is very imperfectly understood; it is not clear, for instance, whether each stores identical facts, or treats memory in the same way.

During sleep the usually frenetic activity of nerve cells in the fibre "bridge" connecting the two halves of the brain is greatly diminished, and it may be that alterations which seem to take place in that communication system may have something to do with the way in which, when we are dreaming, we seem in our very being to differ from our waking selves.

Physical signals that a REM dream is taking place include increased oxygen consumption in the brain, increased adrenalin in the bloodstream and, in men, an erection, which can last for the whole period of the dream. Dr Charles Fisher, at Mount Sinai Hospital, New York, first observed this phenomenon in 1964, though two German scientists had published papers in Germany in 1944 and 1947, noting that a cycle of penile erections occurred in all 17 male subjects observed for 27 nights. Erections had been recorded for 95% of the time the sleepers were in REM sleep. Since the 1960s, similar observations have been confirmed both in newborn babies and in old men; in fact, throughout the whole life cycle. There is not necessarily any relationship, it seems, between the erection and dreams of a sexual nature; sexual excitement seems not usually to be involved. The only kind of REM dream during which erection does not occur, in the male, is one during which anxiety is felt.

If REM dreams are artificially stopped, the erections will continue to occur at regular intervals during sleep, at times when REM dreams might have been expected. This suggests that some internal clock is involved, triggering both dreams and penile erections. There is no reason to suppose that a similar rhythm, probably accompanied by some similar physical manifestation, does not occur in women, but there seems not to have been any experimental work to confirm the fact.

Whatever the physical reason for the disturbances which affect our body when we dream, the question remains – why do we do so?

The most intriguing and perhaps most likely answer is that we dream in order to keep our mental and emotional balance. A great deal of the most recent research supports the theory advanced many years ago by the neurologist Hughlings Jackson (1835–1911) that sleep enables us to sweep away those memories of the previous day's events which we do not need to keep readily available in our minds, and to record those which are of value to us – much as a computer will "save" those things which we wish to keep for constant reference and "forget" or "delete" those things we decide we no longer need.

But there is more to dreaming than this. A large number of dreams are far from nonsensical; and it seems to be the case that this fragmentary type of dream characteristically occurs in the "dozing off" stage of sleep, which is a NREM state. According to another view, our dreams seem to be related to balance and imbalance in our emotional life, correcting or commenting on our conscious state in a language that can sometimes be interpreted. Examination of our dreams – of the events which our dreams "allow" to happen to us when we would perhaps go out of our way to avoid them in our waking life – enables psychologists and psychiatrists to tell us much about our characters, our motivations, the state of our mental and emotional health.

It is almost as though there are two beings in all of us. One of us is living an ordinary, everyday life under the usual pressures, not specially conscious of being any different to most other people, a member of our complex society. The other sees itself as entirely individual, entirely different from any other living person. Different again is the "me" who was once a child. As we grow up, we are all subject to the forming influences of environment and education, and many people now accept the fact that the very process of experiencing the world alienates us from true reality – that we are taught to ignore many of our natural animal instincts and thus get "out of touch with ourselves", as the popular phrase has it. Perhaps dreams are the messages from this lost world, the "subjective" self.

Unfortunately, they are messages in code. We need not be surprised at the fact that such messages exist; any artist knows that inspiration arrives "out of the blue"; a poet will be "given" a line, or even a whole poem; a novelist will find his characters saying and doing things that would never occur to him to say or do. The language of the unconscious can come through clearly even though it uses symbols and images, puns and double meanings, to express itself. The vocabulary may vary completely from individual to individual, for it is built up of individual, subjective experiences. But it is still hard to see why the messages should be expressed in a code which is often so difficult to understand.

But maybe it is not so much that we can't understand as that we *won't* – we either deny that the messages can be important, or we can't be bothered to work them out. This is a mistake. Dreams come, or seem to come, from the depths of our psyche. We receive them without inviting them, but they come through to us in any case because they *must*, and the force behind them (as we have just seen) is almost irresistible. In our dreams, we compulsively talk to ourselves, and we will do well to listen!

Remembering and Recording Your Dreams

Those who fail to recall most of their dreams are undoubtedly missing out on a very interesting part of life, and may indeed in some respects be failing to develop, psychologically, as rapidly as if they were able to bring into consciousness what the dreams are actually saying. The inability to recall dreams may not be due to a simple failure of memory. Psychological tests suggest that some so-called "nonrecallers" may be reluctant to remember their dreams just as they tend to avoid anxieties in everyday life. Non-recallers, it appears, are often more inhibited, more conformist and more self-controlled than recallers. According to the dream researcher Anne Faraday, they are less willing "to confront this dimension of experience – some have called it self-awareness – which manifests a close interest in the inner, subjective side of life". For dreams, as we have seen, are messages from that part of ourselves with which we are usually out of touch, with deep-rooted instincts and tendencies we may not normally acknowledge. Listening to what they have to say can make us more complete, help us understand what may seem to be irrational behaviour or desires.

The very suggestion that your dreams can be of practical help may start a process enabling you to remember them, and if your dream recall is poor it may begin to improve just because you have read these words. It has been shown experimentally that simply being motivated to recall your dreams really does improve your powers of recall. Of two groups in a laboratory, those asked to remember their dreams did far better than those who were not instructed to do so.

So there seems to be a "set to recall" mechanism that can be activated, just as some people can make themselves wake at a given time by telling themselves to do so.

If you have a lively discussion with a friend about what you've been dreaming, you could begin to release your dreams in a truly fascinating way. It may be just as well for you to leave it at that for a few nights; you could find that, very gradually, dreams will start coming back to you – and if so, you've very little to worry about – you are off to a good start, and you can soon move on to considering what the symbols that you can now see occurring in your dreams actually mean to you.

But it's quite possible that things won't be as easy as that; and anyway it's very important for you to develop a systematic approach to recalling and recording your dreams. A really clear and detailed memory of the content of your dreams will help you whether you want to look at them simply for interest's sake, or in order to try to see your way through a specific problem – perhaps a practical one, perhaps one which concerns your personality. If you find yourself living or working under particular stress, or through difficulties, or if you have very important decisions to make, you may care to intensify your dream-work, but it seems to take some time for the unconscious to respond constructively to problems – usually several nights – so you may have to be patient. And even then, your dream comments may seem so garbled that you will have to "prompt" more dreams if you are to get any kind of help at all! For your dreaming self, as we shall see, does respond to such prompting. As you read on you will see how to work your way through your interpretations and get help even from the zaniest of dreams.

*Improving
your recall*

As we have seen, many people claim that they do not dream at all, or at least, that they find it impossible to remember their dreams. If you are a "non-recaller", it is important to convince yourself that you *do* dream *every* night, and that every night you have several dreams. The work done in dream laboratories makes this perfectly clear – it is a biological fact that the REM periods of dreaming occur with each 90-minute sleep cycle for everybody (and less vivid and visual dreams are recalled from NREM sleep) – but it can still seem unlikely to someone who hardly ever remembers dreaming.

Secondly, be quite clear that everyone can train themselves to remember their dreams: it is a matter of technique, of practice. We no more *have* to forget our dreams than we *have* to forget any of the many facts or incidents that take place every day of our waking life. We are selective about the daytime facts and events we consciously store in our memory, and similarly our mind appears to censor our dreams – sometimes more thoroughly than we might wish. On the other hand, dreams can persist in the memory as long as anything that "really" happens to us: Freud was often told by his patients about dreams they had dreamed a quarter of a century earlier, and he himself claimed to recall a dream he had 40 years before the time of writing.

There have been various theories as to why many people so easily forget their dreams. Early investigators have suggested that some dreams might simply be too weak, too insignificant, to remain in the memory. Others may have been forgotten because they were too random – in waking life we tend to remember facts, names, incidents, because they are part of a sequence of events, or at least are related to some recognizable area of our lives. Dreams are often random: there are no surrounding incidents which make them easy to remember and so they "fall to pieces" as soon as we try to touch them.

Some dreams do indeed seem to be of this fragmentary sort. It has been proposed by researchers that a particular type of dream takes place at the very beginning of sleep, the so-called "hypnagogic" dream. This usually consists of random, fragmentary images that are rarely retained in the mind for long. Dr Anne Faraday has suggested an interesting technique for capturing such "dreamlets". The onset of sleep decreases muscle tone, so that if you go to sleep lying on your back, with an arm propped up in a vertical position, balanced on the elbow, as sleep approaches the muscle tone will decrease, and your arm will fall and wake you at about the time that these "weak" dreams are coming through.

These "dreamlets" are by their nature hard to remember, being perhaps little more than a mental form of radio "noise". But as Freud wrote in *The Interpretation of Dreams*, people often forget their dreams more or less on purpose: either because they are simply not sufficiently interested to make an effort to recall them (no "set to recall") or because perhaps they are a little frightened at what they might learn from them.

The memory of a dream may be repressed at the actual moment of waking, an event that typically gives rise to the feeling that you *know* you have been dreaming but can't recall any of the details. But repression is of course not the only reason for the failure of recall. It has been experimentally established that anyone awakened from a dream is unlikely to retain the dream unless he or she stays awake, with the dream in mind, for at least ten minutes. This gives time for the memory trace to form. Otherwise all memory of the dream will be wiped out through the action of the NREM periods of the sleep cycle.

The cyclical nature of the human sleep pattern means, as we have seen, that everybody normally enters the REM period of dreaming sleep several times a night. Most of these dreams are never remembered at all; the ones that are remembered occur when the sleeper awakens directly from a dream, and stays awake long enough for the memory trace to form. So, apart from spontaneous awakenings at night, most recalled dreams happen in the long period of REM sleep that rounds off the last part of the sleep cycle, before you get up in the morning.

S. T. Coleridge (1772–1834) wrote down his celebrated poem "Kubla Khan" after a laudanum-induced dream. Its fragmentary nature is due to a visitor interrupting the poet's recall.

Dreams are fascinating, and one need no more be frightened of them than of any other means of self-knowledge. No one need do without the fascinating information and help they can offer.

Get into the habit of saying to yourself, "I remember one of the dreams I had last night", rather than "I had a dream last night". The best tried way of training yourself to remember your dreams is to keep a pad of paper and a pencil by your bed, and immediately on waking from a dream to make a note of it. You don't at that stage have to write it up in detail, but if you can jot down a few words – just a note of the main elements of the dream – where you were and, most importantly how you felt (i.e. frightened, elated, amused or whatever) – you will find yourself, later on, able to remember the dream more fully. If you are going to study your dreams seriously, you should later write them out in detail from your rough notes. You will usually find that even if your memory is sketchy at first you'll remember more about a dream as you describe it in writing.

This is a sound approach and indeed an extremely enjoyable one. To encourage yourself, get a special notebook for the purpose, and pay particular attention to your work in it: all this will help clear the mists. Later,

The Arrival of New Words, by G. Segantini, summarizes the kind of dream that may emerge in the course of non-REM sleep. Fragmentary, elusive, yet full of apparent significance, such dreams often prove tantalizingly hard to recall.

when you are coming to terms with what the dream actually means for you, you can write your individual interpretations and comments – perhaps in a different coloured ink. You will then be able to see at a glance your conscious reaction to your dreams, and even if this seems in direct contrast with what seems to be their unconscious meaning, there may be a connection.

It is best, when you wake after a dream, to move about as little as possible: try to remain relaxed, within the mood of the dream; reach out in a leisurely way for your pencil and pad: above all, don't strain too much to remember every detail – let the dream come to you, rather than trying to chase after it!

Nonrecallers may find what we have so far written to be sufficient to put them on the "royal road to the unconscious mind", as Freud called it. A more drastic method is to set your alarm at 90-minute intervals through the night, and to write down at once what was in your mind before waking. In this way, as Dr Faraday points out, you will probably not only pick up materials from the REM states, characteristic of dreams, through which the sleep cycle passes, but may also catch some of the stranger, perhaps deeper, dreams that occur in the NREM periods of the sleep cycle.

However, too many dreams may be as hard to handle as too few. You may find that at first you will wake up at all hours of the night to make notes on your dreams. This certainly means that you collect a large number of dreams on which to work, but it will also mean that your sleep pattern will be seriously disturbed, and you may find the process rather exhausting. We often need help from our dreams at a time when we are under a certain amount of stress: for instance, when we are in doubt about a line of conduct, about our feelings for someone, or about some important aspect of our life. Here we need to see people and situations in a way that will come through clearly in our dreams, often presenting us with a new perspective, a new understanding. But at such times we also need good, sound sleep. If this is your situation, you must simply do what you can to keep a balance. It may be that, having had a few disturbed nights as a result of your investigations, you will settle down and find that you recall your dreams naturally when you wake up, refreshed, in the morning, and this really is the ideal state of affairs. You should still keep that pencil and paper at hand, and make your rough notes – it does seem to be the very best way of developing good recall – and you should still develop your notes more fully later on.

In doing that, however, you must be very careful from another point of view: it can sometimes be the case that we embroider our dreams in recalling them, and while this is no doubt an excellent exercise for our imagination it

Albrecht Durer painted and described this dream in 1525: "I saw this appearance in my sleep, how many great waters fell from heaven. The first struck the earth about four miles away from me with a terrific force . . . I was so sore afraid that I awoke from it before the other waters fell. . . . So when I arose in the morning I painted above here as I had seen it. God turn all things to the best."

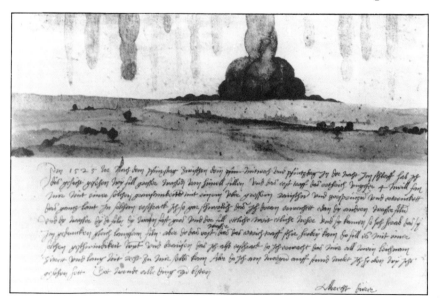

can distort the dreams, so that in the end we place more importance on the incidents we invent than on what we really dreamed. Record what you dream, and not what you think you *should* have dreamed! (Incidentally, some people like to record their dreams in the present tense: "I am standing on the deck of a ship . . ." They find this is easier than using the past tense; this is something you may like to consider.)

If you hate writing, or just don't think you're good at it, you can draw or paint your dream. This different approach can be equally successful – you'll be going through the same basic process, and indeed you may well make a more thorough record, since it's likely you will take rather longer to produce a picture (no matter how good an artist you are) than just to write your dream experience down.

Get on good terms with your dreams

This next stage will stir up a mixture of feelings in you – and one of them may be embarrassment at what we suggest you should do. Some analysts consciously use the embarrassment of their patients in order to drag dream memories from them, and to interpret them, but if you are working alone on your dreams, it is more likely to inhibit than help. So try not to worry about it; for if you do, you'll interrupt the positive flow from your unconscious to your conscious mind, and your progress will be blocked. If you are a practical, materialistic type the chances of embarrassment are greater, but you may have to come to terms with it if you are to make progress. Remember that any tendency to feel a fool as you go through the process is only superficial; you can practise the exercise when everyone else is out!

Basically we have to learn to *talk to our dreams*; we have to get on good terms with them. The process is rather like playing a game of chess with yourself, the sort where the board is set out and you move from one side of it to the other in turn, first playing white, then black. In coming to terms with your dreams a similar process is involved, and for those readers who are finding their recall slow, or the process in any way difficult, we suggest the following method, used by Gestalt therapists and analysts for many years.

The idea seems to have come originally from Dr. F.A. Perls, one of the most influential of Gestalt psychotherapists. Suppose you have had a dream that you can recall, but which somehow just doesn't make sense. Put two chairs facing each other, and sit on one of them. Be yourself, look straight at the empty chair – in which your dream or an image from it is supposed to be sitting – and simply hold a question-and-answer session with it. You ask the question, then directly move to the other chair to let the dream answer. It's quite possible that you'll feel foolish to begin with, but you'll also find that the system really does work surprisingly well, given a chance. The conversation may go something like this:

Dr Frederick A. Perls, Gestalt therapist, who developed the "empty chair" process whereby fragments of the dream material are isolated and worked through.

"Why can't I understand your real meaning?"   *"Because if you do, you won't take any notice of what we're trying to tell you!"*

"If I try to trust you, will you help me?"   *"We might, but you are putting up resistance."*

"So what must I do?"   *"Lower your resistance."*

"But take last night's dream: what can you mean? I've never been to Edinburgh."   *"Then what do you associate with Edinburgh?"*

"Well, I once had a girlfriend whose mother came from there."   *"And what was her attitude to you?"*

"Well . . . ."

And so on.

Should some particularly vivid symbol occur in your dreams, you can address it specifically. It may be a symbol which recurs in various dreams, under different circumstances. This may make it difficult to interpret. If so, your conversation could go something like this:

"What on earth are you, a pot of honey, doing in this particular dream?"

"Well, you should worry – you like sweet things, don't you?"

"Yes."

"But you haven't noticed that each time you see me, I'm a little more empty?"

"So?"

"You're gorging on the honey in me, and the supply is fast running out."

"You mean I'm being self-indulgent?"

"Right! I wouldn't mind so much if you were spreading the honey round a bit – what about giving some to other people rather than hogging the lot? There'll soon be none left, and when someone else hungry for something sweet comes along, there'll be nothing for them."

It is usually the case that a recurrent symbol, just like a recurring theme, is telling you something important. By questioning it in this way you can gain yet another perspective.

If the meaning of a particular dream still eludes you, you can ask for *another* dream to be "sent" to help you interpret the first. This very often has an excellent result. Again, incidentally, try not to be worried by the rather strange situation in which you are asking yourself to send you a message! The connection between the conscious and unconscious you is, unless you are extraordinarily well balanced, likely to be a tenuous one; you have to send a fairly strong signal in the direction of your unconscious self in order to be reasonably sure of a reply!

Don't hesitate to argue with your dreams, but *do* listen to what they reply, and remember that the answers you get will be in immediate reaction to what is actually going on in your unconscious, which in itself is most revealing.

The second method of talking to your dreams is perhaps less embarrassing but can be equally rewarding. When you have settled down in bed and are just beginning to feel really drowsy, strike up a conversation with your dreams in much the same way as I have described. You don't have to speak out loud – just "to yourself", as it were. Many people find this approach just as effective, and it's certainly one to which you can graduate once your dream studies are really under way.

The Language of Dreams

In every dream there are numerous images, and when interpreting your dream it is important to realize that "you" may not always only be "yourself". You can become other people and even objects, so it is important when assessing your dream to look at it from all points of view. For instance you might be having a conversation with a friend. Think of being yourself, but also of being the friend in the dream – this will give you another perspective on it. Think too of being one of the objects in the dream – perhaps a book, a piece of fruit . . . The idea may seem ridiculous, but when you put yourself in the place of the object (as we have suggested in the previous chapter on recalling dreams), and consider what is happening to it, being done to it, how it is being used, then apply the action or circumstance to yourself, you may well see that your dream is using the symbol to illuminate, in a new and fresh way, the situation in which you find yourself. What is happening to that object, people's attitudes to it or use of it, may be significant. The object will of course usually have some connection with you: for example, a writer might become a pen, or a manuscript, in his dream. Freud called what happens in this type of dream displacement.

An important question to ask yourself is how you felt in your dream. Were you happy? Frightened? Worried? Were you showing off, being boss? Were you cowering, or afraid? In this way you can relate to your conscious feelings in your dreams; they will probably be telling you something important about your reactions to situations in your everyday life.

If you have any difficulty in coming to terms with this admittedly somewhat difficult concept, ask your dreams for more help and a greater clarification of the situation (see p. 47).

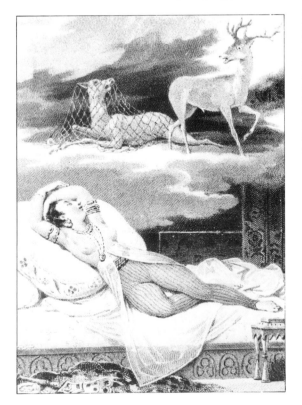

The Dream of the Sultan's Wife, a 19thC French illustration, exemplifies the way that an object in a dream – in this case the captive deer – may actually represent the dreamer. Freud was one of the first to notice this "displacement" effect, which he discussed in his *Interpretation of Dreams*.

Many of our dreams are so muddled and confused, it is as if our unconscious is having a sort of spring clean. As we have seen, various theorists have suggested that one of the main functions of dreams is to sort through the literally millions of sensory impressions that we receive throughout our waking days, and to file the important ones; the other, random, impressions are wiped from consciousness, and these muddled dreams may be, as it were, the used tape flipping past the window of the computer. Depth analysis should no doubt sort out a lot of garbage, but in general really muddled dreams are probably relatively unimportant, and should be allowed to go away; any image of real importance will hang about in your memory, forcing you to consider it more deeply. After all, if you try to sort out every incident in every dream, your sleeping life will take up hours of your waking life next day, you will probably get tired and irritable, and progress will be hampered. Recognition of what one might call "the rubbish dreams" isn't always easy, but you will probably find that in due course you will instinctively know which dreams are important and which are not. Your decision, one way or another, will be the right one for you.

Symbolism and punning in dreams

Both Freud and Jung believed in a collection of universal symbols, stretching across time and distance – symbols which were common to all mankind, and resided in what Jung called the collective unconscious. Sometimes, as we see elsewhere in this book, the notion ran away with them: almost every psychologist now recognizes that Freud's tendency to regard all oblong objects as phalluses and all hollow things as vaginas became ridiculous. And indeed, we would hold to the view (firmly advanced by the most modern dream analysts) that an image in a dream has a meaning individual to the dreamer. Yes, we all live in the same world, and so some symbols and images will be interpreted, broadly, in a similar way. Yet even the most obvious one

The symbol of the cross may well carry different meanings according to culture and circumstance. A dream illustration (*left*) by the French artist, J. Grandville, suggests confusion and deceit. The fiery cross of the Ku Klux Klan (*above*) is a familiar racist symbol. But the primary Christian meaning of the cross (*opposite above*) still predominates in the West.

will have different meanings for different individuals, not only because of personal experience, but because of upbringing, culture, environment. Take the Christian Cross, for instance; it will not only mean something different to the ardent Christian and his atheist friend, but to their mutual friend, a Jew, the symbol will have a different complexion altogether. In the A to Z Alphabet, we refer to symbolism and mythology where the symbol concerned seems specially universal, and the symbolic meaning may be strong enough to load the personal signature with an additional patina.

Puns form a tremendously important part of the symbolism of dreams; we dream in them a very great deal (the A to Z section will make this clear). The associative nature of the unconscious mind, which deals in symbols and images, has been experimentally demonstrated, so it is not altogether surprising that this occurs. You may dream of being in some place devoid of light. Think about it. Are you "in the dark" over some aspect of your life? Is some specific problem bothering you because you don't know all the facts, can't "see the light"? This is the very simplest example of the punning dream.

You should bear in mind the possibility that any dream you find confusing could well be full of puns. Language comes into question here, of course; some puns could have very different significance on each side of the Atlantic, and certainly in other languages than English. We will do our best to make the necessary allowances in the interpretation section.

Falling Asleep

A great many dreams occur when we are just falling asleep. Sometimes we actually dream of falling, and while this could mean many very different things, it can be the case that we are simply falling asleep – another punning dream, and nothing to worry about. Some people find this dream disturbing, but it may just be that the body is becoming more settled and relaxed, and "dropping off" as the muscle tone decreases.

The stage at which our last waking thoughts become our first dreams of the night is an interesting one, an area of dream interpretation which we would do well to consider in some detail. Try to recognize it when it occurs. The process need not interrupt the pattern of your relaxation and indeed could aid it. The first entry into Stage One sleep is not characterized by REM sleep, where vivid dreams occur. Dreams experienced at this time tend to be shorter than REM dreams, though they are sometimes not otherwise dissimilar. If you can eventually remember your thoughts and the dream pattern that follows, you could very easily get a further insight into your eventual interpretations, for there might well be some important link between what was going on in your conscious mind and the dream that extended it, perhaps having some bearing on how an aspect of your life is developing within your mind. Remember too that a "waking dream" can be triggered off, perhaps by your alarm. If this is the case, do remember that the physical sound of the bell will at least have distorted the dream, and allow yourself time to consider subsequent dreams before coming to any important conclusions about its interpretation. It could be less important than you think. Some experts consider the very earliest impressions that come as you enter sleep – vague images, voices, etc. – to be little more than what Sir Peter Medawar called "assemblages of thought – elements that carry no meaning whatever", or the equivalent of the buzz or "noise" produced by any electrical apparatus.

"Shock" dreams and nightmares

A very simple type of dream, which is occasionally shocking but can usually be easily dealt with, is the dream which repeats a traumatic event in your life – perhaps being mugged, robbed, sexually attacked, or caught in a sudden accident. This is one kind of dream about which there is little mystery; your mind is simply harping on the traumatic event, and as time passes the dreams usually fade. If they persist for more than a few months, perhaps you need to discuss the fact with a psychologist, or at least talk it out in detail with a sympathetic friend.

The Nightmare by Fuseli
shows an incubus seated on
a dreaming girl, with a
ghoulish "night mare" in
the background. The belief
that nightmares represent
possession by evil spirits was
once widespread; modern
research on the frequency
and seriousness of such
dreams has produced
conflicting results.

Originally, the word nightmare came from the Anglo-Saxon and meant "a
female spirit or monster, supposed to beset people and animals by night,
settling upon them when they were asleep". Many cultures shared this belief
in incubi and succubi – male or female spirits who attacked their victims and
might cause nightmares while they were asleep. Some researchers claim that
nightmares – really frightening and distressing dreams – are far less frequent
than is generally thought. Common enough in childhood, it is rare for them
to persist through life, and is usually a sign of some deep-rooted problem.

Ernst Hartman in *A Note on the Nightmare* (1970) has doubted whether such
dreams often happen, but agreed that frightening dreams did of course occur
from time to time. David Foulkes in *Two Studies of Childhood Dreaming* (1969)
pointed out that children often expect their dreams to be frightening, while in
fact they seldom turn out to be so. Ernest Jones, an older but eminently
respectable authority, claims in his book *On the Nightmare* (1909–10) that
healthy people actually never have nightmares – that they are always "an
expression of a violent conflict between a certain unconscious sexual desire
and intense fear". He meant that, for instance, a normally sexed man or
woman might have a horrific dream involving homosexual intercourse, and
be very upset by the revelation that such unconscious desires existed in them.

However, more recent researches have suggested that as many as a million
adults in Britain experience two or more dreams a week that are frightening
enough to awaken them. These usually happen during REM sleep, but
NREM nightmares also occur, nearly always from Stage Four of the first 90-
minute cycle. *Pavor nocturnus*, or children's night terrors, also arise from Stage
Four sleep. Dream laboratory research has shown that these distressing
dreams sometimes appear to be triggered off by a sudden noise, so those
afflicted by nightmares at this time may find the use of earplugs helpful.

A "worry" dream suffered by the British statesman William Pitt, according to the political caricaturist James Gillray. Entitled *Political Dreamings, Visions of Peace, Perspective* (sic) *Horrors*, it well captures the nature of this type of dream.

"Worry" dreams

Dreams in which one is worrying about something are far more common – in fact, most of us experience them from time to time. The worry we experience in sleep may seem trivial compared to our waking problems, or to have no connection with them. But worry dreams should not be ignored on that account, because there is no reason for anxiety to be expressed in a dream unless it is playing some part in our waking life. A close examination of a worry dream will often be specially valuable in revealing areas of our lives about which we are unsure, but to which we have perhaps not given sufficient thought. Freud thought anxiety dreams were in general the result of a wish to repress some desire or emotion, usually sexual in origin, and emphasized that the important thing was to find the source of the anxiety in our waking life. But such dreams may also reflect unconscious doubts and fears about more mundane facts and events of your life, things that have registered themselves in your mind, but have vanished from consciousness.

Sexual dreams

The Victorians, in particular, were tremendously distressed by sexual dreams, especially in adolescence. Professor Orson Squire Fowler, a popular Victorian doctor, recommended that young men should always take a cold bath before retiring, never sleep on their backs, and in extremity, tie a towel around the waist with a hard knot just under the spine (in order to make themselves as uncomfortable as possible, and therefore no prey to lascivious

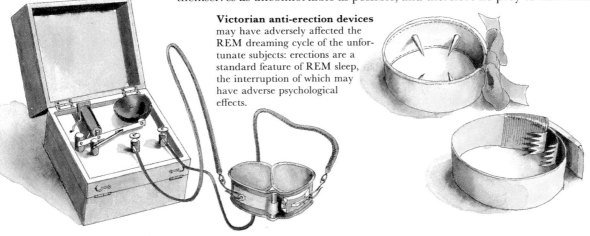

Victorian anti-erection devices may have adversely affected the REM dreaming cycle of the unfortunate subjects: erections are a standard feature of REM sleep, the interruption of which may have adverse psychological effects.

thoughts). Other doctors invented dreadful mechanisms which were locked around the bodies of unfortunate boys, and gave them an electric shock to wake them the moment they had an erection. As it happens, this may well have deprived them of REM sleep and its attendant dreams, since REM dreaming and penile erections are closely connected, as we have seen. Erections also occur in NREM sleep, but are particularly common at the beginning and the end of the REM period.

However, erection is not necessarily connected with sexual dreaming. Nor is the theory altogether convincing that claims sexual dreams are simply the result of sexual tension demanding an outlet: for instance, men who have been so seriously injured as to be incapable of any sexual feelings still report sexual dreams – certainly not the result of physiological sexual tension. And if the release theory is correct, why do so many more men report sexy dreams than women? Surely we cannot now subscribe to the suggestion that women are less liberally endowed with sexual emotion than men? The question is a difficult one – but certainly no one should be worried by an enjoyable sexual dream. At the same time, dreams with an overt or a disguised sexual content are often very revealing, and should be seriously studied.

The "Mood" dream

One of the most interesting, and often moving, forms of dream is that in which a kind of haunting quality – a true "dream quality" if you like – is the chief thing we remember. In many ways such dreams are very vivid indeed, though it is all but impossible to put them into words, for the overall emotion and very unusual and personal images seem beyond language. These dreams are not only important, but may also perhaps sum up our present feelings in an extremely subtle way. They may not always help us to come to decisions – mundane dreams give us that kind of help – but perhaps may encourage our emotions and imagination to develop in new ways, and are thus basically creative. Maybe such dreams are the very embryonic forms of new creative work or the beginning of developments in our lives which will in due course take shape and become important. We should be happy to allow our unconscious to do its work, in the knowledge that in time we will be further enlightened.

Village of Mermaids, by Paul Delvaux, captures something of the unusual spirit of the "mood" dream. Vivid but very hard to describe, these dreams make use of personal images and have a specially haunting quality.

The same elements may reappear in different forms in several related dreams, as in these sleep laboratory drawings of chairs, seen from the side and from above.

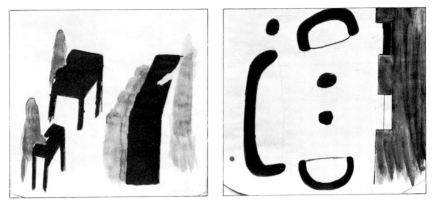

Sequences of dreams

It is very important if you are to get real help from your dreams that you should remember not just to consider one dream in isolation. Experiments in dream laboratories have shown that common elements recur in more than one dream during a given period of sleep, and that on some nights all the dreams seem to express variations on the same theme.

On the other hand, the connections may be "disguised". It may well be that you'll have a series of dreams which seem, to all intents and purposes, totally different, but are in point of fact referring to the same thing. This is because our unconscious will latch on to any convenient symbol and use it to comment on the subject which is most preoccupying it, though we may not in our waking life be conscious of that preoccupation. It is often the case that when we remember a dream connected with something we did the day before – perhaps with something we saw on television, or some casual remark that someone has made – it is because that incident or remark offers a convenient handle for the subconscious and what it has to say to us. The following night, you may dream of something quite different, but as you progress with your experiments you will begin to see that the whole series of dreams makes a lot of sense, telling you, possibly repeatedly, the same thing; in doing so it may be reassuring you, helping you to reach some decision, summing up your problems, or whatever.

Of course you will need to develop the skill and insight to be able to interpret your dreams fully, but we can't too often say that this is very worthwhile, so do persevere. Perhaps, for instance, you have some problem that is getting you down. One night you might dream of carrying a very heavy shopping basket, the next of, say, digging your garden, or of getting involved in some long, complicated situation which means literally nothing to you. The dreams could simply be illustrating your present predicament – echoing your conscious feelings; your basket could be full of your problems; your dream might suggest that you should be trying to dig through the surface of the problems, breaking them down like surface soil; the confusion of events in your dream could mirror the confusion of your present problems, telling you that the first thing to do is to impose an order on them. Different dreams may share an identical mood.

The symbols in your dreams may seem to have nothing in common, but will be trying to make you face up to what's going on. Later on, the theme of your dreams could develop: for instance, you might see "light at the end of a tunnel", open a window, be driving your car and feeling absolutely certain you are on the right road – in which case the chances are that you now know precisely what to do, and, while your problems may well not be resolved, you will be approaching them in a positive and constructive way. If in fact you don't bother to consider your dreams at such a time you would, of course, be in the same frame of mind – but how much more reassuring to know what is going on, to have an indication from your unconscious that you are at one with yourself psychologically.

Fantasies on a Lost Glove (1881), a series of etchings by Max Klinger, anticipates modern dream theory in its use of imagery. A glove picked up by the artist inspires several dreams, romantic (*below*), fantastic (*opposite top*) and nightmarish (*opposite bottom*).

Something else which is worth assessing is how a sequence of dreams may develop as your attitude to your problems changes. A few years ago Julia Parker was commissioned to write a very long series of books which involved producing some half a million words in a relatively short period of time. She had all the material in her mind, but the amount of work involved daunted her. A number of dreams now came to her. The first was of an enormous empty warehouse that she was considering renting. In the second she was in a huge, beautiful building full of lovely materials for craft and art work, which she was buying. In the third dream she had inherited a lot of antiques, and was telling a friend that she was going to rearrange them and use them in some way. The last dream of the sequence found her tap-dancing.

The first dream appeared to her to suggest that she had an open mind and was receptive to what was going to happen, the second that she was gathering her thoughts and ideas together; the third told her she was ready to use all her past experience and knowledge of the subject she had to write about. The fourth was different in context and symbolism, but perhaps the most important: there is a connection in her mind between tap-dancing and typing – a sort of pun. The dream told her that she had got on top of her apprehensions and she was ready to get down to the actual work. Of course, yet again, we must point out that this meaning was peculiar *to her as an individual*. Only you will be able to say with certainty what something similar could mean to you.

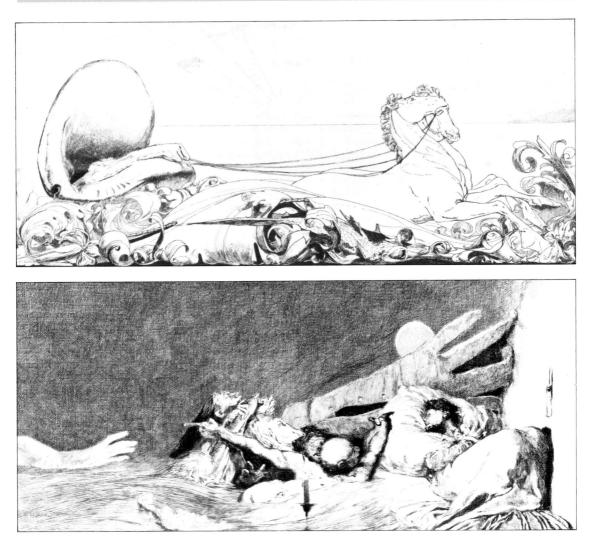

The recurring dream   Most of us from time to time experience recurring dreams. For many, the old favourite will crop up over a period of years, while for others it will return at rather shorter intervals. Basically it seems to be telling us time and time again about something we very much want or need. Don't misunderstand or place too much emphasis on the word "something", for the dream may well not relate to anything material; your need, as symbolized in your recurring dream, could be for love and affection, a better sex life, or most important of all, could represent an attempt to find the solution to a deep-rooted and unresolved psychological problem.

In fact, recurring dreams probably reflect problems of long standing that some external situation or impression has reawakened in the unconscious mind. The dream, each time it recurs, will probably be telling us what stage we have reached in resolving the problem. So it is important to note the slightest difference between the latest dream and its last appearance; a rearrangement of the order of events, changes in the visual content, different emphases, can be significant.

Any recurring dream needs working on in detail. A reference to the interpretation section of this book could get you started along the right lines; hopefully it will do so, but remember that in analysing your dream you should think of it in terms of your overall attitude to life, and your own individual point of view, for it is a manifestation of the very depths of your unconscious confronting your outward personality. Above all, don't just dismiss it, simply saying to yourself, "Oh, I've had that boring old dream again", and forgetting it until the next time it occurs. Neither should you be afraid of a recurring dream. Granted, if it is frightening it may well mean that you will have to face up to something about yourself which is distasteful – perhaps something very repugnant to you, or, even more confusing, something of which you are totally unaware or the significance of which you simply cannot grasp. But you must confront your dream and try to accept the fact that it is very definitely telling you something about yourself, and probably something important.

The best way to start on a recurring dream is to write it up in detail every time it occurs (in greater detail than you might usually record your dreams) and to examine very carefully the subtle variations in it. Each time the dream occurs, you will probably understand a little more clearly what it is trying to tell you (and, by the way, if it is a rather frightening dream, it will frighten you less the closer you come to understanding its significance).

Even if you can relate your recurring dream in detail, do not neglect to write it up every time it happens, and to think about what is going on in your life around the time the dream occurs. It may be that over a period of time you will discover that a distinct pattern emerges. For instance, the dream may occur when you are due to visit your mother. Even if it seems to have absolutely nothing whatever to do with the way you relate to her, the dream may be trying to tell you something important about your relationship. But in many ways it is the subtle *changes* in the dream that are of vital importance to you.

Dreams as warnings

William Cavendish-Bentinck, Duke of Portland, who helped to organize the coronation of King Edward VII in 1909, recorded in his memoirs a remarkable dream which took place when the plans for the ceremony were already well laid. He wrote:

> *The state coach had to pass through the arch at the Horse Guards on the way to Westminster Abbey. I dreamed that it stuck in the arch, and that some of the Life Guards on duty were compelled to hew off the crown upon the coach before it could be freed. When I told the Crown Equerry, Colonel Ewart, he laughed, and said, "What do dreams matter?" "At all events," I replied, "let us have the coach and arch measured." So this was done, and, to my astonishment, we found that the arch was nearly two feet too low to allow the coach to pass through. I returned to Colonel Ewart in triumph, and said, "What do you think of dreams now?" "I think it's damned fortunate you had one," he replied. It appears that the state coach had not driven through the arch for some time, and that the level of the road had since been raised during repairs.*

Here is a truly remarkable example of the warning aspect of dreams. The ancients believed that a chief purpose of dreams was to warn: dreams were messages from the gods. The very first dream book to have survived, the so-called Chester Beatty papyrus written in Egypt in 2000BC, detailed the symbols by which the gods warned of coming events; priests – "Masters of the Secret Things" – were appointed to interpret such dreams. While we may not take such a fatalistic attitude today, it is certainly true that it is wise never to ignore a warning dream. It may be that you will find the dream has no significance, but once in a while – like the Duke of Portland – you'll be very glad indeed you took notice of it. You may be unlikely to be setting up a coronation, but you might be arranging your daughter's wedding! More simply you might dream that your dog's lead breaks, that the brakes on your car give way . . .

It seems likely that such dreams as Portland's may be the outcome of observations and impressions that the dreamer has made in waking hours, but has either forgotten or not consciously noted: that is, his eye will have told

The assassination of Archduke Franz Ferdinand, 1914, was foreseen in a dream by the archduke's former tutor, Bishop Lanyi, who tried to get a warning through to the victim. Such apparently prophetic dreams may reflect unconscious knowledge or may be mere coincidence, but there is no doubt that "warning" dreams not infrequently "come true".

him, as he looked at the arch, that it would be too small for the coach, but he could have dismissed the idea without taking note of it. Many apparently prophetic dreams can be accounted for in this way, since they can be shown to refer to something which the dreamer has once been aware of but has pushed to the back of his or her mind.

This is yet another area in which dreams can help us, either by suggesting what may be going to happen, or simply by suggesting actions we might take. Remember too that if you dream about an area of your body, it can often mean that that part of you needs some kind of attention. Our dreams often carry warnings of illness, and aches and pains experienced in dreams can be valuable clues. The evidence also suggests, more and more firmly, that in sleep we can in some way tap both psychological and physiological signals that may pass unnoticed by any doctor, and even by the most sophisticated medical equipment.

However, one warning; if the dream is really evil in context – if what it suggests to you is an action or a series of actions deeply repugnant to you or likely to cause harm to others, you must examine it really carefully, and if you remain confused it may well be necessary to consult an analyst, who will study your dreams in depth with you. This is of course the ultimate way to learn about yourself.

Waking from dream

How often we have to say, when relating a dream, "Then I woke up, just as it was getting interesting." How sad it is! Your favourite dream idol is just about to embrace you, in the most romantic of settings, when you are suddenly wide awake. This may seem a little strange: such dreams, on the face of it, appear to be obvious wish-fulfilment dreams, and yet we so often wake before they are fulfilled!

It was Freud who first suggested that dreams were almost always the dreamer's attempt to satisfy, if only while asleep, ambitions or objectives which for some reason he or she could not fulfil in waking life. But his theory was mainly directed at dreams which many dreamers would find objectionable; he believed that in dreams our unconscious brings to our attention wishes which we would find offensive if they came to the surface while we were awake. There are holes in this theory, which later dream-explorers have emphasized: for instance, it is hard to see how a "shocking" or a "worry" dream can have anything to do with wish fulfilment. The general tendency among modern psychiatrists is to disregard the wish-fulfilment aspect of a dream except where it is obvious, and to concentrate on the general state of mind of the dreamer, and consider the dream in that context.

So we are left with the problem of why we so often wake just before the climax of an enjoyable dream. Is it perhaps that our dreams are teasing us? Or is this kind of dream telling us we haven't as yet achieved all we want out of life – we haven't in point of fact fulfilled our dearest dreams? What more obvious punning dream could one have? Similarly, if some delightful dream story comes to a natural end, and the story – romantic or otherwise – is complete, so that we may even find ourselves as part of the very dream relating it to a friend, this may be a reassurance that we've "made it" in some way. Should you have this truly delightful dream experience, ask yourself, "Have I arrived? Have I, at long last achieved my objectives?" This may well be the case, your dream a true reassurance.

To sum up, this book will just get you started on the road of dream interpretation. You will soon see that the long interpretation section that follows is quite different from any other you might have come across in popular dream books. This is aimed at *you*. *You* have to work to make this book work for you.

If you move on to study more advanced books on the subject, you will discover whole worlds that we cannot develop here; but this is your beginning, and certainly, as you actually refer to and use the next section, you will learn more and more, for while the questions are geared towards making you think about your own individual reactions to your own individual dream symbols, we also, when and where possible, put the symbol into an historical, symbolic and mythological context.

It is all too easy to rely heavily on one basic meaning of a symbol – even well-trained analysts fall into this trap, imposing their own interpretation of a dream on their patients. And while, of course, they are in an excellent position to know precisely what any individual symbol will probably mean to a patient with whom they have been working intimately, there may sometimes be a tendency to impose preconceived ideas.

Because you are working on your own, you can only put your own interpretation on your dreams, provided you answer the questions honestly, and do not accept them as suggestions as to the meanings of your dreams, but clues which might enable you to discover those meanings. There is no better way to dream interpretation, off the analyst's couch. But if you are deeply unhappy about a dream or series of dreams you should of course get professional help. You don't after all attempt to treat serious physical symptoms yourself; you go to the doctor. Similarly, if you honestly feel that your dreams are telling you distressing things and if, having asked for their help, you get no reassurance, you could need professional help. This will only be the case for a very tiny minority of readers; for the majority, the examination of your dream life will open up a whole new area of experience and fulfilment which will be rewarding and extremely worthwhile.

The Dream Directory

Using the Dream Directory

As we have pointed out, your dreams are completely individual to you, so there is no way in which you can be told by a book just what a dream, or a symbol in a dream, means. Interpretation is a do-it-yourself affair, and that is what this book encourages.

Following the suggestions in Chapter 5, you will have jotted down the main essentials in your dreams. Now decide what seems to be the most important element of it – the story, the mood, a particular character, even an inanimate object. You will find for the most part that this is not nearly as difficult as it seems. Often you will know, instinctively, the aspect of your

---

Dream Example

The following dream is dreamed by a man.

You dream you are running down a dark tunnel which, after a while, leads into a courtyard in bright sunlight. Around you is a magnificent castle, with turrets and battlements. You don't feel in the least threatened by it, but begin exploring the building, climbing staircases, which always seem to be outside the building. You begin to look for a way in, but at first cannot find one. Then you come across a doorway with a massive door which looks threatening or forbidding. However, when you put your hand to it, it swings easily open, and you walk inside, into a wide and light corridor, at the end of which you see a chair set on a platform; as you get nearer you see it is a throne, with a woman

sitting on it. You are afraid to approach, but you walk slowly towards it, and see that the woman is someone you know and admire, but find forbidding. As you reach the steps to the throne, however, she gets up and walks to meet you, takes you by the hand, and leads you through a door onto a wide terrace, with a magnificent view over wide and open countryside. You can see below you a house, and recognise it as your home; from it, you see many roads leading across the countryside, twisting and turning, disappearing behind hills, and out of view across the horizon. The woman points downwards, and you see below you a road leaving the castle and leading straight to your house. She takes your hand again, and begins to take you down a stairway leading to the castle entrance. You wake up.

dream on which you must concentrate. If, after some thought, an important element seems meaningless, then shift your viewpoint, and think about some other aspect of the dream – trying to relate it to your real – waking – life.

When you have come to a conclusion about the most important element of a dream, look it up in the dictionary section of the book. Perhaps (since it is obviously impossible to include in one book absolutely every situation or object that may occur in a dream) you will not find it, even under a synonym or related entry. In that case, turn to the next most important theme or object; it may well be that this will give you a clue to meaning – and atmosphere is often as important as theme: if you dream, say, of a clock breaking down, it may be that the element of disrepair, the idea of breaking, may be as important as the fact that it is a clock that expresses it.

Under the relevant entry in the dictionary, you will find a number of questions which should suggest a number of ways of approaching the dream, and which will lead you to decide what aspect of your waking life the dream

Dream Analysis

Going through your notes, you underline the words or phrases which seem important. You are most interested in the *woman* who appears in the dream; in waking life you don't know her very well, and though you find her attractive, she does not seem specially interested in you. Obviously the surroundings in which she appears to you in the dream are important. You look up *Buildings*, and find the suggestion that in dreams they often represent areas of our personalities. A *tunnel*, it is suggested, is sometimes a sexual symbol, so maybe the whole dream – since you approached it, as it were, through a tunnel – in some way refers to your sexuality? You come out of it into bright sunlight, which seems to suggest that you were going in the right direction.

What of the *castle*? It isn't a threatening building. Does it, as the dictionary suggests, represent your own personality or libido? And if so, does the fact that you begin to *explore* it, climbing upwards as you do so, suggest that you are beginning in waking life to explore an aspect of your personality, or your life, that has previously been neglected? You are looking for a *way in*, and that certainly seems to support the idea that you could be searching for some element in yourself previously unexpressed. And when you find a way in, the *doorway*, it seems at first unlikely to allow you to pass through – yet when you touch the heavy door, it opens easily. Is your unconscious telling you that some apparently difficult aspect of your inner life is more accessible than you think.

Now comes the corridor – not this time a tunnel – leading to the throne, on which sits the woman at the centre of the dream. The lightness and openness of the corridor suggest "ease of approach" again – and the fact it is a corridor rather than a room suggests that you are led, or impelled, in one direction. The throne clearly suggests that you find the woman somewhat inaccessible, even "above you"; but she comes down to your level and takes your hand, leading you out into the light again, where a remarkable view is seen – every aspect of which

suggests an opening out – of the landscape – and the opportunity to explore the unknown (the *roads* leading in many directions). Just before you wake, the woman is leading you towards home.

It is impossible to take the interpretation any further without actually being the dreamer whose dream we have described. But it is at least possible that he feels a strong but probably so far largely repressed attraction to the woman in the dream (the tunnel may indeed signal the sexual part of that attraction); but that in some way she seems remote and unapproachable. The dreamer's unconscious is probably telling him that while she seems too "different" to him to make a good relationship possible, it is likely that she could open out his life, showing him new aspects of it – and that she would respond positively to an approach.

But beware – always beware – of the simple approach; dreams are extremely, puzzlingly, often infuriatingly subtle in making any statement. It may be that our dreamer has been on the wrong track in regarding the woman in his dream as the woman he knows in waking life, or thinking her apparent motives in the dream have much to do with her attitude in "real life." The dream may not refer to her, and his relationship to her, at all. His unconscious, through the dream, may be referring to elements of her personality as elements which he should cultivate in his own inner life. These could well have reference to the "anima", the feminine side of his nature, which due to upbringing and background he is repressing. The apprehension he feels towards her in the dream may be an apprehension about his own sexual nature, or unwillingness to accept it. Yet this too must remain only the most tentative suggestion, at least at first. Question and requestion every interpretation you make before you accept it. You will find that just as in acupuncture, the feeling of the needle striking the right place is unmistakable, so the "right" interpretation of a dream strikes an unmistakable chord once you hit it.

refers to – whether it is an emotional situation, another person, some decision you have to make (or have made), and so on. It is important to look at your dream from many angles, to "walk around your dream". Follow up every trail the dream suggests, every clue thrown out. "Become" every important object in the dream which seems, possibly, to symbolize something significant, and look at the dream from its point of view.

Very occasionally a dream will seem totally opaque. Don't worry about this! the meaning may occur to you suddenly hours later. Or, infrequently the dream may simply be a sort of fantasia, meaning little or nothing.

Dream Themes

As we have emphasized, dreams are full of symbols which can only be interpreted in the light of our own individual experience – our upbringing, our environment, our personality as a whole. But much of the experience of mankind, certainly in the western world, is held in common, so if we were able to stray for a moment into our neighbour's dream, we would at a very shallow level recognize our surroundings: we might be in a city or townscape, in the countryside of our native land, amid a crowd of our contemporaries or on a beach or river bank, but we would be in a world we knew.

Similarly, certain themes occur in many dreams: dreams in which we are flying or falling, in which we are caught embarrassingly undressed, in which a major disaster is taking place or in which we are chasing or being chased by someone or something.

We have taken 16 of the themes and situations which seem among the most common, and suggest how you should look at them in order to see them as part of your own singular dream, rather than as a mere background. There are of course a good many more, and these have necessarily been chosen somewhat arbitrarily, but they are among the most discussed by the dreamers to whom we have talked.

Always remember, however, that though it is important to recognize the landscape in which the dreams are set, or the circumstances in which they occur, there will always be all-important individual symbols within the dream. The artists we have invited to illustrate these themes make the point beautifully: for instance, every reader of this book might have a dream in which the weather was an obviously important main theme – some may dream that the wind and rain actually intruded into the room in which they are sitting: but perhaps only one, the artist who painted the picture on p. 75, will have dreamed that an avocado plant is growing out of the seat of an ordinary chair. Similarly, the other paintings suggest an overall background theme within which symbols are set or symbolic events occur.

While it is the individual symbol or event which will probably remain sharp in your memory, and possibly be the first thing you will vividly recall on waking, it is very important to remember also the overall atmosphere, and within the A–Z reference list you will find that we often refer you to this background or theme. If, for instance, you dream of being chased, it is not only the monster chasing you which it is important to recall and name: the countryside through which the chase takes place will often reveal the area of your life or your mind which the dream is discussing. A dream in which water is a main theme will very probably be commenting on your emotional state, but the form taken by the water will be significant: the sea – very well, but calm or stormy? Cold or pleasantly warm? And so on.

It is as impossible to generalize about these dream themes as about the individual symbols listed after them. What we have tried to do is suggest ways in which you can look at the overall theme, as well as the individual symbol, in order to place it within the context of your waking and unconscious life, and recognize its significance and importance.

Dream Themes

Pursuit

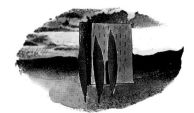

Dreams of pursuit are common, and sometimes very frightening. Big bad wolves, skeletons lurching from cupboards, black dogs, cats, horses, people, supernatural Things from other worlds . . . anything can pursue us in our dreams, sometimes to the point of nightmare. The great thing is not to allow frightening symbols to continue to pursue us through our waking hours, and the best way of preventing this is to discover precisely what they represent. If after doing so we are still dogged by them, this may indicate a failure to come to terms with the basic source of the dream, suggesting that we should build greater inner strength to help us contend with those weaker elements of our personality which are making it impossible for us to turn and face our problems.

Consider two things: if you were being pursued, were you able to out-distance your pursuer or turn and face him, her or it? And indeed what form did your pursuer take? If the dream is a recurring one, you should (as always) make careful notes about how one dream differs from the next, and the way that it develops. It can be significant if the gap between you and your pursuer increases – the chances are that you are actually distancing yourself from your waking problem, because it is becoming less and less important, because you are absolutely determined to escape from it, or simply choosing to ignore it. If your pursuer is gaining on you, perhaps you are getting more and more immersed in the problem, feeling that life is closing in on you so that you have no room for manoeuvre. The dream, then, could signal excellent progress, or be encouraging you to stop and face your problem (with more inner strength than you may be aware of).

Thinking about who or what was chasing you, remember that it may represent a person, a problem, or even an element of yourself from which you are trying to escape. If your pursuer was an animal, try to work out just what that animal means to you in waking life: do you like or hate it; are you afraid of it; do its characteristics suggest someone you know? If your pursuer represents some unacceptable personality trait of your own, you must decide whether to ignore it or work on the particular weakness. Pursuit by hostile animals (try to remember which animal, and what it means to you) has been interpreted as the dreamer's own hostile instincts; or something from which the dreamer cannot get free.

But what if you were chasing someone or something? Again, you must decide what or who your quarry represents. It could be that the dream is emphasizing some personal inadequacy or describing some inferiority complex: you are chasing after a means of becoming more positive. Or your quarry could represent something material which you are striving after – an ambition or objective; it could be helping you assess your progress. If you are failing to catch up with whatever or whoever you are chasing, perhaps you are "missing the boat" in some way? Are others perhaps overtaking you, or are you afraid of that? Maybe you should make a greater effort to catch up – perhaps by working harder, or making a greater effort to achieve a better and more meaningful relationship with your partner. Are you at present feeling somewhat hopeless about some association or situation, perhaps really on the point of giving up? At such times we need reassurance from our dreams: they (perhaps only they, despite kindness and help from friends and family) are in a position to boost our confidence. Be on the lookout for positive symbolism, especially increased out-distancing of your pursuer, or the moment when you turn round to face up to him, her or it.

Landscape

Some of our most memorable dreams, and those we remember with most pleasure, are those in which we find ourselves in a strange and beautiful landscape. Sometimes we wake as though we have been on a refreshing holiday. But impressive landscape need not be the dominant or most important feature of a dream; and even if it is obviously important, do not forget that other features – some of them perhaps "blots on the landscape" – may well merit special attention and interpretation, with the landscape simply forming a background – though an important element in the dream.

If, in your dream, you stood on a vantage point viewing the scene, it is possible that the landscape represented some situation in your waking life which you are assessing before reaching a conclusion. Think of the details of your dream and see if they could be symbols possibly referring to this "overview" aspect of your life. If you are in a busy landscape, where a great deal is going on – for instance a city street crowded with traffic and pedestrians – there could be a reference to your daily life. Perhaps you should ask yourself if you are spending too much physical or emotional energy, or just taking on too much? Were the people in your dream moving freely towards their destinations, or were they snarled up in a traffic jam? Maybe they were scurrying around like ants, getting nowhere.

Alternatively, you may have been blissfully happy in a peaceful rural landscape. But if that situation was changed by a rude intrusion, this is an aspect that needs attention. Perhaps the intruder represents a disruptive problem, or person, in your waking life, something disturbing to your lifestyle or peace of mind. If a desired landscape seemed to recede before you, this may be an indication that you are allowing

desires or ambitions to slip away from you – and a landscape viewed from behind bars, or even from a high window, may represent wishes which you are prevented from attaining (either by some outside obstacle or by your own inhibition. Is there any way of breaking down the barrier?

Your own activity in the landscape could be important. Perhaps you were striding purposefully across the landscape, suggesting confidence and a sense of direction. Or you may have been creeping through it with trepidation: in which case the dream may be the reflection of a lack of confidence, or possibly a warning of overconfidence. Rely on your intuition to see which could be right. Looking down on a landscape from a height may be a warning of a superior attitude to others ("pride comes before a fall" – did you trip, in your dream?) If you are moving too quickly through the landscape, ask yourself whether life is passing you by.

You may have been bogged down in a muddy quagmire, scarcely able to move; obviously this may refer to some waking situation out of which you can see no way. Think about what happened in the dream, in that context: was there some hint of a way out which may apply to your waking dilemma? Some symbol of hope? Do not forget that the landscape can be *yourself*, as though you were a Gulliver over which tiny men were moving. Think of the physical aspect of it: was it rocky and arid, or smooth and lush? Could this find a physical parallel? Do you need to "shape up", lose weight, improve your appearance?

Consider the various elements of the landscape: sea, lakes, mountains; what was the weather like? These may be more or less important, and may have something to say about your emotions and the way you should express them. A landscape dream may well refer to a need to get away from it all, suggesting that you need a change of scene, or maybe a holiday.

Travel

One of the most refreshing and exhilarating dream experiences we can have is of travelling to some distant land, and waking with such vivid memories of it that we feel we have actually been there. It has sometimes been claimed that the feeling of déjà vu, of "I have been here before", stems from just such an experience, and there are records of people having described very accurately places which they have never visited, except in dreams.

Today we would probably explain this in terms of having seen, but forgotten, photographs, films or television programmes about the places we later visit in dreams, but it is nevertheless surprising how often the very atmosphere of a place, even its individual smell, seems familiar to us, and rational explanations are difficult to find.

Dreams of travel, of strange places, are often scene-setting dreams, offering us a background and even a structure for our waking lives. We often venture into the unknown in dreams at times when in waking life we are about to start new work of some kind, or are on the brink of a new relationship, or of making some important change or commitment. While the landscape of your dream, and your feelings towards it, can accurately sum up your waking emotions, the conditions under which you are travelling are equally revealing. You may perhaps be pulling something, or coping with a car which has broken down. Are you, then, trying desperately hard to encourage your partner's enthusiasm for a particular project, or facing up to unwillingness on the part of others which prevents you from being entirely comfortable or happy about the future? If something is hampering you, or cramping your style, it may be that a dream will encourage you to consider the pros and cons of the situation more deeply, warning you of difficulties ahead, and that you are not properly prepared for them, psychologically or practically. If there is no change in prospect, and your dream travels take you far afield, perhaps that is a hint that your lifestyle is cramped and claustrophobic, and that you need change and a broadening of interests and mental stimulation. You could, of course, have a deep longing for travel which you have not been able to fulfil – as a hungry man will dream of food.

What of the horizon, in your dream? Was it clear or threatening? Did it open out, as usual, as you drove towards it, or was something preventing you from reaching it? Perhaps you were secure in an aeroplane, "up in the clouds" (a pun, maybe); if so, are you sufficiently down-to-earth? Escapism in waking life is often symbolized in dreams of travel.

Consider your mode of transport. Your *car*, especially perhaps if you are a man, is more than just that: it is often an extension of the personality, and often suggestively sexual (the body seeming a part of you, and protruding ahead of you as you sit in the driving seat. A motocycle, even a *bicycle*, can have the same significance). Someone colliding with your car in a dream, damaging it, maybe someone attacking your personality – or perhaps just "knocking you". Someone who tells you your car is dirty, or too old, or worn out, may well represent your unconscious suspicions about middle age, or a slipping image. If you are lovingly cherishing your car in your dream, does this reflect a narcissistic tendency? – "I love me!" A woman having the same dream may find it refers to her general expression of love and affection.

The embarrassment of not having a ticket or the money for one may (like dreams of *nudity*) relate to some kind of inadequacy or apprehension. And if you arrive at your destination (you obviously passed "go!") the dream could indicate a certain degree of self-satisfaction. If not, ask yourself whether it could not represent, rather, a beginning.

Disasters

Dreams of disasters often qualify as nightmares: we wake up in a cold sweat and find it difficult to get to sleep again – often afraid of slipping back into the dream. But the disaster is unlikely to be quite what it seems.
Of course such a dream may be telling us something, and possibly something important; so approach it in a logical way, and try to take a cool view of your feelings during the dream, and when you woke from it. Be severely practical.

After a disaster dream, remember first that the dream may simply be summing up your physical state: the onset of the menstrual cycle may prompt a woman to dream of blood, or a need to urinate may prompt a dream of flood! More subtly, a dream of a volcanic eruption might signify some skin eruption, the onset of a boil. At a deeper level, such a dream could refer to the breaking into consciousness of some formerly repressed emotion. In some of these cases, you can disregard the dream as probably not worth further consideration, though in the last case it would clearly be worth further examination. Your state of mind during the dream may provide clues to its importance. Was the disaster tragic, terrible, enjoyably spectacular? Or was it a farce? The success of "disaster movies" suggests that one side of us positively relishes such events.

If you dream of crashing your car, or of something that could certainly happen in waking life, rather than something fantastic happening to yourself, your partner, children, or pets, then you could certainly make any checks suggested by the dream – dreams have been known to refer, for instance, to a slight softness in the brake pedal of a car which the most careful of drivers has ignored. As we say elsewhere, dreams can warn us by "reporting" facts which our concious senses have failed to notice, facts which remain at a subliminal level of consciousness.

Disaster dreams can reveal private anxieties: buildings crashing to the ground suggest the collapse of material aims, objects and ambitions, and could be a warning that we are spending too much, or that in some way we (as represented by buildings which are personal to us, such as our homes) are "falling apart". So consider your situation, and watch for further signals in further dreams. Similarly, a dream of being buried could signify that you are being swallowed up by commitments, or a dream of an earthquake that your waking life is not as secure as you might think. Such dreams are probably focusing on a specific important problem, whether of a psychological or physical nature.

Because dreams of disasters – earthquakes or fires, famine or epidemics – can be depressing, it is important to remember that dreams seem to have little sense of proportion: a dream of a handsome building crashing in ruins can merely allude to some incident in the love life of an architect friend, or a dream of a battle at sea can refer to a family argument about which seaside holiday place you should visit next summer! Here, as everywhere, never take a dream at its face value – search for the underlying meaning (which may be less worrying than you think).

Disaster dreams may, and usually do, allude to personal concerns. Can they sometimes be genuinely predictive? In her book *The Dream Game* (Temple Smith, 1975, p. 160–1), Ann Faraday excellently sums up the proper attitude to "warning" dreams:

Dreams certainly can give us important practical warnings but these can almost always be traced directly to the heart's subconscious detective work based on small impressions or subtle vibes, picked up by normal means during the day, which the waking mind was too busy to register or perhaps did not want to know. Dreams that seem to give warnings of a more dramatic and paranormal nature "come true" only in a tiny minority of cases; for every uncanny story that gets written up in the press, there are thousands of equally vivid dreams about friends dying, air crashes, floods, war breaking out, or presidents being assassinated, which are never literally fulfilled.

It is when we dream of disasters that most people wonder whether their dreams may be precognitive: vivid dreams of crashes or assassinations do sometimes come true: four or five people claimed to have dreamed of the assassination of President Kennedy. But remember that we all dream several dreams a night; considering the population of the Western world and Mr Kennedy's prominent position, would it not have been amazing if no one at that time had dreamed of his killing?

Weather

If you are conscious of the weather in a dream it is probably important; but make sure that it is indeed a key symbol before you concentrate on considering its meaning. It may simply have a bearing on your physical state: thunder and wind may even be an expression of gastric problems (we speak of "having the wind")! If there is rain, it may relate to simple thirst or dryness. Obviously if you dream of excessive heat or cold, and then wake up to find yourself perspiring under too many bedclothes or shivering because you have thrown them off, the dream may mean nothing more than an expression of your physical feelings!

But weather dreams can be much richer in symbolism than this. Everybody's moods are affected by the weather, and the words used to describe moods and weather are often interchangeable. So the language of dreams makes frequent use of weather imagery. If the sun is shining, for instance, and you are conscious of warmth and happiness, then your dream is probably one of reassurance. Your unconscious may be confirming that you are functioning positively, both in physical and psychological terms (the sun is a symbol that relates powerfully to our general wellbeing and vitality). As always, your feelings during the dream are of essential importance. A dream in which you feel that everything is right (and sunshine and warmth confirm the fact) is probably telling you to carry on in your present course and signals inner contentment.

Dreams in which the weather plays a major part often relate to a problem or area of life which is particularly centred on the state of your emotions – whether they are warm, cool, stormy, passionate, hot or torrid. A snowy landscape, for instance – especially if your dreaming self was reluctant to tread on the white pristine surface – may have a bearing on your attitude to virginity, or at least purity. Perhaps you are reluctant to become emotionally or sexually involved with someone, in your waking life. But if you find yourself in a hot, scorched desert landscape, this could vividly describe a feeling of frustration or unfulfilled passion – there is a very clear connection between heat and sexual desire. Chilly weather in the dream may express a similar symbolism. Frozen lakes or icebergs tend to symbolize "frozen" emotion, so the question you should ask yourself, if such a potent symbol emerges in your dream, is how close you are to "thawing"; or, if you were admiring and enjoying the icy landscape, whether you want to thaw! You may be a Snow Queen or King by nature – but is that desirable? If ice is a recurring symbol,

maybe you should consider your emotional life in general, and whether you are allowing yourself to express your feelings in a truly satisfactory manner. Could they, for some deep-rooted psychological reason, be frozen? In a recurring dream in which climate plays an important part, you should look out for changes as you work on your problems – either through self-analysis or in therapy.

If the weather in your dreams is turbulent, this too may well be reflecting your inner feeling. Perhaps in waking life you are being buffeted by other people, or their unhelpful or uncertain attitude to you may be affecting you more than you consciously realize. Perhaps some area of your waking life is in a state of turmoil, translated in dream into storm or hurricane. Quarrels can be described as "stormy"; if the storm passes, this may be reassuring; perhaps you should consider attacking your problems head on, turning your face to the wind, so that you can work your way through to a quieter and more productive existence. If you were sheltering from a storm, should you distance yourself from your problem, or seek help from others? The form of shelter you seek may symbolize a supportive friend or relative.

Dreams dominated by the weather are always worth serious consideration, and they often afford clues as to our next move or action. Changes in the weather are especially important, for then the dream is probably encouraging you to reassess feelings and opinions. If you run into a storm in your dream, do not be over-concerned; the chances are that this is an encouraging hint that you should express your anger or be stronger and more assertive in waking life; even if, in the dream, you were afraid of the storm, your fear may relate to an inhibition which makes you fearful of speaking up. Consider the situation: if you are still apprehensive, encourage your dreams to help you further (see p. 47). Changes in the weather can also relate to decision-making.

Birth, Death and Change

One of the strongest and most magical forces in our dream world is that of transformation – animals change into birds, fish become tigers, buildings dissolve into water. In dreams, as in fairyland, anything can happen, and often does – it may be that our childhood encounters, in books and bedside stories, with beautiful queens who turn into ugly witches, frogs who become princes, genies emerging from bottles, have something to do with the readiness with which our limitless imagination is ready to turn our dreams into a kaleidoscope of changing images and symbols.

Transformations of this kind almost always seem to signal psychological changes in our waking lives: if we are riding a horse, which becomes a cat, which then turns into a dog, this may well be a comment on our changing attitudes to a particular problem or situation with which we are struggling to come to terms. If we are holding an object which becomes soft and malleable, and then slips from our grasp, it most probably symbolizes an opportunity – or even life itself – which we are allowing ourselves to miss, or to pass us by. The transformation of any vivid or colourful object into something dull or elusive may indicate lack of assertiveness or concentration in waking life.

Like all kinds of dreams, a transformation fantasy can be an extremely lively and clear form of shorthand, and once you understand its significance and meaning can offer very vivid comments. A heavy burden may, for instance, change from a lead weight to something just as heavy but immeasurably more desirable, and could indicate a changing attitude towards our responsibilities. The suddenness of such transformations, in dreams, seems to have no relation to any waking time scale – it is as if dreams have not time to be leisurely; a sudden change in a dream may be commenting on a very gradual one in waking life. Because of this, and because the images are often brilliant but sudden and mutable, it may be that, particularly with transformation dreams, we will need an above-average number of question-and-answer sessions (see p. 47) to unlock the symbols.

Transformations can be frightening, and perhaps the transformation from life into death is most frightening of all. A dream that you, or someone else, is dead should not be taken as a warning, though of course there is nothing to stop you enquiring about that person's health, or looking after your own. No, a dream of death is probably yet another signal of change, perhaps deep-rooted psychological change, which your unconscious has probably noticed before you are aware of it. The very fact that you see such a change in someone else means that you are so closely in tune with him or her that you would probably be able to be of great help to them at what may be a crucial and disturbing time. Follow your intuition. Such a person may mean a very great deal to you – whether as friend or enemy. It is possible that you may identify with a major trait you recognize in his or her personality, and it may be this to which the dream of transformation is referring: are you about to, or should you, change?

Just as dreams of death are often disguised transformation dreams, so are dreams of birth; but in these, the transformation is from nothingness into being, and usually they signal a different kind of birth: the birth of new ideas or projects – which we may regard as "our babies".

Fire

Our level of enthusiasm and energy, and indeed our whole outlook on life, may be under scrutiny when we dream of fire. In our waking lives perhaps we are confronted with some kind of challenge, and if the fire in our dream is a welcome one, the dream may be encouraging us to approach difficulties more positively.

Certainly it will be encouraging us to continue in the course we are pursuing. If we are lighting a fire, this would seem to be a hint that we should get started on some project – but the course of the fire, how it burns, should obviously be watched.

Our attitude to fire may say something about our general approach to life – how confident or fearful we are; the degree to which we express the emotion of anger. In certain contexts it can be related to other passions, passions positively directed through love and sex (which, again, can be all-consuming or obsessive). Passion can however be intellectually orientated, and fire dreams may be saying something about the controlling of intellectual or esoteric interests. Religious fervour and creativity are aspects which fire can illuminate.

Dreams in which fire plays an important part may, then, be encouraging us to be more daring and assertive, more enthusiastic, optimistic and positive. They may be inviting us to be more physically energetic. If the fire seems out of control, we may need to develop caution, prudence and self-control, to take a more relaxed attitude to life – in fact, literally, to "cool it".

A dream in which we emerge safely from the fire, phoenix-like, may be of special importance: your unconscious will probably be reassuring you of your ability to overcome difficulties or setbacks, or of some kind of rebirth (see WATER, p. 80 and BIRTH, DEATH AND CHANGE, p. 76). A dream in which you and your family are sitting around a *hearth*, or a camp fire, may be a signal of reassurance and inner contentment, of the warmth of family love and togetherness.

Do not underestimate the creative element symbolized by fire – think of the part it plays in forging. A dream in which fire plays a major part could be encouraging you to express yourself more positively, through creative work – goading you on to be more energetic and enthusiastic, increasing your self-confidence as you do so.

If we find ourselves, in sleep, playing with fire – maybe with *fireworks*, or with lit *matches* (holding them as long as we can without "getting our fingers burned") – we could obviously be experiencing a punning dream. How are you "playing with fire" in waking life? Are you involved in something which is more dangerous or risky than you consciously realize? In dreams, remember, we can sometimes be more far-sighted than when we are awake! A dream of an uncomfortably hot fire, incidentally, may simply be echoing the late US president Harry Truman's words: "If you don't like the heat, get out of the kitchen!" Should you withdraw from some situation that is troubling you? Or should you wait for the pressure to ease?

The *sun*, the most potent source of fire in mythology, often refers in dreams to our psychological state, at whatever level of development it has reached. There will probably be a symbol somewhere in your dream pointing to the area of reassurance – although the dream may be a general one, simply underlining the fact that your enthusiasm, energy level, general outlook on life are high, and inner contentment justified.

Water

Our deepest emotions, intuitions and instincts are in question or under examination when our dreams use the symbolism of water; they may be either reassuring us or making us conscious of deep-rooted conflicts and phobias. They may be encouraging us to dive to the bottom of our problems, to allow our emotions to flow more freely, to stop confining them behind some sort of dam or within too narrow channels. Or maybe to seek an emotional re-birth, to give expression to some deep, creative urge.

Dreams of the *sea* are often concerned with birth and the womb; we should always consider whether we are not trying too hard to escape from our problems by losing ourselves in fantasy or pretence ("back to the womb"). Other dreams – perhaps of deep *lakes*, stagnant *pools*, *waterfalls*, *fountains* – have their individual meanings, but there is usually a reference to our attitude to our independence of thought or action – whether we are "in full flood" or in danger of drowning through over-enthusiasm. Any dream in which water is being confined or compressed is perhaps a danger signal telling us that we should release ourselves in some way, give our emotions more freedom – though the opposite can be true, and an unchecked flood may be hinting that we should be more restrained. If we are *swimming*, are we doing so effortlessly, or struggling? And how does that relate to our current waking life? If we are *sinking*, perhaps we should examine the rock bottom of our problems and consciously consider how we can rise to the surface again.

The temperature of the water may be significant: is it pleasantly warm, or are there icebergs? If so, this may relate to a too cool emotional life. Storms involving water may relate more directly to inner stress than similar storms only involving winds. Lack of water may, obviously, relate to a "dry" emotional life, or a spiritual drought. Water often seems to relate to our imagination, and dreams involving this element may invite us to be more imaginative, to nurture original ideas; psychic ability and esoteric interests may be ripe for development.

Our personal attitude to water is probably crucial in interpreting all dreams of this element: if we love the water, are confident and happy as a part of it, our dreams will be different from those of people who hate and fear it.

Water may represent the fluid, unformed aspect of the dreamer, and yet in many dreams of water the dreamer sees his or her reflection. Water is thus a potent image of the unconscious, reflecting the self from a surface that may be calm or disturbed, placid or tempestuous. How you see yourself in the water can be important, but remember it will be a mirror image.

But what if, in your dream, you were diving through an underwater tunnel to emerge into daylight? A general interpretation would certainly suggest that this was a dream about birth. And it will most likely be signalling a desire to be re-born in some way, to re-create yourself – maybe physically: do you need a course of exercise, or a change of diet? Or maybe psychologically. It would not be surprising if "born-again" Christians had experienced such a dream. To dream of giving birth, if you are a woman, may certainly signal a desire for parenthood; but it is as likely to be about a desire to bring some creative idea to full fruition, to create something (not necessarily human life). The nature of the thing, or idea, you need to express in this way may reveal itself in other dreams: if not, invite your dreams to be more explicit! (*see* p. 47).

The image of water as a purifying agent should not be ignored: Shakespeare used it memorably in *Macbeth*, and if, like Lady Macbeth, you were trying hard to wash your hands clean, or some other part of your body, this may be significant – you may be trying to rid yourself of something unpleasant: in your attitude to others? Or your general behaviour? Such a potent symbol should not be difficult to decipher. On the other hand a vision of a beautiful running *stream* of fresh water should be a rewarding and encouraging symbol; bathing in it could mean that you are preparing yourself, in waking life, to move on in some way to new, fresh areas of life (much as we will clean up before going out, or to work.)

Baptism and rebirth are symbolized by water, so dreams involving water may have much to do with the feeling that you are ready for some fresh start in life, or a desire to change old habits or an existing lifestyle. Experiencing such dreams, it is wise to try to relate them to religion and matters of the spirit.

Clothes and Nudity

One of those dreams that almost everyone has at some time or another is of being naked, often in the company of other people who are quite conventionally dressed. Writers about dreams often ally this dream to sexuality, suggesting that it refers perhaps to sexual inadequacy or guilt. This is by no means necessarily the case. Indeed, such a dream can be a simple suggestion that your clothes need attention: you may unconsciously be bored with the style to which you have to conform (if, for instance, you work in a conventional office); or perhaps you should check your zip-fasteners or buttons!

But of course there are circumstances where there could be a sexual connotation. If, for instance, you are a young man and dream you have lost your trousers, this may be a firm hint that you are concerned about your sexual prowess or performance. If no one around you is in the least concerned at your trouserless state, the dream is a reassuring one: you are unduly worried! If, in your dream, lookers-on are aghast or expressing disgust, then maybe you should try to relax a little more with your partner, try to be less self-critical; or perhaps your partner is less sympathetic than you might wish. If this sort of dream is really worrying, and recurs over a period of time, it may be as well to look in detail at your relationship; you may need professional help or objective advice.

But, as always, the circumstances of your dreams are important: were you perhaps at a party, or at work? If so, the chances are that you are vulnerable or feel in some way "exposed" at work or leisure, particularly in relation to colleagues or friends: those you may especially want to impress.

There is sometimes a link between dreams of nudity and personal probity – a naked body suggest the "bare facts", the undisguised truth. But what if you are positively enjoying your nakedness – sunbathing or swimming, maybe? Once more, think of the context. Or what if you are acting out a role as a stripper? Are you, then, out to shock, in waking life? And if so, are you just out to attract attention, or do you really feel that the people around you need shaking up a little? Be honest with yourself: you may be an exhibitionist of the first order, and showing-off may be natural to you. The dream could be warning you that you are going too far. If it is attention you are seeking, perhaps from the opposite sex, are you setting about it in the right way? The dream, or subsequent ones, will almost certainly make this clear, or warn you about your line of action and its possible consequences.

Sometimes we dream we are donning some special or totally "different" garment. Are we trying to become someone other than ourselves? If so, who? Are you turning into a wolf in sheep's clothing? If you are buying (or better still, making) some totally original style of garment for yourself, perhaps the dream is suggesting that you should change your image. If the garment in your dream was very outlandish, maybe the dream is a warning – especially if you were wearing it with pride and pleasure, and some authority figure declared it "unsuitable". You may, then, in your waking life be putting on a tremendous act, pretending to be someone entirely different from your true self. But if your new outfit felt right and looked good, you may be starting out on some new line of action, or have come triumphantly through some inner change, maybe in your opinions or attitudes, and are perhaps ready to face the world with them. The dream will then of course be offering you support and increasing your self-confidence.

Remember that in real life accessories – sun glasses, *handbags* (beware of "old bags", which may refer to yourself or some unpleasant acquaintance), *belts* are all image-extenders, and within the context of your dream could fulfil a similar purpose. Think of them in this light; they may reveal a perhaps less important but still interesting facet of your personality.

Flying

Most people at one time or another have dreamed that they are flying. It is not surprising, for human beings have always associated the flight of birds with freedom — from being earthbound, from reality, from the forces of gravity. In such dreams we can be sitting in aircraft, parachuting, or ballooning. We can also, however, become a bird or in some way defy gravity and float and soar in the elements.

Freud, as he did with so many other dream symbols, made a positive connection between flying and sex — the effect of sexual desire, orgasm, even life in the womb. However the connection is not exclusive and it would be a mistake to give it undue prominence. The association between dreams of flying and sex can be based partly on physiology (some researchers have made a firm connection between the release of sexual energy and dreams of flight) but it is also very reminiscent of the freedom of expression which is an essential part of a good sexual relationship. Bearing this in mind, it is possible to place some interpretations on certain aspects of flying dreams: the dreamer as a bird hunted by other birds or being shot at by a human hunter, for example, may indicate a fear of being caught or trapped inside a relationship; alternatively, the simple joy of flight is too close to the simple joy of good sexual expression to be ignored and a dream of a happy flight may indeed be interpreted as an expression of the wish for, remembrance or celebration of a joyful sexual relationship.

However, dreams of flight can be associated equally well with other areas of experience. You may have been flying "high" because of some real achievement; you might have been looking down on a landscape or interior – can you associate the place with somewhere you know in real life? – in reality you may be on top of a situation, or you may have been trying to escape from something or someone – what did you see below you? Were you afraid of falling, and if so can you connect your dream with some perilous feat you have to achieve during waking hours?

How were you flying? Were you soaring above the land, the clouds, with a feeling of freedom and release? Or were you making small hops, just clearing hedges or fences? Was your flight sustained or partial? Were you, perhaps, climbing a mountain and flying only when you came up against a barrier, a precipice? Was your flying dream associated with falling, another common and often related dream?

Were you dreaming of actually being a flying machine of some sort, or a bird? This could be interpreted to mean that some aspect of your dream is less connected with flying than with the sort of machine or creature you have become. Perhaps an angel?

Elderly people dream of flight relatively more frequently, perhaps because they harbour a stronger desire to rid themselves of everyday problems. This, of course, can apply to any age, but the old may be responding consciously or unconsciously to a growing restriction on physical movement and want to release themselves from this inhibition and to distance themselves from it or from other burdensome problems or difficulties which are keeping them "down to earth". Perhaps those of us who find such dreams recurring should seek new ways of fulfilling our lives through the development of new interests.

Food and Drink

Dreams of food and drink may have a simple physiological trigger: it may well be that if you are on a diet you have a few dream banquets, just because your body is signalling to you that it is missing the luxury of your normal, untramelled menu! And of course hunger is itself a strong motivation towards dreams of food, and the greater the hunger the more poignant the symbols – a perfect example of wish-fulfillment in dreams.

But having said that, the significance of dreams of food when we are not dieting ourselves, or suffering from hunger, is another matter. There may be a question of self-discipline, especially if parents were strict with us about eating every scrap of food on our plate when we were young. In such dreams we may be being encouraged to exert more self-discipline, or at least to restrain ourselves in some way (not necessarily connected with food). If, in dream, we are nibbling or being over-selective about food, perhaps there is a relation to an emotional involvement in waking life: we may be holding back somewhat. Or

perhaps we are "picking away" at a particular problem, working on the surface detail rather than really getting down to it. If, in the dream, you were sitting down to a regular banquet, you should consider whether you are ready in your waking life to enter wholeheartedly into some enriching sensual experience – can you recognize in yourself a deep inner desire, even lust, to do so? Gorging on food may represent a hunger for some other, personal, form of nourishment – affection or security.

When we prepare and give food, in waking life, we are often expressing love, and there is a very deep

symbolic connection between the two. If you are preparing food in your dream, compare the manner in which you do so to the way in which you express your love – to partner, family, friends. Are you unstinting with the ingredients? Is the food rich and generously served? Or are the portions dry and skimpy? Perhaps you were serving food to many people, in a famine area. Was there enough to go round? If not, the dream may be warning that you are emotionally drained. There could be a reference to finance: did you have to pay for the food? Money and food are often allied; is there a reference to your buying, or seeking to buy, love or friendship? Greed for food has, sometimes, a sexual reference, and the shape and colour of the food may be amusingly suggestive: bananas, asparagus, tomatoes (they used to be called "love apples").

Drinking is often suggestive of physical pleasure; the drinking of water may relate to a need for purification of the spirit as well as cleansing of the body. If the food or drink in your dream revolted you this may relate to an element in some waking situation or relationship, and your attitude in your dream, or the way in which you dealt with the situation, may be highly significant. Dreams of bread often relate to the development of psychological wholeness, coming to terms with oneself, the way one functions as an individual. Follow up such dreams in real detail, for they may well help you to assess your progress in life.

Fish, Flesh and Fowl

There are no strict rules for dream interpretation, but animal dreams are very often taken to represent the basic "animal instincts". However, another way to approach dreams of animals, fish or birds is from the point of view of the creature concerned. Consider it in detail; its appearance, size, behaviour, how it relates to other species and its own kind, whether it seemed to you to be sympathetic or repulsive. Whether or not you are specially interested in zoology or ornithology, you may have picked up, unconsciously, some facts about the creature which show in your dream.

Pigeons, for instance, may seem rather dirty and troublesome – but they are superb parents, if poor nest-builders. A dream of pigeons may therefore be more warm and reassuring than you may think. But there may be other references: Freud believed that the bird was a phallic symbol, and dreams of a flying bird signified a burning desire to be good at the sexual act.

You will not, of course, take any notice of "dream-book" interpretations of dreams of animals – that it is lucky to dream of an elephant, and so on. Nevertheless, some of the traditional interpretations have a surprisingly universal basis: in Hindu mythology, for instance, there is an *elephant* god – the genial, popular and rotund Ganesha, guardian of banks and bringer of prosperity. Dreams of elephants may sometimes conceivably share this symbolism. You may also actually admire elephants, their gentle strength, their relaxed, easy life which perhaps symbolizes luxury well-earned by hard work, and this admiration may work through into the dream imagery. Elephants also have notoriously long memories!

Snakes are feared by many people, and the symbol of the serpent is potent in Christian civilizations. It often symbolizes psychic and spiritual energy, latent forces that can be destructive if not allowed expression. The coiled serpent in Hindu belief is the spiritual energy that must be awakened, and brought to fulfilment, by yogic practices. Alternatively, the serpent represents Earth forces, as with the Python of the ancient Greek oracle of Delphi. Though slain by the Sun god Apollo, the Python continued to speak ambiguous prophecies, through the intermediary of the priestess, for a thousand years.

Fear of snakes is very ancient – Jung believed that it was innate. This dread of snakes (or worms, or similarly shaped creatures) can reveal, in waking life as well as in dreams, a fear of the penis, or, in men, sexual guilt. The snake may be some particular *colour*: try to relate it to colour symbolism (a green snake, sexual jealousy; a red one, sexual energy; a blue one, spiritual energy, and so on). Your attitude to the snake, in your dream, is obviously important. Again, the beauty and power of the *horse* can have sexual overtones, but any dream of a horse may also refer to inner power, energy and progress, to "riding out" problems or overcoming difficulties. Unconscious references to power (sexual and otherwise) can be found in dreams of a *bull*, while the *cow* will perhaps refer to the maternal instinct. The *lion* has been taken as the symbol of unbridled desire, not necessarily sexual; it often appears in dreams of middle life.

Recognition and identification of the dream animal's behaviour will usually reveal at least one point with which the dreamer can identify, and it should be possible to extrapolate from this. It is worth mentioning the hybrid mythological creatures which sometimes invade our dreams – Chiron, half-man, half-horse, for instance; or Pan, half-man, half-goat, or the mermaids and mermen of legend. Even if you cannot consciously remember the significance of these creatures, it may be worth researching their stories – the unconscious mind is infuriatingly clever at hoarding useful symbols from very casual reading or conversation, and using them to make a point. Dreams using mythological subjects can be warnings, especially if some change is in process in your waking life and the way ahead is unclear.

Sex

It is easy – and often rather a temptation – to interpret almost any symbol in any dream as relating to sex or our attitude to it. Happiness and fulfilment in a positive expression of sexuality is vital to us all, but nevertheless it is easy to over-emphasize the theme, as many Freudian analysts have done.

Some people are disgusted or ashamed by obviously sexual dreams. But *we* are the creators of our dreams, and if we are disgusted by them, we are disgusted by our own nature – for sexual dreams most often discuss the way we would like to be expressing our sexuality. So if dreams remind us of our animal nature, we must decide just how we feel about that nature – whether we need to express it more positively, change it, or turn its energy to other use. If you are shocked by a sexual dream, consider it in this way – and consider too whether you may not need to relax into sex a little more. The dream may be leading you to a happier sexual life, more natural and more enjoyable for yourself and your partner.

Dreams in which we are actually making love are relatively rare; but since dreams express themselves more often than not in code, and since analysts of most persuasions agree that sexual symbols are often present in dreams, it is reasonable to consider the possibility that almost any symbol in your dreams *could* be telling you something about your sexuality – revealing an unsuspected aspect of it, confirming a predilection, reassuring or warning or simply celebrating.

Aspects of your dreams which are apparently unrelated to sex may make some important statement about an area of your waking life in which sex plays an important, but not all-important role. They may be commenting on simple "togetherness", for instance; or if they express excitement, danger, heat or passion, they may be inviting you to consider whether you should not change your attitude to sex. A feeling of abandon, in a dream, of the rejection of inhibitions – not necessarily sexual – may be prompting us towards a more fulfilling sex life, while if we are being scolded or feeling small, we may be being made aware of inhibitions we do not know we possess. Violent behaviour, or dreams in which aggression or domination over others are stressed, may also have strong sexual overtones, and may be warning us about our lack of consideration for our lovers. Dreams of coldness or ice can relate to frigidity, as can restriction of movement.

Sexual imagery in dreams need not be blatant and obvious: it can be very beautiful – the beauty of flowers and growing plants, the textures of velvets or silks, the tactile shape of an object, all these may be making a sexual statement – and just as forcibly as the obvious dreams of flying, climbing stairs, falling factory chimneys or trains rushing into tunnels! Yet even in such obvious symbolism we often receive a spiritual message, too, for the sexual and spiritual sides of our natures are rarely completely disassociated. Our psychological development tends to relate closely to a fulfilled sex life, and our dream symbols tend to remind us of the fact. Remember too that there is a difference between dreaming of an object which obviously represents a penis, and a "phallic symbol", for the phallus can strongly represent the power of creation, of healing and fertility.

Think about dreams you have had over the years; it will be surprising if one really vivid dream memory does not relate to your sexuality. It may have been crucial to your sexual development – and remember, this does not simply take place at puberty: in one way and another, our sexuality changes and develops until our death. A really important dream which has struck you forcibly, but seems not to be related to any obvious waking situation, should always be considered as a possibly sexual dream; and if you remember it in vivid detail, is probably important to you. Think about it now in the light of these comments: the chances are that it is signalling or suggesting a development in your sexual personality.

Environment

The environment, the setting of your dream, can often be very important, though as usual you will have to try to weigh up for yourself just how important it is to the specific dream you are seeking to interpret.
When buildings play an important part in the dream, these may well be reflecting particular areas of our personalities – for in dream symbolism it can be the case that we are the buildings themselves. A very ornate, highly decorated building may relate to the rather flamboyant image we present to the world; a very modern building may comment on our feeling that we must be right up to the minute – perhaps in fashion, but perhaps too in our attitude to life.

Awe-inspiring buildings such as cathedrals, castles, mansions, may relate to ambitious aspirations, especially if we are looking up at them. Were you climbing to the top of a building? Try to remember if you were frightened or elated. Did you feel inspired by the vision? Alternatively, you may be getting carried away by your ambitions. Are they in proportion to your abilities? If you were building something in your dream, this obviously may relate to some project in waking life: had you firmly established the foundations? How sure were you of success? The dream could have much to say about your general attitude to life – a dream of a palace and its "marble halls" could warn you of pomposity; one of an ivory tower could obviously be about remoteness and "untouchability".

Freud was not alone in suggesting that a house was a strong image of the human body with its various orifices, and this is an obvious possibility. Freud also considered that the climbing of stairs was always a sexual image, and in his view passages too had a sexual context. If you feel this may be a possible construction of your dream, consider the manner of your ascent: confident, frightened, difficult, easy . . . But it is worth remembering Freud's insistent emphasis on sex as a background to most dreams. It is possible to feel that dreams of rooms, passages or windows (which are extremely common), may well relate, like the buildings in your dreams, to different areas of your lives.

Many people dream of discovering new, empty rooms in houses that they know well – behind an existing cupboard door will be an undiscovered space. In our experience this has usually indicated that the dreamer is ready for a new intellectual challenge, ready to expand the mind in new direc-

tions, and deeply wanting (perhaps needing) to do so. The symbol of emptiness waiting to be filled is clear enough, and such a hint should be taken! See Julia Parker's series of dreams related on p. 56. Such a dream sequence is by no means uncommon, and tells us a great deal, adding to our confidence. Two buildings played an important part in Julia's dream: a huge warehouse and a beautiful building with artistic associations.

If doors in your dream house are firmly shut and cannot be opened, windows blacked out or bricked up, with notices saying NO ENTRY, you should ask yourself what is blocking your waking progress: it may be an element of your personality, or some basic inhibition. The no-go area could represent something to which you are not yet ready to face up: hammering on a door may symbolize a feeling of claustrophobia, or a need to break a pattern. Here, a sexual meaning is certainly possible; only you can decide whether this is likely.

Dreams of different rooms can relate to different areas of your waking life, according to the nature of the room: if you were in a kitchen, cooking, perhaps you are "cooking up" some plan? If you are in a prison cell, you may be feeling guilty, or feel that you should be punished for something. Finding yourself in a hospital room may hint that you need rest, though not necessarily medical treatment.

Dreams in which we are very conscious of exploring the interiors of buildings, interested in different rooms and their contents, almost always seem to be related to challenge and a need for fulfilment, with our personalities involved as thoroughly as our wish to be materially successful. They can tell us a lot about how we should approach the future, with reference to our need to conquer new worlds.

Colours

Research seems to show that most people dream in colour much of the time, but that it fades quickly from memory unless there is some special reason for remembering it. Sometimes a colour can strongly represent a person – someone perhaps who often wore it. And if a colour repeatedly occurs in a series of dreams, it is well worth spending some time working out to whom, or what, it is drawing your attention.

It is probably true that most people are not strongly conscious of the part colour plays in their dreams, and it has been suggested that undue attention to colour or lack of it can indicate, depending on the colours emphasized, either extraversion (if someone boasts of the glorious colours in their dreams) or introversion (if someone asserts they always dream in black and white). In general, people not keenly aware of colour in their waking lives may not "need" colourful dreams, while it seems that artists, or people to whom colour is important, are more likely to be aware of it. Ania Teilhard (in her *Le Symbolisme du rêve*, 1948) suggests that coloured dreams are evidence of great animation in the unconscious, and show special vitality in the dreamer.

Certainly many people are conscious of colour: they will dream of a vividly blue sky, a bright red dress, a deep black void, and colour does sometimes seem to place an additional emphasis on a particular dream symbol. Colour symbolism has a recognized history, and colours, it is claimed, are often related to the collective unconscious, so even the associations made by ancient or non-European cultures can be significant. See how these might apply to any strongly coloured symbols in your dreams. Here, as always, the *tone* of the dream is vital.

Red This is in general a positive colour, representing activity, joy, festivity, passion and sexual excitement. But blood lust, anger, vengeance, martyrdom and cruelty are also possible associations. The Hindus see red as representing the basic energy force of life, creativity and expansion; for the Mayas it presaged victory and success, and for the Chinese the joy, happiness and warmth of a benevolent sun. Christians have used red as symbolic of Christ on the Cross, but also of love, faith and power. In our time red often means danger, and says "Stop". A dream in which red plays a vital part may, then, be warning you; or may be suggestive of gaiety and vivacity.

Blue Inner spirituality, justice, truth, intellect, peace, chastity, magnanimity, piety have all been associated with the colour blue. In Christian cultures it is above all the colour of the Virgin Mary, the Queen of Heaven, the great mother figure, so fidelity, faith and eternity are also suggested. In dreams, it seems likely that blue as a predominant colour encourages us to slow down, relax, to be more meditative and contemplative.

Yellow Bright yellow represents the light of the sun – intuition, faith and pure goodness; American Indians and Hindus both think of it as the light of life, of immortality. But dark, muddy yellow symbolizes treachery, faithlessness, secrecy, betrayal, treason, avarice. Saffron yellow, in Buddhism, stands for renunciation, humility and lack of desire. There are powerful associations between yellow and the abstract idea of health, so you should relate dreams in which yellow plays a dominant part to your general wellbeing.

Green This is the colour of vegetation and of nature in its simplest forms. It is chiefly the colour of hope and gladness, paradise and abundance; at the same time it is the colour of unripe corn, of our naive "salad days, when we are green of judgment". So folly and innocence can also be symbolized. Vernal green is the colour of immortality, but also the colour of jealousy (associated too with the unseen supernatural forces of fairyland). In Chinese symbolism it is associated with "the beginning of great work", and so reassuring for anyone starting a new and important project.

Black and White Almost every culture associates white with a positive force, black with a negative one. In dreams, either may bear on any transformation or change which you are considering or for which your unconscious is preparing you. Black, the colour of protest, also represents a void, and in many cultures death and the underworld – and so, often, something "underhand". The white flag is the flag of surrender and truce, but white is also equated with simplicity, spiritual authority, chastity and the purification of the soul. A white-dominated dream may therefore suggest that you see yourself as "untouchable", distanced from problems.

Crowds

Dreams involving crowds are, on the whole, complex and difficult to explore, for they can involve many areas of our personalities. As usual, it is important to decide which of several possible trails to follow when starting to interpret the symbolism of such a dream, and as usual your own feelings are crucial. A very common emotion in such dreams is one of claustrophobia, of not being able to get away. This may have a direct reference to your lifestyle, or may relate to your age and to the emotions and expectations you associate with it.

You may be a busy wife and mother, almost entirely preoccupied with domestic chores, with looking after the children, but crying out for greater freedom of expression through the development of interests which are more intellectually demanding than your present role supplies. You may be a man at work at the same desk or bench every day, longing to be able to expand and grow, intellectually. Or you may be out of work, so that your days are boring and apparently useless, and you cannot escape from that depressing pattern. Within you are many people, and all of them, you feel, deserve a voice, room to move about and express themselves. The other selves which are now crowding your dreams may have taken some time to gather together and demand a voice, which is why such dreams tend to declare themselves in middle life, and may indeed be part of the menopause, male or female with all its stresses and changes.

On the other hand you may be much younger, and a natural rebel who for some reason cannot strike out against routine in the way you wish. In all these cases the crowd could represent the circumstances which are inhibiting self-expression, preventing escape. For the wife and mother, the busy businessman, the crowd will represent the many areas of the personality, the many abilities, which deserve attention and fulfilment. So they should think very hard about how they are spending their time and energy; the chances are that if they are to develop as persons they will have to make time for self-expression and the creation of new interests.

But of course dreaming of being one of a crowd may refer to a need to conform, and if you feel quite content being swept along with your fellows the chances are that in waking life conformity is your most natural means of being at peace with yourself – though other symbols within the dream may confirm or deny this, and you should concentrate not only on your own feelings in your dream, but on the attitude of the people around you, and what the crowd was actually doing. Sometimes crowd dreams relate to everyday problems, and the way in which we attempt to cope with them. A dream crowd in which we are helpless, which tramples over us, can be drawing attention to the fact that in waking life problems are getting on top of us, or that we are failing to put up a fight. A dream of an orderly crowd may again be speaking of conformity, or perhaps a need for the blessing of society (is the crowd actually a *congregation*?).

If the crowd seems to involve a team element, with everyone "pulling together", are you happy to be a part of this united effort – or are you trying to break away on your own? Are you basically a team man (or woman) or a loner?

If the crowd seems to suggest "the establishment", does it refer perhaps to your parents or someone in a position of authority – teachers, authorities at work or in society, and the way in which you are trying to relate to them or perhaps to impress them? Were you addressing the crowd, making a political speech, preaching? If so, begin to think of the dream as relating to your inner need for power over others. If the crowd was impressed, you may well be in a strong position to sway others, in your waking life, and perhaps you should exercise this capacity – you may be ready for more responsibility. But if the crowd is restive and unresponsive, may you be getting just a little pompous in your waking life? Delighting in addressing a large crowd may say something about your pleasure in gossip.

The reaction of the crowd may indeed be crucial, so try to think seriously about its behaviour and attitudes, especially if the dream may be about various facets of your personality, for then it may have helpful tips to offer on your future personal development. Think in a challenging and positive way about crowd dreams, allowing yourself room to move and breathe.

The Dream Alphabet

Your emotional response to the situation and symbols in your dreams may be crucial to interpretation; yet the emotions you feel in your dreams are virtually impossible to interpret in a reference section such as this. Before looking up the principal symbols in the following pages, then, consider how you felt about them. Pleased? Disappointed? Unhappy? Ecstatic? Frightened? Sexually aroused?

Since so many dreams sum up our waking feelings, the emotions we feel in them can put us on the right track when we turn to interpretation. You will not find adjectives in the A to Z section: it is for you to apply the appropriate adjective to your dream, as you consider the symbols and what they may mean. If in your dream your emotions seem to mirror those in your waking life, the dream is likely to be a reassuring one. If they are opposite – if you feel unhappy about a person whose company in waking life gives your pleasure, then perhaps the dream is inviting you to question your or their motives.

If on reading the entry under the chief symbol of your dream, and thinking about it, you come to the conclusion that the suggestions we make have no validity, but that there is some other significance – splendid! The purpose of this book is not to interpret your dreams for you, but to make you think about them in such a way as to come to your own conclusions; if these are arrived at only by a process of rejecting our suggestions, they have nevertheless been reached, and our purpose accomplished!

a

abandoned Had you been abandoned in your dream? If so, by whom? Someone you respect? That could suggest that some area of your personality is telling you to rid yourself of a problem. Rather differently, if you were "abandoned" in the sense of behaving in a loose manner, you may need to express yourself a little more freely.

abdicate Are you "giving up" something important in your waking life? If so, do you really want to do so, and is the sacrifice really worthwhile? Or is it being made on someone else's behalf? Were you forced to abdicate, or was it your own idea? Think very carefully about your decision.

abroad Was the country you visited in your dream pleasing? Were you excited by it, or apprehensive? The dream could be summing up your feelings about your attitude to life. If the country is strange to you, are you about to start some new project? There may be a suggestion that you are in need of a new challenge or stimulation. See LANDSCAPE (p. 68).

accident The accident in your dream may refer to some mistake in your waking life; think about the context of the accident, and try to connect it with any situation in which you are involved. The people involved in the dream accident may be significant. Are they, in waking life, likely to interfere with you or obstruct your progress? Be specially cautious should the dream situation occur in waking life.

acid Have you made any acid remarks lately? Acid is corrosive: is something "eating away" at you, or have you been making particularly biting attacks on someone? The dream may be suggesting that you externalize problems; perhaps you need to speak strongly to someone else.

acrobat Have you been showing off lately? Perhaps you are seeking approval from someone. Were you confident in your dream, or did you fall? If so, the dream could be a warning. Acrobatics and sexual intercourse can be linked; Freud suggested that children's delight in acrobatic performances "is a memory-image, often unconscious, of an observation of sexual intercourse, whether between humans or animals." In adults, there can be sensual memories of wrestling or acrobatic games between children. But it is often difficult and sometimes painful to make the connection between such images and our later, waking lives.

acting Are you "playing a part" – not entirely sincere – in a personal relationship? Acting could imply some form of pretence, and the dream may be telling you to be yourself. The part you were playing may be important – a hero, villain, or comedian. Is this how you see yourself, or do you feel forced into the characterization you assume in waking life? Do you long to remove the costume and make-up and "be yourself" rather than play some role? This is what the dream may be saying.

admiration Were you admiring someone, or were you the object of admiration? the dream may suggest you have become vain, or aspire to be like the person you are admiring. If you admire someone who in waking life you rather dislike they may perhaps have some qualities you would do well to adopt. See *hero/heroine*.

adventure What sort of adventure? Ask yourself whether *violence* was involved, or *romance*, or *sex*. And what was your attitude to it? Broadly speaking, is your daily life lacking in the quality expressed in the dream? Perhaps you need more adventure.

advice Whether you or another character in the dream was giving the advice, the chances are that this is your unconscious giving *you* some sensible instruction and counsel.

affair Did you enjoy this dream, or did you feel guilty? It could be encouraging you to improve your love and sex life; of course it could also be a warning. Perhaps some aspect of your life is getting out of hand, and you need to exercise more self-control. Or are you longing for greater freedom of expression?

age If you were younger, or older, in your dream, your unconscious may be telling you to be a little younger in heart and outlook, or, on the other hand, to be more sensible and worldly-wise. Maybe you should change the pace of your life. The time of day in dreams can represent the age of the dreamer, especially when a child – a quarter past five can mean the age of five years and three months. But dreams are timeless, and often a reasonable time-scale simply does not exist or matter.

air raid Are you being "got at" in some way? If you were in a shelter, are you being over-protective, or do you feel claustrophobic in any way? The dream could represent frustration, or others' aggression.

alarm This could, obviously, be a warning dream (see p. 58). What sort of alarm was it? Be cautious in whatever area your dream suggests.

altar The dream may not necessarily have anything to do with religion, but could refer to someone (or something) for whom you have great respect. Are you being more humble than necessary? It could be yourself you are offering on the altar! Or perhaps you need to develop humility. Maybe there is a pun here (see p. 50) suggesting you should change or "alter" something in your waking life.

angel See FLYING (p. 84).

anger The dream could goad you into being more assertive. If someone else was angry with you, he or she might represent an aspect of your character you dislike. Think about the way you feel towards the other person in real life. Does he or she represent the feminine/masculine side of your personality?

animals Dreams of animals often reflect our most basic instincts and reactions. In working on such dreams be sure to relate your conscious

angel *The angelic power*, Gustave Doré

a

feelings to the animal symbol, and make a particularly careful assessment of the dream as if *you* were the animal. Some animals give us love and affection, and in turn we express many basic instincts in looking after them. If you dream of your *pet*, it is important to remember this. You must decide how your feelings in the dream relate not only to your pet in real life, but also to people in your immediate circle. If you have children of your own, the animal in the dream could represent them, or indeed anyone close to you, or even someone you would *like* to be close to you. In which case perhaps you should begin to get to know that person better. *Herds* and flocks sometimes occur in dreams! Ask yourself if you were frightened or intimidated by them. If so, how does this relate to your friends' attitude to you? Are you simply doing what everyone else is doing, following a "herd instinct", going with the crowd? If so, your dream may be telling you to be more of an individual. Wild animals in a jungle may represent problems: were you hunting the animals? If so, the dream could be reflecting some kind of search – for perfection, perhaps, or excitement. Are you taking risks at present? See also FISH, FLESH AND FOWL (p. 88).

apartment See *rooms*.

apple In most Western cultures the apple is associated with the Fall of Adam and Eve in the Garden of Eden, and so with "sin" (by which sex is usually meant). A particularly delicious apple might suggest an acute sexual appetite, or that you are ready to taste the full fruits of life. Obviously there could be an association with anyone sharing the fruit with you. Jung noted that "the theft of an apple is a typical dream-symbol that occurs in many different variations in numerous dreams".

appointment Was your dream about keeping an appointment or breaking one? The person with whom you made the appointment could be important. Perhaps the dream is telling you to face up to your problems.

archaeology Is the dream telling you to consider or consult your own past? Or perhaps you are in a situation in which you could be about to make a mistake for the second time. Do you lack a pattern in your life? Archaeology digs up the past – perhaps you need to root out old problems. See Jung's dream (p. 23) for a detailed analysis.

arm See *body*.

argument An argument in your dream may be an inner debate between two aspects of your own personality, represented by yourself and another person. Try to remember who the other person was, and what he or she was like. Was it a parent, or someone for whom you have respect? Perhaps the dream is telling you to be sensible and practical, or scolding you for not asserting yourself, or trying to shake you up in some way.

armour Maybe there is something you are protecting yourself against. Are you about to do battle in some way? Or perhaps, in taking precautions, you are concerned with acquiring greater confidence and security. The dream could be reassuring.

arrest Were you arrested? You may feel guilty about something; or possibly the dream is telling you to stop. If you were making an arrest, is there someone of whose actions you disapprove, or someone whom you think should be warned?

arrow A male sexual symbol, of course – Cupid's arrows are swift and deadly! So who were you shooting at, or who was aiming his bow at you? But there are other possibilities: are you putting ideas to other people? If so, try to remember if the arrows in your dream were on target or landing in unknown territory. Were you shooting at a person or at an object? Perhaps you are trying to rid yourself of something you dislike.

artist Were you painting a picture? Perhaps you are seeing your problems as clearly as the painting represents its subject – or as unclearly, if it is a bad picture. Do you think the dream is telling you to be more creative?

ashes It is certainly possible that this could be a very depressing image indeed: dead, lifeless, grey ashes. But were you raking out dead ashes, ready to light a new and spirited fire? If so, like dreams of DEATH (see p. 76), this could be a symbol of a new beginning as much as of a dead past. On the other hand, you may be trying to rake up the past. Has some aspect of your life disintegrated? Have you just ended some phase or relationship?

audition

Sarah dreamed: *"Someone invited me to play Principal Girl in a pantomime at the London Palladium. I was pleased, but thought they were crazy. At the hotel where the audition was held, I could not find the right room, but finally saw through a glass door another girl being auditioned for the part. She was not very good, failing pathetically to improvise dance-steps to some lively music. She then made a mess of Hamlet's 'To be or not to be . . .' I knew I could do better, was encouraged by those who had invited me to apply, and eventually got the part."*

At the time of the dream Sarah was learning to play a musical instrument which she found very difficult. She decided she was both girls in the dream, which mirrored exactly her ambiguous feelings about the new interest. Her stronger, more assertive and confident inner self "got the part", and this encouraged her to continue her studies with renewed confidence. Note the presence of authority figures who invited her to contend, reassuring but also testing her.

astronaut The dream may be encouraging you to be more ambitious, to "reach for the stars" in some way. Were you in a spacecraft? How secure did you feel? If you felt inspired and uplifted, this could mean spiritual progress in waking life. Do you want to "take off", or to escape from reality?

audition See *Dream Analysis*.

automobile See *car*.

autumn Dreams about autumn, the falling of the leaves, are often related to the approach of old age, or one's fears about this. They tend to occur in middle life. Such dreams, though often melancholy, are rarely deeply sad, and seem to be offering reconciliation with the idea of age as part of the natural cycle of nature.

avarice See *money*.

axe Are you "for the chop", about to lose your job? It may be that your unconscious suggests you should cut yourself off from something.

baby See *child*.

back Consider the possibility of some physical ailment in your back. Or perhaps there may be a suggestion that you are not sufficiently forward-looking in your waking life. Are you tending to live in the past? Was your back bare? If so, did you feel insecure (see CLOTHES AND NUDITY p. 82)? Are you receiving sufficient "back-up" from partner or friends? If your back was breaking under a burden, perhaps you are coping with too many responsibilities. Are you sufficiently aware of what might be going on behind your back? Or perhaps you have some reason to feel specially pleased with yourself, i.e., a "pat on the back"?

backwards Was everything moving away from you? Did you take some kind of retrograde step in your dream? If so, your dream may be telling you to hold back from some current decision or action, or else that you are shrinking from some element of your waking life that must be faced.

badge Was this being pinned on you? And for what? Have you done something recently of which you are particularly proud? Are you about to identify yourself with some new interest or cause? See *medal, investiture, honour*.

bag Were you putting articles "in the bag"? Are you in waking life putting things aside, or perhaps gathering up knowledge? Or perhaps some "old bag" is involved in all this. Your dream may be telling you that you are not looking as good or as young as you could be!

bake See *cooking*.

balance If you were performing some sort of balancing trick, did you feel secure or insecure? Did you actually lose your balance? Perhaps your dream relates to your sense of judgment at present. Is someone else's life, or your own, "in the balance" in some way? Or are you faced with an important decision?

baldness Women: have you suffered a lack of self-respect lately? If your head had been shaved in the dream, are you ashamed of some recent action? Men: did the dream depress you, relating to your fears of lack of virility, or increasing age? And see *hair*.

ball If you were playing ball, the dream, particularly for men, may have a sexual connotation. Were you enjoying yourself, or shrinking from a fast bowler or pitcher? Was your skill being applauded, or were you always dropping catches? Think about your sex life in the light of the dream. Is it successful, rewarding, fulfilling, or are you missing out?

ballet See *dance*.

balloon If a balloon escaped your grasp, perhaps you are allowing good ideas to escape you. If you let it go, and admired its flight, you are perhaps on the edge of an intellectual breakthrough. If it burst – forget it! Was it a "hot air" balloon, and might that relate to your thinking?

band Were you playing in one? Perhaps you have been "blowing your own trumpet" lately, or perhaps the dream may be encouraging you to do so. In waking life, are you feeling tied down or restricted, unable to play your own tune? Or were you the only one out of tune?

bandage Did you feel the bandages were constricting, or protective? Apart from the suggestion that some part of your body needs care and attention, the dream may refer to someone (perhaps yourself) who is being over-protective.

bank The dream could well be reassuring, unless your waking attitude to banks is apprehensive. Are you beginning to store up experience? Perhaps you are feeling more secure, both emotionally and financially. If you had an overdraft, or were robbing a bank, perhaps you are drawing too heavily on the resources of family and friends.

bankrupt If you felt ashamed and degraded, is anything happening to you in waking life that has the same effect – and might it be the result of your "over-spending" in some way? If in the dream you were despairing, you may have been overworking, or expending too much energy so that your resources are drained. Perhaps you should recoup those losses.

banquet See FOOD AND DRINK (p. 86).

baptism Are you committing yourself to something of great importance? The dream may be reassuring you that you are ready to do so. Or perhaps you are making a new beginning.

bar Perhaps this could be a punning dream suggesting that something is coming between you and what you really want to do with your life. Are you feeling held back from something good? On the other hand, if you were drinking or ordering drinks at a bar, perhaps you are currently making plans or reaching decisions. Or if you were refused a drink, you may not be ready to move ahead.

barn See ENVIRONMENT (p. 92).

baseball See *sport*.

basket The contents of the basket will probably be the important image in the dream. But possibly you could be the basket itself, the dream commenting on your protective instinct or attitude towards investment. Have you put all your eggs in one basket? The dream may suggest you should be more self-contained. Perhaps the basket gave way under the strain. If so, are you under pressure at present?

bat (cricket or baseball) A bat is a possible phallic symbol, and it should be fairly obvious whether this was so in your dream. Were you delighted by your skill with it, or upset because you could not hit the ball? Did you even break it? See *sport*.

bath If you were rigorously cleaning yourself, perhaps there is something distasteful in your waking life which you wish to rid yourself of. Warmth and comfort seems to suggest escapism. WATER (p. 80) is also involved, and may relate to the womb, so perhaps your dream hints that you are trying to escape from reality and your problems.

bats Bats often inspire fear, and tradition says that the fear is of the bats getting tangled in your hair – and *hair* is a potent sexual symbol. There is usually a claustrophobic element (bats tend to live in caves, in darkness). You may be afraid to face some element in your emotional life.

battle Did you win or lose the battle? Perhaps you are putting up some sort of fight for your rights. Is someone trying to take advantage of you. Maybe you should be more (or less) aggressive. Decide whether the dream is warning you or trying to strengthen your confidence.

bear Perhaps this was a punning dream on the burdens you have to bear at present? How are you bearing up under them? Do you want to bare your heart in some way? See *animals*.

beard Men who dream of their beards being cut off may have a castration fear, or other anxiety; for women, a dream of growing a beard may refer

b

bats from *Los Caprichos*, Francisco Goya

to something unpleasant entering their consciousness. How did you cope with the situation in your dream?

bed Sometimes the physical state of the bed and bedclothes can prompt a dream (see p. 20). But there may be a punning application: are you putting some project "to bed"? If you dreamed of being in a comfortable bed, you can probably "rest assured" about a problem preoccupying you. The bed can also sometimes represent escape. See *bath*; the symbolism could be similar.

bedfellow A dream about being in bed with someone need not be sexual, unless that element is overt. It may be a dream about partnership, or it may relate to some inner conflict, in which the bedfellow represents an element.

bees Busy bees may be a reference to the pace of your present work; perhaps you enjoy being very busy, but consider whether you are achieving as much as you could in view of the amount of time and energy you are spending. You could be over-concerned about some serious problem, perhaps imagining that it is more important than it really is – i.e., there is a bee in your bonnet. Remember the old superstition that you have to tell the bees the latest news; are you missing out on something going on around you? See *hive*.

beggar What is lacking in your life? Maybe you are crying out for something – love and affection, perhaps. The beggar probably represents some part of you or an aspect of your life.

bell A tolling church bell often symbolizes death in Western belief, and may represent loss or deprivation. But bells can also be joyful. If you were ringing a bell, it seems likely that you are being prompted to spread some kind of news or attract attention in some way.

belt If the belt was tight, it suggests a sign of constriction. What are you "keeping in" and why? If it fails to keep your trousers up, see CLOTHES AND NUDITY (p. 82).

bet The dream may be commenting on your attitude to risk-taking. If you won the bet you are probably confident; if you lost, perhaps you should be cautious or try to develop more self-confidence. But what are the stakes?

bigamy Are you nursing some guilt complex, perhaps about relatives? The dream could warn of complications ahead, perhaps especially if you are engaged in an illicit affair. Your unconscious may be saying, you can't have it both ways.

birds Obviously a great deal depends on the type of bird in your dream, but equally much depends on whether you were menaced by them, whether you saw a flock or a single bird, whether they were free or caged, and if the latter whether they were in an airy aviary or a cramped, undersized cage. These are all questions you should answer, remembering, as always, to put yourself in the position of the bird or birds if that seems a possible solution. In waking life, are you "caged" in some way? Are you the "bird in the gilded cage"; possessing everything you want except the freedom you crave, unable to express your independent spirit? Are you rather happy to be in a cage, secure from the restlessness of the world, pleased to be constricted within the physical and mental home erected around you by your family or other contemporaries – the flock? Or if the birds in your dream were free, did you admire and envy that freedom? Maybe the antics of the birds delighted you; if so, perhaps you are being rather "flighty" in waking life. Smaller, garden birds may well be related to your home and family life. Were you feeding them? See FISH, FLESH AND FOWL (p. 88).

birth A dream of giving birth may mean you should take a pregnancy test! But, of course, you could be giving birth to an idea, or starting a new project which will be "your baby". The dream is underlining the fact, and prompting you to nurture and care for it, helping it to develop in the way you want it to go. You may not as yet have given your idea consciousness, a separate life of its own, and the dream may then be of pregnancy leading to birth. But perhaps you were attending a birth, or were even the midwife. If so, the new inspiration could still be your own, but the dream may also be inviting you to help out with someone else's project or idea, or represent a cry for help of some other kind. Some dreams are of being born, and if so perhaps you are about to make a new start in waking life. See BIRTH, DEATH AND CHANGE (p. 76).

bite Have you "bitten off more than you can chew" in waking life? Or if you bit your tongue, have you been speaking out unwisely or prematurely? What you were biting is obviously significant – and if you were bitten, who or what bit you. *Fear* and antagonism could be elements.

black Blackness, darkness, very often relates to ignorance, so think about your attitude during the dream – were you attempting to find your way through it? With success? Or were you entirely lost? Perhaps there is some important area of your waking life where you have insufficient knowledge or confidence. And see also COLOURS (p. 94).

blessing This may well be encouragement from the unconscious, or approval, or a go-ahead for some action.

blind Not to be able to see one's way in a dream (see *black*) can be very frightening, but it is usually a constructive warning: you may be losing your sense of direction in waking life (think of the circumstances of the dream). Are you blinded by the effect of someone else on you?

blonde If you are a woman, but not blonde, were you admiring one in your dream? Dark-haired women sometimes, consciously or unconsciously, equate blondes with success and glamour. So is some specific blonde your ideal or dream woman? Are you thinking of becoming a blonde in real life, and changing your image? Maybe this dream is focusing on your true aspirations, telling you how far you got in achieving them. Did it come to a satisfactory conclusion, or did you wake up before you actually reached the climax? If you are a man, the blonde may also represent some non-sexual object, something (as well as someone) which you need to possess.

blood Blood is above all the symbol of life, energy, vitality – so if it is in the context of illness, do not ignore this. Women sometimes dream of blood if they start to menstruate while asleep. If blood is flowing from you, perhaps you in waking life are feeling "drained", and should look for ways of conserving energy. If the blood in your dream frightened you, are you in waking life afraid to face up to facts, or to some conclusion about "life", particularly your own? The dream may relate to some very basic principle with which you are having to deal. Are you channel-ling your energy as positively as you might? Are you in control of what is going on in your life? (blood sometimes symbolizes inner truth; consider this, especially if you couldn't stop the blood flowing). Blood flowing from others may indicate a cry for help, spiritual, emotional or corporeal. Blood as part of a dream of *violence* is another matter.

blow Were you blowing something in your dream (see *band*)? Perhaps it was a violent dream in which you were dealing someone a blow. Or, if you received the blow, perhaps you have had to cope with a shock of some kind. If a wind was blowing, are you trying to speed up the pace of resolution of some issues in your life?

boat Depending on your state of mind during the dream, you may be "all at sea", happily cruising, or "rocking the boat". You may have felt secure, but perhaps your boat was leaking. Were you mending it? If so, what are you trying to make good or patch up in your waking life? Ask yourself if you are under any heavy emotional stress at present, in stormy waters, or just drifting with the tide. See WATER (p. 80).

body Dreams of various parts of our bodies belong into a category of their own. Often the dream may do no more than refer to a physical position you have got into during sleep, causing pressure or discomfort in the affected part. But a dream that some part of your body is in pain may well be a warning of some physical problem, even before it is medically observable (see p. 58). Such "warning dreams" are often based on information stored in the unconscious.

bomb Is a bomb about to go off in some way in your emotional life? Or perhaps the dream symbolized a need for survival, or a bleakness "after the bomb". Alternatively, you may need to take explosive action. See DISASTERS (p. 72).

books Ask yourself if you were interested or bored by the book or books in your dream. A reference book may be telling you to "refer" to past experiences. Or perhaps you are learning a great deal about yourself at this particular time. Is the dream warning you to take your present situation more seriously? If you were in a library, were you intimidated by being there? The dream may be suggesting that you fill in some gaps in your education. If you felt confident and knowledgeable, and were searching for a specific book, how does that fit in with your waking life? A single book may possibly symbolize the Book of Life – wisdom, learning, revelation.

b

boot Are you being kicked around, or kicking someone else? Or perhaps the dream was telling you that you are getting "too big for your boots". Were you confidently striding out in your boots? You may have been "given the boot" in waking life, or perhaps fear the possibility of it? There also is a strong connection between footwear and sexuality. Were these sexy boots? If so, was the dream referring to exhibitionism? See CLOTHES AND NUDITY (p. 82).

bottle It is possible that you are "bottling up" your emotions or opinions. The dream may be encouraging you to release them. Perhaps it was describing prudence and foresight on your part, especially if you were storing bottles or bottling fruit! If they were wine bottles, the dream might refer to sexual over-indulgence?

bough Did it snap? The dream could be warning that you are taking on too much. Are you emotionally insecure at present?

boundary Perhaps your dream is saying "thus far and no further". Or are you accepting unnecessary restrictions on your freedom of thought and action?

box Were you shut in the box? If so, it was a dream about restriction, being boxed in. But perhaps you were opening it. If so, what was in it – something pleasant or unpleasant? The dream may refer to some aspect of your character. Why were you taking the things out of the box? Try to relate them to your waking life. Was the box rather like Pandora's, one which contained a secret not to be revealed? Are you involved in some sort of cover-up? Perhaps the dream is questioning your approach and motives.

bread See FOOD AND DRINK (p. 86).

breakage Try to remember your feelings during the dream, whether you were having a rewarding, or somewhat violent smash-up. Perhaps you are thinking of ending a relationship, or a phase in your life. Were things collapsing and breaking around you, while you were in no position to do anything about the situation? This may sum up in some way your present position. Are you in a "state of collapse" or "near breaking-point"? The dream could be warning you that you are perhaps living and working under more strain than you realize.

bride Women: if you are single, this may be a wish-fulfilment dream. Or have you some feeling that you are "pure" or "untouchable"? Could

the dream relate to your virginity, real or not? Men: Who was the bride? Someone inaccessible? Or a "bride of Christ" or similar virgin figure? Did someone prevent the marriage? The dream could be saying something important about your attitude to women, and how it might be changed.

bridge Is your present life in a state of transition? Ask yourself whether the bridge was secure, and whether you crossed it confidently. Or perhaps you were about to throw yourself off it (see FLYING, p. 84). Another possibility is that you are trying to bring two elements of your life together, bridging some gap. The dream could well assess your real attitude to the problem. If you were playing bridge, how did your partner react? Are you making some kind of deal, or putting some proposition to others? What sort of hand had you? There could be a clue here to your present situation, see *cards, gambling*.

broadcast Dreams about giving or receiving messages are always interesting and sometimes important. Have you something you want to tell the world? Are you desperate to speak out, to make your voice heard? See *messages*.

brother See *family*.

bubbles Light-hearted ideas, pleasure, fun – but how disappointed were you when they burst? See *balloon*.

buds The symbolic growth of your personality might be the unconscious's message here, a certain unfolding or development, a flowering. If the buds faded, maybe you need to work on the weaker elements of your personality.

bug see *insect*.

buildings see ENVIRONMENT (p. 92).

bulb Plant bulbs: see *buds* – but perhaps the reference here is to material growth. Electric light bulbs: does the dream refer to some sudden awareness – to your "seeing the light" in some way? Are you "switched on" or off?

bull The bull obviously often has strong masculine sexual connotations. Are you trying to strike up a sexual relationship with someone new? If so, are you perhaps being too forceful? Is your sex life as rewarding as it might be? Are you even somewhat obsessed with sex? Were you frightened by a bull in your dream? Don't forget that "bullshit" can refer to something worthless, silly, objectionable. See *animal*.

bulldozer A warning dream, maybe. Are you less caring than you should be? Bulldozing your way through life? Or is someone crushing *you*?

buoy Could this refer to some hope or eventual security? Are you trying to keep yourself optimistic?

burden If you were ridding yourself of one, the dream may be prompting you to relinquish some responsibility. If you were happy about it, fine – the dream is reassuring you. If it was too heavy, maybe you are too involved.

burglar Check the security of your home! Alternatively, the dream may be saying that you are taking too much from others, in some way, or vice versa. What have you to lose? Try to recall the other characters in your dream.

bush Were you hiding in it? If so, are you evading some issue in waking life? Alternatively, if the bush was flowering, this may be a symbol of personality development.

business Dreams of a business in which you are involved may relate to your private life and its problems. The people you are dealing with in the dream may represent aspects of your own personality. Is the dream telling you to be more cunning, clever, cautious, daring? Have you something to sell? Are you making the most of your abilities? Ready to take some risk? Searching for security in your waking life? Was the business in your dream thriving, or failing? Or is the dream commenting on the pace of your life, its general busy-ness?

butcher As always, the mood and circumstances of the dream are all-important. Were you buying from a butcher, or engaged in butchery? If the latter, are you "carving up" someone, or engaged in some fairly vicious plot? If you are buying meat, your body may be crying out for more protein. What meat were you buying, and what does that animal represent to you?

butter Nutritious, rich, even luxurious, butter may represent the good and sensual things of life. Was there plenty of it, or did you have to spread it thin? The dream could relate to a longing for pleasure, or a lack of it. The colour of the butter may be significant: was it a really rich *yellow* (see p. 94)? Or was it rancid?

butterfly If the accent is on lightness and prettiness, is the dream warning you that you are being too superficial or flirtatious? If you are hunting a butterfly, you may be in search of a little more fun in your life; catching and killing it may suggest that you feel you are too superficial in some area of life. Mounting a butterfly may have a sexual significance for a male – not only possibly rape, but capture and repression (the butterfly is dead). A butterfly is something beautiful that emerges from something ugly: is the dream persuading you to change your life in some positive way?

button Are you tightly buttoned-up, or unbuttoned? There seems almost certainly to be an emphasis on your general psychological attitude. If the buttons restrict you, perhaps you should relax more; if they barely hold your clothes together, maybe to the point of *embarrassment*, perhaps a little more formality would be no bad thing. If you are sewing on a button for someone else, perhaps there is someone who needs assistance.

buying What are you buying? Was it in stock? Or "coming in soon"? Or unobtainable? Perhaps you are awaiting developments in some area of your life, buying time in some way. If the purchase was satisfactory, the dream was probably signalling inner approval of some recent transaction or decision. But any unease or delay, or the feeling that you have overspent, may indicate that you have doubts, that you have bought rather more than you can cope with; even a sense of guilt, i.e., are you in some way "buying someone" with gifts or praise?

C

cabaret The enormous success of the film *Cabaret* suggests that almost anyone dreaming of this kind of entertainment has in mind something rather *louche* and *risqué*. Are you in waking life too intent on sensual satisfaction? Or, if you were really enjoying yourself with a sense of release, should you be giving more time to this kind of relaxation? Check your mood.

cabin The sea is an extremely potent symbol (see WATER, p. 80), and if you are in a ship's cabin, closed away, it may be that you are in waking life hiding in some way from what it represents, perhaps some emotional element in your life. If there is a storm, and you are feeling frightened and disturbed, you may be taking refuge in waking life from some situation which causes you concern – it may be, from some display of emotion, or from a situation in which emotion might be called for. Get up on deck and feel free!

cactus Cacti are pretty but prickly! There may well be a sexual implication, for the cactus is almost too obviously a phallic symbol. The cactus possibly had a nice flower, but you may have been afraid to touch it because of a fear of being hurt. Cacti flower and fade very suddenly: are there implications of potency here for a male dreamer? Alternatively, are you, in waking life, in a prickly situation?

café FOOD AND DRINK (see p. 86), and a choice of it, may sometimes suggest a dream about decision-making and discrimination, though there is often a connection between food and sex, the satisfaction of desires. What choices confront you in waking life? Is there a suggestion of waste? If you own the café, what have you in stock – on offer? Is your café busy, or empty?

cage Restriction, inhibition, being prevented from leading your life as you would wish to live it, are all possibilities if you are a prisoner. Some area of your personality is perhaps crying out for release, for free expression. Since you are in a cage rather than a prison, your public image seems in question: is someone "keeping you in your place"? But perhaps you feel secure in your cage? Or are you imprisoning someone? Characters in the dream are, as always, very significant. But the prisoner could still be yourself: a sexual partner may represent the sexual aspect of your life, an employer your working life, and so on . . .

cake "A slice of cake" could refer to a particular aspect of your personality, how you express yourself to others, how you share out your life and energy. Or perhaps you were greedy for more cake, or just the icing. Are you trying to have your cake and eat it? The dream may hint at selfishness – unless you were baking for others.

calendar Dreams symbolize *time* in many ways. Are you concerned about how time is flying, or even running out? What date was on the calen-dar? Did it represent the past, present or future? The symbol may be imposing a time scale or setting the context for other events or actions.

camera Cameras in dreams seem almost always to represent oneself ("I am a camera"), the view through the lens being perhaps more detached than a view through the naked eye. So dreaming of photographing something or someone may well indicate a desire to see it or them more detachedly, less emotionally, than we are able to do in waking life – to get a situation or a person really in focus. If the camera failed to work properly, or the picture did not "come out", you may be avoiding an issue.

camp Out of doors and in natural surroundings, a happy dream of a summer camp may indicate a need for relaxation, a change of scene, or for more freedom than you may have in your working life. Unhappiness, homesickness or loneliness may be associated emotions, however, and may relate to family life and the feeling that you are being shut out from it.

can If in the dream you were opening a can, you could well be into a period of self-discovery (though what if it was a can of worms?) Or there may be a punning aspect to the dream, probably reassuring – i.e., you *can* do it.

cancer A dream that you are suffering from the disease is by no means premonitory (though if you are uneasy, get a check-up). A cancer is a "growth", and the dream may refer to something unpleasant attaching itself to you – a fast-growing obsession, for instance, which may be having a malignant effect on your personality. Is some aspect of your waking life posing a threat to your wellbeing and happiness?

candle Obviously a possible phallic symbol, but also a symbol of wisdom and understanding. The flame or absence of it is probably significant. If you are a man, was your candle burning brightly, or guttering out? This is possibly a reference to your hopes or fears about your potency. Otherwise, is your religious faith in question? If the candle went out, leaving you in darkness, this may be a hint that you should study more deeply a subject that means much to you.

cane Any dream of a cane is likely to refer to aggression of one sort or another. Who was being caned? If it was you, who was doing the caning? Someone who may want to put you in your place in waking life? Or someone about whom you feel guilty, and who might want to punish you? If you

C

were using the cane, it may have been on someone for whom you feel contempt or anger; their reaction will be significant, especially since you will be in the character of a father figure; and in that case, the dream will be of power.

cannon Who was shooting at whom? As a weapon, the cannon obviously suggests a dream of antagonism. But possibly the suggestion here is that you are "going great guns"! Freud, of course, believed the cannon to be a phallic symbol. See *gun*.

captive See *prison, cage*.

car Being in the driving seat suggests control, confidence. But what if you were in an *accident* or *collision*? Ask yourself if there was a destination, or what kind of *road* you were driving along. See *chauffeur, driving*.

cards Playing cards suggest chance, but also skill. Were you playing against someone – someone with whom you are in competition in waking life? How did the game go? Does the dream suggest you should not rely too much on luck? See *gambling*.

caretaker Were you looking after a building? If so, what did that building represent (see ENVIRONMENT, p. 92)? If someone else was the caretaker, could it have been someone who may be in some way shaping your life, keeping an eye on or taking care of you?

carnival A dream to enjoy, if you were just having fun: maybe it reflected your natural enjoyment of life at present. But if you were looking on, and felt left out, life could perhaps be passing you by. See CROWDS (p. 96).

carpenter Are you "making enough of yourself" – of your personal attributes? If you are a man, and were making something for something else, remember that sharp tools can have a sexual connotation. If you are a Christian, could there be a reference to spirituality, to Christ the carpenter?

carpet Was the carpet beautiful, or useful, or just worn-out? Walking along a carpet could refer to your progress – are you apprehensive about your next move, either because it seems too ambitious or just another shuffle in someone else's well-worn steps? On the other hand, there could be a feeling that you are facing trouble – "on the carpet", in some way. What would be the best way of coping with this?

carry See *burden*. But if your arms were aching in your dream, check for muscular or rheumatic pains. And see *body*.

carving What were you carving? A large cake, or joint, could refer to sensual pleasure (but also see *butcher*). If you were making sculpture, was it of someone? If a "graven image" is there someone – or something – you idolize? The dream may simply suggest you should be more creative.

castle Are you being over-idealistic, building "castles in the air"? Alternatively, remember the saying: "A man's home is his castle". But also see ENVIRONMENT (p. 92).

cat To many people there can be something mysterious and even slightly uncanny about a cat (after all, they were traditional companions of witches). But they are also highly sensual creatures: could the cat in the dream represent a beautiful object of desire? Was it purring and contented? Were you fondling it? If it was showing its claws and snarling perhaps your unconscious is suggesting that you should be more assertive in waking life. Or perhaps it was a criticism – have you been "catty" recently? See FISH, FLESH AND FOWL (p. 88).

cathedral The dream could obviously relate to your religious beliefs, or objects of respect and reverence. Could the building be a symbol of someone or something you find particularly inspiring or admirable? Perhaps there is a suggestion that you need spiritual development and security (see ENVIRONMENT p. 92).

cattle Are you "one of the herd"? The dream may suggest that you should develop your individuality, and care less about what others think. See *herd, animals*.

cave A cave is an obvious symbol of female sexuality Alternatively, perhaps you were sheltering from someone or something. Were you reassured? You may be in need of greater support or security; but consider too how good or how bad you are at facing life's present problems.

cellar The dream may be encouraging you to go in for self-analysis – to see what is in the basement (see Jung's dream, p. 23). Think about your basic drives; perhaps you could uncover some rich potential. What was in the cellar? Maybe something unexpected. If you were afraid, in your dream, was it of the dark, of the unknown areas of possibility in your life?

cement A reference to consolidation? Of a friendship, your finances, or in your career?

cemetery Sometimes we dream of our own grave, a dream which may refer to lost opportunities or "dead" plans or projects. Were the dead rising from their graves? Give yourself another chance in some area of your life. But of course, this could simply be a mourning dream.

cesspit The symbolism of dreams can be very direct. Are you "in the shit" in some way?

chain If you were in shackles, the dream may refer to drudgery in your everyday life. On the other hand, if your chain was of rich gold, perhaps you enjoy your present commitments. Was there a weak link which broke? Examine your present plans minutely! Or maybe you are working less thoroughly than you should.

chair See *seat*.

chalice Rich in symbolic meaning, this dream image is associated with the heart, and in Christian myth contains the blood of Christ. Were you offered a chalice in your dream? If so, you could be on the brink of considerable psychological development or inner contentment. Perhaps you should consider your religious beliefs. The chalice may represent the Holy Grail: are you searching for something to give your life greater meaning?

chalk A piece of chalk could have an association of schooldays with teacher and blackboard. Have you recently come through a learning experience, or perhaps you need a lesson? Are you seeing "the writing on the wall"?

champagne Do you need more fun, pleasure, luxury, excitement in your life? Or is the dream warning you of too much concentration on those elements, or of over-indulgence and even perhaps extravagance?

chapel See *church*, ENVIRONMENT (p. 92).

chasm Falling into a chasm could represent some trap you see ahead of you, but may be disregarding; it could represent depression or other negative feelings. You could be about to take some kind of leap which is risky, but might provide a solution: did you land safely?

chastity Is the dream making a statement about you and your attitude to sex, or telling you that you simply "don't want to know" about some problem? Perhaps you feel you should "keep clean", stay uninvolved.

chauffeur If someone else was the driver, did he or she represent some helpful friend giving you guidance at present? Or if you were at the wheel, are you helping to steer the course of someone else's life in some way? Was the drive smooth, risky, too fast. See *car*, *driving*.

cheat Who was cheating? If you, did you feel smug or guilty? This could be a warning dream. Obviously, your feelings and attitudes during the dream are the key to its meaning here.

cheering Have you gained additional self-confidence recently? Your unconscious obviously approved of something about you, whether you were cheering or being cheered!

cheese Is the dream suggesting economy (cheese-paring)? Was it "hard cheese", inviting you to make the best of things? And see FOOD AND DRINK (p. 86).

chicken Are you "chickening out" of some option? Are you over-concerned about your partner, children, friends and in danger of being a "clucking hen"?

child Consider the circumstances of the dream carefully. Did the child represent yourself, or some immature aspect of your personality? Did you love and nurture the child, watching it develop, or did you scorn it? Was the child desperately trying to get away from you, or to attract your attention? Perhaps the child symbolizes a developing idea or concept. If so, how healthy was it? Do you want children? If so, this could well be a wish-fulfilment dream of a very straightforward kind.

chimney An external chimney may be a phallic symbol; the inside of it, a symbol of female sexuality. If you are male, and were frightened by the darkness of a chimney, this may indicate

C

fear of sex. But perhaps you were climbing it. If there was a glowing fire in the chimney, the sexual probability is strengthened.

chocolate Maybe a wish-fulfilment dream, if you are on a diet! But the dream could be commenting in general on your attitude to luxury and good living. The colour may be significant, perhaps representing a dark-skinned man or woman. See FOOD AND DRINK (p. 86).

choir Heavenly, or otherwise? Harmony or discord? And how does this relate to your waking life? There may be something you want to join in, or simply enjoy observing or listening to in a detached, uncommitted way.

choking There is a possibility that someone or something is blocking your progress in waking life. Alternatively, a part of your body may be affected. See *body*.

chopping Probably a dream of antagonism, but there could be a punning element. Are you trying to cut problems down to size?

Christ The dream may, obviously, be commenting on your religious beliefs; but consider whether the Christ figure may relate to a living human being – your father, perhaps, or a father-figure. In principle, an encouraging, reassuring dream; perhaps you have recently learned humility. This is by no means necessarily a sacred revelation, though in historical times it was often considered so.

Dream Analysis

child

On March 6, 1815, Mary Shelley, the poet's wife, found her baby dead. Two weeks later, she recorded in her diary:
"Dream that my little baby came to life again; that it had only been cold, and that we rubbed it before the fire, and it lived. Awake and find no baby. I think about the little thing all day . . ."

Mary Shelley's unconscious may have been trying to reassure her of her baby's immortality (Shelley himself was an atheist). The fire symbol seems important; probably a reference to rebirth – she would have been familiar with the Phoenix myth.

Christmas Sentimentality apart, a dream of a cosy traditional Christmas may well be asserting strong traditional values, family unity, general friendliness and good humour, generosity, optimism. Could it be dropping a hint that you should be less Scrooge-like? Are you, in waking life, preoccupied with your childhood, or otherwise nostalgic? If there was a reference to presents, this may be a statement about experience gained or good advice offered or received. Think about the nature of any gifts in your dream. There could be a focus on cold, loneliness and lack of feeling – especially if you dislike Christmas, or resent the hypocrisy of those who ignore the less fortunate while tucking into their own food and wine.

church The dream could be saying something about your beliefs and faith. But if you were specially inspired by the beauty, loftiness and dignity of the church, there could be a reference to admired psychological characteristics (see ENVIRONMENT, p. 92). Your personality as a whole, and your potential, may be in question. Perhaps you are capable of further achievements, given greater faith in yourself? Are you in need of greater support? Have you sins to confess, or to be forgiven?

churchyard A rather more traditional symbol than that of the *cemetery*, Wandering among unknown graves suggests a search for something. Your own identity? Or simply new challenges? The age of the churchyard may suggest the support of past experience.

cinema What film was showing? Try to refer it to your own life at present. Was the audience enjoying it? Could you see the screen (your motives) clearly? Were you acting in the film? – if so, are you "putting on an act", and not entirely true to yourself? See *acting, theatre*.

circle The circle, or *mandala*, is a strong symbol of wholeness; if it was complete, the dream could be making an important and very positive statement about your own wholeness and self-containment. If it was imperfect or incomplete, perhaps the dream is suggesting you should work on yourself, explore your personality.

circus If the circus ring was strongly featured, see *circle* and *mandala*. If it was crowded with performers, is too much going on in your life at the moment? What was your reaction to the various acts? Are you "clowning around" a little too much? Or in danger, walking a tight-rope? Are you the caged animal or the ringmaster?

city Were you lost, or was the city well-known to you? Are you reaching important decisions in your waking life, seeking greater order, or to compartmentalize your life in some way? Was city life crowding in on you? Consider simplifying your schedules and lifestyle. But perhaps the city was orderly and prosperous: a statement perhaps relating to self-satisfaction. See ENVIRONMENT (p. 92).

class Many people dream of finding themselves back in a class at school. Perhaps this was a nostalgic dream about your classmates at school or college. Was the dream rebuking boastfulness, warning you not to try to appear to be someone or something you are not? Are you getting out of your depth in some way? But dreams of social class may refer to inferiority or superiority complexes.

claw It depends on the animal whose claw featured, and its attitude. There could be a reference to "clawing back", to someone or something draining your emotional or physical resources, or holding you back.

clay If you were moulding clay, perhaps you are trying to give new shape to your life or personality. Any object you were trying to make may refer to an aspect of yourself, or some characteristic of another person whom you are trying to influence.

cleanliness The dream may be suggesting that you "come clean" about something; but it could be making a statement about your attitude towards sex. Is there any aspect of your life that needs cleaning up? See WATER (p. 80).

clergyman Still a typical father figure to many people. Your dreams may be suggesting that you need counselling or guidance. Or are you yourself tending to preach too much at other people?

cliff Were you looking up at a cliff, or attempting to climb it? Are you much concerned with material progress and how you are to reach your objectives? Are you in some kind of "cliff-hanger" situation, with your security threatened in some way? If you were exhilarated by your climb, the dream may be reassuring; but it may also be cautioning you against a fall.

climbing What were you climbing? Were you making progress, or getting nowhere? How secure did you feel? Your dream may well be saying something about your present position in life or at work.

cloak Were you under a cloak of darkness, or hiding yourself inside some protective garment? This could refer to your hiding your emotions. Do you wish to disguise your feelings from someone, or indeed hide from reality? See CLOTHES AND NUDITY (p. 82).

clock Is your dream making you more aware of time slipping by? Or encouraging you to be more punctual? Maybe the time has come for you to make a change. See *calendar*, *time*.

closet See *cupboard*.

clothes See CLOTHES AND NUDITY (p. 82).

clouds Are you "up in the clouds" (see FLYING, p. 84)? But perhaps there is a note of warning, if the clouds were heavy and foreboding. Maybe your waking attitude at present is pessimistic, or you are unnecessarily depressed. The dream may be suggesting that you are not viewing some situation or problem as clearly as you might; your thoughts may be cloudy.

club Dreams of a social club may refer to almost any area of your life in which other people are concerned, so the *kind* of club is obviously important. It should tend to be a reassuring dream. But the club could be a *weapon* used on someone, in which case anger or even cavemannish behaviour may be in question. The club suit in cards (or Batons or Sceptres in the Tarot pack) represents action and assertiveness, and is associated with power.

coal Coal has a long symbolic association with good luck, in spite of blackness and dirt; so with its relationship to the earth, we might think of it as representing the good results of hard work.

coast Was the coast clear? If so, the dream is probably telling you to go ahead, coast along at a leisurely pace. Or are you being complacent about elements in your waking life?

coat See CLOTHES AND NUDITY (p. 82).

cock The sexual connection is obvious; but the dream could also refer to a somewhat pugnacious, proud young man. Have you something to crow about?

code This could refer to the unravelling of waking problems or complications. Did you succeed in breaking the code, or did it baffle you?

coffee The dream could be suggesting that you are in need of some sort of stimulation, of "waking up". If you were drinking coffee with friends in a pleasant atmosphere, this would seem to suggest a reasonable level of inner contentment.

coffin Such dreams often suggest we are laying some idea or project to rest – perhaps because it has been completed. So who or what was in the coffin? There could also be a reference to an aspect of your personality with which you have finally come to terms, especially if the body in the coffin is someone with whom you identify. If you were trying to escape from a coffin, perhaps you are in need of greater freedom of expression and a less claustrophobic lifestyle. See *burial*, *funeral*.

coins See *money*.

cold Cold is an image of frigidity, emotional coolness, even the death of emotion. Are you behaving coldly to someone at present, or should you "cool it" in some emotional relationship? The dream could be a comment on your sexuality, or on the lack of response of a lover. The oncoming of winter (see WEATHER, p. 74), the cold stopping the growth of plants, hints at a restriction in personal emotional development. If in your dream you touched someone or something and it was cold when you expected it to be warm maybe you should consider distancing yourself from whatever that symbol represents to you. But of course, the dream may simply have arisen from physical cold in your bedroom, or the bedclothes falling off you (see p. 20).

college If you dreamed that you were back at college your dreams may be suggesting that you are in need of greater intellectual stimulation and challenge; but it is often true that when you dream of the past your dreams are hinting that there is a strong desire to live life as you once did. Maybe you are reluctant to face changes.

collision See *accident* and DISASTER (p. 72). Ask yourself what you collided with, and what it represented to you. Were you the active or passive partner in the accident? A clash of wills or opinions may be indicated. If you survived the collision, the chances are that you will meet opposition firmly – head-on; but there could be a suggestion that you should curb impulsiveness.

colour See COLOURS (p. 94).

comb This may have been a punning dream, referring to present problems or the *minutiae* of detailed work – work you have to go through with a fine-toothed comb. There is a strong association between hair and sexuality. If you were combing your hair, there could be a reference to hard thinking about a current relationship; or perhaps you want to get someone "out of your hair".

combat See *battle*.

compass A reference, perhaps, to your direction in life. If you were steering a course with a steady compass, avoiding hazards, the dream is a reassuring one. If the compass was swinging, your direction uncertain, there may be a suggestion that you should change course. Referring to other symbols in the dream, there could be a suggestion about future actions.

competition Your dream is probably reminding you that you are competing with someone in waking life – a consideration of the sort of competition in your dream may give you a hint about this (see *games*). Have you some get-rich-quick plan on your mind, which seems to offer good rewards for little effort? If you win a prize, this could be a wish-fulfilment dream.

concert If you were very much involved with the performers at a concert, there could be a suggestion that you are being over-emotional in waking life, carried away by enthusiasm, out of touch with reality. But there could be an inspirational element in the dream which may relate to creative work and your ability to do it. If you were performing, there could be a comment on your exhibitionist tendencies (see *crowds*).

confectionery The icing on the cake? Dreaming of sweet things might suggest too much concentration on frivolous, unimportant matters; too much pleasure and not enough work. Or are you eating too much sweet food?

confession Presumably there is something you should get off your chest in waking life, something you should tell someone. Such a dream, with a priest involved, suggests guilt. If you were absolved, your feelings of guilt are probably ill-founded, though the dream could be a warning of the consequences of an action of whose morality you are uncertain.

congregation Almost certainly, a congregation represents the force of public opinion; if you were a member, reacting with the others, this could be a sign of complacency – perhaps a warning that you are not thinking for yourself. You may be uncertain about some aspects of your personality, especially if you were intimidated by important members of the congregation.

congratulation A sign of self-approval, whether you were receiving congratulations or handing them out; probably a reference to some recent action or achievement.

conjurer The chances are that you have been "up to tricks" recently, behaving deceptively; or perhaps you are under an illusion. The kind of trick may indicate the sphere of your life the dream is questioning. A warning could be involved, especially if the trick failed.

conspirator Your own feelings and the other characters are obviously important here. Were hiding, stealth, plotting involved, perhaps cold-blooded deception? Possibly a warning dream, especially if it ended in disaster.

convict A condemnatory dream: symbols within it may associate it with some action or attitude of which you unconsciously feel guilty or ashamed. See *cage, prison*.

cooking A possible reference to your creativity, a need to express it more fully – unless you are "cooking the books". Perhaps your maternal instincts are in question. Should you be more concerned with other people, less self-centred (see FOOD AND DRINK, p. 86)? Or have you got something cooking?

cork A cork popping from the neck of a bottle has often been, in films, a symbol of male ejaculation, and this still seems the most likely reference. A floating cork could suggest that you are keeping afloat amid your problems.

corn In general, a symbol of richness, growth, fruition, maturity. The dream may refer to your present state of physical and emotional development. If the corn was green, there may be a suggestion that you are naïve or over-innocent; if gold and ready for harvest, the dream should be reassuring, for your outlook should be mature. See *harvest*.

corpse See *coffin, funeral, burial* and BIRTH AND DEATH (p. 76). Always remember that the body, even an identifiable one, could represent an aspect of yourself.

cosmetics Disguise, hiding, "patching up", trying to "make good", "filling in the cracks", doing a cosmetic job on something. This really could be a warning dream: are you ignoring reality, trying to be what you are not? Though the dream could be encouraging you to take more pride in yourself, smarten up your image.

cottage See ENVIRONMENT (p. 92).

counting Are you in some way obsessive? Counting every penny, calculating the extent of your partner's love for you, always engaged in asking yourself "how much"? This could be a warning dream. Much depends, of course, on what you were counting. Perhaps you should be more concerned with quality than quantity. There could be a hint that you should be more relaxed, less completely disciplined.

court A court implies judgment. You may be over-concerned with other people's attitudes or opinions, feeling that they are always judging you; this could be a dream of insecurity. Conversely, if you are presiding, you may always be holding others in judgment. Are you in some way "courting disaster"?

cow Often the symbol of motherhood or maternal instincts. Is there a comment on the relationship between you and your mother? Have you been a "silly cow" recently?

crack The appearance of a crack in a dream – in a wall, a piece of china, even the ground – may well be a symbol indicating tension, and you should try to apply it to your waking life: is there some way in which you are likely to "crack up"? Whatever was cracking in your dream may well represent an image or aspect of yourself.

cradle Any dream involving babies is more than likely to be one relating to creativity, unborn or newly conceived ideas which are ripe for development. The cradle is a symbol of care and nurture; if it was comfortable and secure, the dream is a reassuring one; if it tipped over, watch out for difficulties ahead. Or the dream may refer to the saying that "the hand that rocks the cradle rules the world"; it may be commenting on your matriarchal attitude.

crash See *accident, collision*.

cream Were you "the cat that got the cream"? You may get away with it. Cream is rich, luxurious; are you too self-satisfied or too self-indulgent? See FOOD AND DRINK (p. 86).

cripple Whether you were crippled, or dreamed about a cripple, you need reassurance, support, in some area of your life; some part of you, perhaps psychologically, lacks strength or even health. The dream is perhaps encouraging you to develop self-confidence.

crocodile Much depends on your attitude to crocodiles in waking life, but don't forget the traditional associations with the crocodile. Have you been shedding crocodile tears about some action you should genuinely regret? Or perhaps you are trying to swallow someone whole – to "welcome little fishes in with broadly smiling jaws"? Are you being too "snappy"? Have you bitten off more than you can chew?

cross Though the cross has appeared in many religions from the most ancient times, the Christian symbol is an enormously powerful one, suggestive of immortality, pity, or even unjustified and cruel punishment. There is also a connection with the tree of life and nourishment. Any dream involving the cross is almost certain to have religious overtones, and its interpretation will probably depend on your personal attitude to the Christian religion.

crossroads The chances are that you are currently involved with a decision which will affect your future life. Consider how confidently, in your dream, you chose one way or the other – and the condition of the road ahead. Confidence in your dream may reflect a sound decision; uncertainty may suggest that you are not yet ready to make the decision with which you are faced. See LANDSCAPE (p. 68).

crow Perhaps this is a punning dream suggesting you have something to crow about. But sometimes crows have magical associations, so consider any tradition you may have heard as a child: as a crow was always said to be a symbol of death, there may be a comment on the death of an idea or some personality change. But don't get old wives' tales out of perspective.

crowd See CROWDS (p. 96).

crown If you were being crowned, there may be a reference to some position of command or power which you are called on to fill. But maybe you simply feel a sense of achievement, not necessarily material. Possession of a crown may suggest possession of a splendid secret, or of some valuable information.

crucifix See *cross*.

cruelty The dream could relate to an inner conflict. Perhaps you have a need to come to terms with certain aspects of your personality you recognize as negative (remember, another person in your dream may represent this); or maybe you are being unjustly cruel to yourself, needing to be less harsh on yourself in some respects, especially if, in the dream, someone else was being cruel to you.

crush If you are in a crush, or some part of your body is being crushed, it may be that some aspects of your personality need greater expression; try to allow yourself some psychological space or fresh air. Are you coming to terms with less desirable characteristics, and crushing them? If so, the dream is a reassuring one. Have you developed a "crush" on someone lately? See CROWDS (p. 96).

crutch In waking life, are you getting enough support from those around you? The dream could be summing up your present situation: i.e., you are playing a supporting role. You must decide whether this is giving you enough satisfaction and fulfilment.

crystal It may be that the dream is referring to your seeing your problems with real clarity. If you dream of an object in cut crystal, there could be a reference to many facets of your life. One colour in the rainbow spectrum may have been prominent (see COLOUR, p. 94). Were you crystal-gazing? If so, and you felt nervous about it, be careful not to rely too much on intuition. If the process seemed reassuring, the dream will probably be so. The formation of rock crystal suggests the development (crystalization) of your personality; snow crystals may refer to something ephemeral. Does the name Crystal have any particular association for you?

C

cuckoo The dream could well suggest you are not facing up to your responsibilities, or that you have behaved rather stupidly recently. You may be intruding on other people's lives – "a cuckoo in the nest".

cup The cup is an ancient symbol of the feminine principle: the dream could be saying something about your emotions. In the Tarot, the Cups suit refers to love and happiness, so you could question yourself about this sphere of your life, as your dream may focus on your present attitude towards your partner. But perhaps you were washing up a lot of cups: if so, are you cleaning up some aspect of your love life or its expression? Perhaps "your cup runneth over" – if so, your present inner contentment is probably justified.

cupboard There could be something you feel a need to conceal. You may not be facing up to problems as you should – perhaps you are hiding some sort of skeleton in your cupboard. Think seriously about what is going on within yourself, or you could be storing up more problems for the future. If the cupboard in your dream was a larder, or full of beautiful things which gave you a sense of satisfaction, excellent – but don't slip into a self-satisfied state of mind.

curse Against whom was the curse directed? If at you, and it made you feel apprehensive, the dream may be a warning invoking caution. Should you bear a grudge against someone else, the dream may simply be expressing it. Women can disregard this dream if they awake to find that they have "the curse".

curtain Was it a "final curtain"? If so, your dream suggests that you may have to accept "the end" – perhaps of something in your waking life that has been a little unreal or theatrical. Personal development and revelation could be the meaning if your curtain was going up. Whatever was revealed, whether on a stage or screen or through a window, will be the key symbol for you to interpret. If hanging or making curtains, the suggestion is that you might have something to conceal – or something you wish to stress, "frame", dress up in some way.

cushion Are you perhaps trying to cushion yourself, or someone else, against some blow? If you are relaxing on comfortable, sensuous cushions, ask yourself whether you are being complacent, self-satisfied, even sybaritic. On a simpler level, your dream may be suggesting that you need greater creature comforts in waking life, which may be unduly hard.

cutting This could be a punning dream, or perhaps a dream of division. Is there something you should "cut out"? Should you "cut back" financially? Have you been "cut up" about someone's actions? Think about what cutting instrument you were using – a sharp, efficient one, or a blunted and inefficient one. Sharp instruments can have a phallic reference.

d

dance Dances and dancing feature in many dreams. Perhaps the dream is saying that you are leading someone a dance; and while you may be in control, ask yourself if you are being over-assertive (especially if you were "leading"). If dancing means much to you, the dream may be commenting on your aspirations in life; high leaps in a dance dream could share some of the characteristics of FLYING (see p. 84–5). If you were dancing at a crowded, busy disco the dream could refer to your lifestyle, which may need revitalizing or perhaps simplification.

danger Danger lurks in many dreams and especially in nightmares (see p. 51). A danger dream could also be a warning dream of some kind, so take time out not only to consider the full context of the dream, but carefully to consider all aspects of your waking life.

darkness There is perhaps a reference to your present state of mind, which may be somewhat depressing or pessimistic. If "the darkness before the dawn" seems relevant, your unconscious is hopeful and encouraging, the outlook probably less bleak than you think – perhaps there was light at the end of the tunnel, or stars or a moon in the sky, in which case your aspirations and hopes are positive (see COLOURS, p. 94).

date This could be a pun: a dream of the fruit (the date is passionate and sensual) may refer to a coming date, or newly developing relationship. A dream of a calendar date may or may not be significant: is it a date you should remember for some reason, but have forgotten? The unconscious can correct lapses of memory in this way. Or there may be a reference to the past: try to recall. Your dream attitude to the date may be summing up your waking feelings (apprehension, happiness, sorrow) about a coming or past event of importance.

daughter A dream of your daughter could be taken at face value, but your dream could be commenting on any relevant aspect of your personality, especially if you and your daughter disagree violently about something – or if there is something about her you greatly admire, for that matter. There could be an element of wish-fulfilment, if you see her achieving something which is an unfulfilled aim of your own. Dreams of a nonexistent daughter may similarly be wish-fulfilment, or a projection of the feminine aspects of your personality (whether you are male or female). See *family*.

dawn The dawning of a new day is a potent symbol, but perhaps in this case something has just "dawned on you". The dream could contain a realization of personal development, and is in general very positive, especially if you were watching the sun rise – a hopeful dawn.

deafness Were you deaf because you did not want to hear? You may for some reason be purposely cutting yourself off from the outside world. Maybe you are in need of peace and quiet, or don't want to be a part of whatever is going on. Check that your ears do not need medical attention (see *body*).

death See BIRTH, DEATH AND CHANGE (p. 76).

debt You may be demanding too much of other people, or they may be drawing on you more than they should. Some kind of imbalance in your life may be in need of correction. Have you to "get even" with another person, or do you have to "pay up"?

deck If you are conscious of being on the top deck of a ship, or the lower deck, this could be a dream about social insecurity. Or there could be an implication that you are "decking yourself out" for some occasion; a suggestion that you are showing off or trying to attract attention to yourself – warranted or not.

decoration If in your dream you were redecorating, this could be a suggestion that you should "put your house in order" (see ENVIRONMENT, p. 92). Perhaps it is a statement about your personal image, which may need rethinking. If a particular room is being "done up", try to think what significance that room has for you.

deer Remember the possibility of a punning dream referring to someone dear to you. But the deer is also a symbol of gentleness and meekness: a comment on your, or someone else's behaviour. See also *animals*, FISH, FLESH AND FOWL (p. 88).

defiance Consider whether in your waking life you are suffering inner unrest because you are either acting against your conscience or being prevented from doing what you know to be right. Examine your motives. The person you were defying, and the reason for your defiance, will probably point to the dream's meaning. It may be suggesting to you that you are not allowing your emotions, the more sensitive, passive, feminine side of your nature, more play.

demolition A statement of finality, of the breaking-up of some situation or relationship, the end of existing conditions. Consider what building was being demolished, and what it means to you in waking life (see ENVIRONMENT p. 92).

demonstration This dream is probably encouraging you to speak up for your rights; or perhaps forcefully drawing your attention to some important issue you have been purposely disregarding. Take notice: the dream could be indicating an action or attitude which is really important to your inner contentment.

depression People who feel irrationally depressed during the morning have often had a depressing dream, but forgotten it on waking. Remembering your dream, you will be able to examine and interpret it, thus rationalizing the depression and throwing it off. Think especially, of course, about what depressed you in the dream, and its waking significance.

descent Descending stairs, or a mine? Sinking through water, or parachuting? You may be striving, in waking life, to examine a problem "in depth", and profundity is certainly suggested, though you may also be sinking into despair. There will surely be symbols in the dream which will suggest its source – and if not, you should ask for another dream to clarify the meaning (see p. 47). If your descent is followed by ascent, then the overcoming of difficulties is suggested.

d

desert Aridity, dryness, heat – all suggest a comment on your present emotional state, which may be parched and lifeless. But remember that heat often suggests sexuality. Or perhaps you feel you have been deserted. See LANDSCAPE (p. 68).

design A dream of a design or pattern is almost certainly a comment on your psychological wholeness, the overall design into which the many aspects of your individuality fit. If you were making a design, you may be experiencing a period of development or reassessment, perhaps preparing the future in some way. Contemplation of a finished design may suggest a reliance on predictability, on fate. Has someone got designs on you?

despair A feeling of deep despair in a dream may, of course, reflect a waking attitude about some aspect of your life, or even life in general. But elements in the dream may help you to throw a new light on this, if you try to analyse them, turning to the concrete images in the dream.

destruction The dream could suggest self-destruction; or there may be something going on in your life which is in some way injuring you. See DISASTERS (p. 72).

detective You may be seeking the truth, possibly about yourself in relation to your feelings and attitudes. The dream could be encouraging you to use your intuition more freely. Do you detect that something is wrong? Here too could be a statement concerning your attitude to small details, which might be giving you cause for concern or taking up too much of your time.

detour You are probably searching for a way round your problems, but you should ask yourself whether you are not procrastinating over a decision, or taking unnecessary evasive action.

devil, the Traditional "wickedness", temptation, desire, or any of the seven deadly sins may be in your unconscious mind with a dream like this. Equally, you may be nursing some guilt complex, knowing that all too soon "the devil will have his due". Most importantly, you should decide whether or not your dream devil was the devil in *you* – most likely, he was. Think about your attitude to him, and do not forget to consider the sexual implications. If your attitude was positive, your dream may be warning you that you are "going to the devil".

diamonds The purity of your dream diamonds may well be a comment on your conception of your own perfection (or otherwise)! If you were buying a diamond, the dream could be saying something about material security ("Diamonds are a girl's best friend"). If you were given one, decide whether this was a wish-fulfilment dream, perhaps focusing on a need to deepen or improve your emotional relationship.

dice games Consider whether the dream was suggesting that you are taking too many reckless chances at present, or was reassuring you in some way. Or it may have been commenting on something important at stake in your waking life. Your "number could be up", or even, perhaps, you have been "talking crap".

dictator A reference to some oppressive authority figure in your life seems likely – or to the assertive areas of your own personality. Your inner "dictator" (perhaps an inhibition of some kind) may well be holding back your potential and preventing you from leading a really fulfilled life. Give your "underdog" a chance. Think about your attitude to your father, and its possible relevance to this dream.

digging What you were digging for and what you actually found are probably the key symbols; but consider whether the dream was making a statement about your getting to the root of some long-standing psychological problem, since it could well be suggesting that you are ready to uproot it. If the digging was hard work, do you think there is too much drudgery in your life? If so, you could consult your dreams about what rewards this could bring you in future.

diplomat The dream could be suggesting that you should cultivate tact, or perhaps weigh up some situation in your waking life with special care. Consider too whether your diplomat represents an authority figure, or what he as an individual means to you.

direction Had you a good sense of direction in your dream, or did you change direction suddenly? Perhaps you are ready to make changes in your waking life. Decide just how reassuring or worrying your dream was. See also *crossroads*, LANDSCAPE (p. 68), *travel*.

dirt The dream could have sexual overtones – parents often stupidly refer to their children's early sexual activity as "dirty", and the idea can stick. If you were repulsed by the dirt in your dream, there could be a suggestion that you don't want to know about various areas of your own sexuality. If you were making mud pies, and enjoying it, this could refer to a readiness to enjoy sex. A rebuke for such activity might indicate that you are not really wholehearted about some sexual activity you have in view.

disappointment The nature of the disappointment is crucial. If the overall effect of the dream was to make you feel depressed on waking, and there was a reference to some event in your waking life about which you are apprehensive, take steps if possible to make real disappointment less likely. Perhaps you have been let down in waking life, or some inner weakness has got the better of you.

dice *Death and Death-in-Life*, Gustave Doré

disaster See DISASTERS (p. 72).

discomfort If the discomfort was physical, seek medical advice and reassurance (see p. 59). On the other hand, the discomfort may refer to some moral or psychological attitude in waking life, so look for symbols which will reveal the dream's real intent.

discovery A dream relating to psychological development and the revelation to yourself of perhaps unsuspected areas of the personality – depending, of course, on what was discovered. The important thing is to relate this to your waking self. The dream may be reassuring, or a warning: only you can decide which.

disease Unconscious observation of symptoms may very well mean that this really is a warning dream: perhaps of some physical ailment (see p. 59). Don't ignore it. But remember, the word is dis-ease, so question yourself about what is making you uneasy or uncertain at present.

disfigurement Your dream seems to hint that you are scarred in some way, so there is a chance that for some reason you are or have been suffering. How are you going to heal yourself? If, in your dream, you saw the disfigurement develop, is this a comment on present changes going on within your personality which may be detrimental? If the disfigurement was healing, then you could be coming to terms with some injury.

disgrace A dream of being in disgrace is probably making a statement about some guilt feeling; it is as if your dreams were scolding you for your actions. If in your dream you were inwardly confident that you were in the right, and felt unjustifiably disgraced, it may suggest that you try to be more assertive, and to stand up for what you know to be right both for yourself and others.

disguise The chances are that you are hiding from something in your waking life, perhaps declining to face up to reality, or acting out of character. You may well be playing a game of pretence with yourself, or trying to be someone you are not; if so, ask yourself what is your motivation.

dish The dream may suggest that you want life served up to you on a plate; but perhaps you were like Oliver Twist, asking for more, and if so, more of what? Greater love and affection, possibly, or emotional security? The dream could be punning, of course: is your eye on some "dishy"

potential lover? If you were washing dishes, there could be a comment on domestic drudgery or boredom in your life. Breaking dishes may indicate some release of tension, and no doubt the dream will, perhaps unconsciously, have reassured and calmed you. The dream symbol of the dish of a telescope could relate to your attitude to universal truth and spiritual development. See *bowl*, FOOD AND DRINK (p. 86).

dishonesty This could be a statement about the baser side of your nature; you may well be failing to face up to something unpleasant. It may be worth seeking guidance from your dreams (see p. 47) to help you to develop greater understanding of the problem. Ask yourself whether or not you are taking an easy way out of a tricky situation.

dismissal Your dream may be encouraging you to "dismiss" something from your mind, in which case it should be reassuring. Perhaps having completed a project, you should now forget about it? But maybe the dream reflected some form of rejection in waking life? If so, how deep is your involvement? You could also ask yourself whether there is something which you desire to be rid of, or simply to escape. If you feel shame at being dismissed, see *disgrace*.

dispute See *argument*.

distance If you see something in the distance it possibly represents something (or someone) from which you should distance yourself, or from whom you feel distanced. It could relate to your objectives in life: are you steadily achieving them, or are they receding? Perhaps there was a reference to something unattainable, or apparently so? Distance may also represent alienation or loneliness, in which case perhaps your social or emotional life needs attention.

distress Did your dream focus on some unhappiness in your waking life, or was your distress due to confusion or concern? If this is the case, the dream could be a warning. Try to calm down a little and view your situation constructively. Do you worry irrationally? If so, your intuition or ability to approach your concerns in a practical and methodical way will help you through your difficulties.

ditch Maybe you are feeling less confident or desirable than usual at present because you have been "ditched". If you were "ditching" unwanted items, the chances are that you are experiencing a psychological spring-cleaning, getting rid of silly minor problems or characteristics that do nothing for you, and cause concern. A long furrow or ditch across a field may be making a statement about your sense of security and the sort of routine you follow especially if you were walking along it. How you felt – bored, content, secure – is important here. Do you need to irrigate your ditch – i.e., enrich your life in some special way?

diving Perhaps your waking life is entering a particularly adventurous or exciting phase; if so, the dream may suggest that you are "diving in at the deep end", and offer a warning. WATER (see p. 80–1) is involved, so your emotions may be in question. Think particularly carefully about this if you are about to commit yourself to a new partner. But here too is a colourful dream symbol for any decision-making. See *descent*.

divorce There is no need to assume that this dream foretells a divorce! It is probably suggesting that you divorce yourself from some problem, some opinion, some aspect of your life that is unproductive or unrewarding, "dead" or "over" in some way – one that may well have been having a more adverse effect on you than you realize. Of course you should be careful to decide just what part of your life or thought is indicated by this dream: if someone else is being divorced, what do they mean to you? This may indicate the area of your life in question.

doctor You may be in need of physical or spiritual healing. A great deal depends on your relationship with your doctor in waking life; if you find him or her attractive, you could be merely enjoying a delightful dream fantasy! But your dream may be suggesting that you need some counselling. Follow up any suggestion your dream doctor made. If *you* were the doctor in the dream, perhaps there is something you need to "doctor" or repair? Your dreams could be reassuring you that you are now "much better", in some way, than you were. Were you taking your own temperature – i.e., assessing your feelings or emotional reaction to some waking situation?

dog The dog, "man's best friend", can be a very potent dream symbol, but of course everything depends on your personal attitude towards dogs. If you love them, perhaps your dream dog represents someone dear to you. If you are afraid of dogs, then the dream may be a warning one. Within those general suggestions there are a lot of possibilities, many of them based on puns. Have

d

dog *The dog walks the man*, Grandville

dogs

Julia dreamed: *"All four dogs I have owned in my life (three of them now dead, and one alive) came running up to greet me, alive and happy."*

This brief but beautiful dream was extremely consoling, and the memory of it still elates her. At the time it was comforting and reassuring, for all her dogs have been close friends, and even a part of her. The dream was very probably stressing the support she was getting from people close to her.

you been "playing the dirty dog" in some respect? If your dog was lame, perhaps the dream was symbolizing the help you are presently giving (or failing to give) to someone else. Guard dogs could symbolize your need for protection. "Going to the dogs", "the dogs of hell" and "the dogs of war" speak for themselves. Are you "barking up the wrong tree"? And see *animals*, FISH, FLESH AND FOWL (p. 88–9).

doll In general the reference is likely to be to some sort of immaturity. If you are a man, the dream could sum up very pungently an oldfashioned and adolescent attitude to women. If you are a woman, the probability is that you are being warned to take yourself and your role rather more seriously. There could be a suggestion that you lack assertiveness; or, depending on the dream's content, that you are being exhibitionistic. The reference could be to your maternal instincts. If you have children of your own, is your attitude to them as adult as it might be? If you are a young mother, remember the saying that "a woman's first baby is her last doll".

door A door can be a very beautiful and meaningful symbol, especially if it is opening, when it usually represents personal development and awareness, or the suggestion that you are about to cross the threshold of a new phase of your life or to start a new and important project. If the door was closed, or closing, you should ask yourself whether you are at a point at which a phase of your life is ending, and should turn towards the future. If a door was slammed in your face, perhaps you are feeling "shut out" of something, or by someone, ignored or shunned by other people. See ENVIRONMENT (p. 92–3).

double It sometimes happens that you see your own double, or *doppleganger*, in a dream. Seeing a vision of yourself, your own ghost, as it were, in waking life has always been considered an extremely unfortunate experience; in a dream, it seems most likely that your unconscious is commenting on your own view of yourself and the attitudes and actions for which you must take sole responsibility. You may also ask yourself whether in some way you are "a ghost of your former self" – i.e., as happy, healthy and fulfilled as you once felt. If the answer is no, then you should either talk your problems over with a friend, or seek professional counselling if the situation seems really critical. If you have by now become good at dream interpretation, subsequent dreams may offer you sufficient help to enable you to turn a corner. More simply, a rather complex non-verbal pun could be involved: are you in some way "doubling up", perhaps unnecessarily. Asking for a double helping would seem to indicate that. See *ghost*.

doubt It is always difficult to measure emotion in a dream – they can be monstrously over-emphasized. But if you were conscious of doubt, this can probably be interpreted literally: you are possibly in doubt about something in your waking life whether you are acutely conscious of the fact or not. If you doubted someone else, try to decide what he or she represents in waking life. Could the dream have been referring to your powers of intuition: "I doubt if that will happen"?

dove Above all, of course, the dove is the international symbol of peace; but in a personal dream this can be a personal symbol, referring to peace within your own environment. Is this lacking at present? Or have you acquired greater peace of mind recently? Did you release the dove, like Noah, to enquire about your present situation? Or did it fly towards you and alight on your hand? The dove is much associated with love. Could it relate to a personal relationship? Or was your dream one of wish-fulfilment, an enjoyable fantasy?

down See *falling, feathers*.

dragon Your dream dragon could be saying something about your sexual drive (there is a strong association with fire, and therefore passion). Do you tend to consume your partners? It might be a good idea to reassess this sphere of your life and needs. The dragon slain by St George represented powerful urges, both personal and universal. There is a strong traditional connection between the dragon and the mother-in-law – did your dream hint at this? Or at some other dragon figure? Dragons when tamed are not entirely lacking in charm, and can even be led on a silken rope, the attractive pet of beautiful women. Does that make sense to you, whichever sex you are?

drain If you were unclogging a drain perhaps you are resolving some waking problem that has been blocking your progress. If the drain was filthy and repulsive, ask yourself whether you need to face up to certain aspects of your life and personality that you find unpleasant (see *dirt*). The drain symbol could refer to your energy level, or to some person who is "draining" you. Or are you, at present, throwing money – or talent – "down the drain"? Whatever is being drained away is obviously important.

drawing To dream of drawing, if you cannot do so, is perhaps an invitation to be more ambitious in your efforts: perhaps you should try to draw in waking life! But the subject of your drawing is probably more important, and your attitude towards your work. If you were drawing a person, but kept "getting it wrong", perhaps you misunderstand that person in waking life. There could be a reference to waking plans, if you were making a "working drawing" or drawing a plan

or map of some kind. Could there be a pun on drawing a cheque or perhaps a winning ticket in a lottery.

dream You may need to ask yourself whether your dreams are not suggesting that you are living in a "dream world", and refusing to face up to reality. If you were "day-dreaming", there may have been a focus on an unattainable wish; if so, think about it, and try to consider your desire in a practical light.

dress Any dream in which the focus is on something you are wearing is probably making a statement about your image, so see CLOTHES (p. 82–3) and *image*; but perhaps your dream was also hinting that you are not being true to yourself, or that you need to change in some way. Think in particular about your opinions and reactions. If you were "dressing up" in your dream, perhaps you should take more pride in yourself and your achievements in waking life. If you were trying to climb into someone else's dress perhaps you are attempting to emulate her in some way? If you are strongly aware of the colour of the dress, that may be an important clue to the dream's meaning. A man who dreams of putting on a dress may obviously be receiving a comment on his sexuality.

drifting Possibly a simple dream statement that you are drifting somewhat aimlessly through life. There is more than a hint of contentment (unless the situation distressed you); but dreaming of being "adrift" – that is, forced into the situation – is another matter, and you should think about the direction, or lack of direction, of your present life. WATER (see p. 80–1) is so strongly connected as a symbol with emotion, that the reference may be to your emotional life. It is important to decide how aware you were in the dream of the ENVIRONMENT (p. 92–3). If the drifting was associated with the knowledge that you were completely lost, you may be in a state of indecision in waking life.

d

drink A dream of being thirsty can simply be the result of your wanting a drink. But it could relate to your enjoyment of other pleasures, especially if the dream drink is a sensual wine.

driving The dream could relate to a "driving force" – in control of waking situations, or unable to control them, depending on how well you controlled the vehicle! Your attitude and reactions in the dream are, as usual, crucial – whether you were bold, apprehensive, confident, terrified . . . Were you in a chase, or evading enemies? If so, perhaps you could be distancing yourself from opponents or problems. The type of vehicle you were driving could relate to your personality in much the same way as a building can. Was it efficient, well-tuned, luxurious, beaten-up or broken down? Did it respond well? See *automobile, car, chauffeur*.

drowning Perhaps you are drowning in a sea of problems or difficulties, or under emotional stress? Ask yourself if you are drowning in self-pity. If you are in a depressed state, about to go under for the third time, maybe you should consider some sort of therapy (see WATER, p. 80–1). Or are you drowning your sorrows?

drum Perhaps a punning dream: do you want to drum up action in others, or drum someone out of your life? The former may relate to yourself, of course – perhaps you should be more assertive, even aggressive, in waking life, especially if you were drumming your way into battle. But perhaps you were a drummer in a pop group? Are you playing someone else's tune, in waking life? There is something unmistakably sensual about drum rhythm, and indeed about most musical instruments; that may give you a hint. Drums also are used to send messages.

drunkenness A dream of being drunk may suggest that you are trying to escape from reality, or are simply out of control of a situation. Think about your attitude to other people and your general behaviour pattern: drunkenness can be a serious insult to the company you keep.

duel Just as in an argument the dreamer can be both people concerned, so a dream of a duel can refer to some inner disagreement – in some way, you may be at war with yourself. At best, there may be some area of your personality, some behavioural trait with which you are at odds. At worst, you can be in a state of inner conflict which urgently needs resolution. Can you identify your dream opponent as representing an aspect of your life you want to annihilate? If this seems improbable, the dream may simply be relating to your attitude to that person in waking life. There could be a pun on *dual*ity, and a reference to your love life, in which case it seems likely there is some tension which needs resolution.

dwarf Has someone made you feel small lately? Or does the dwarf in your dream represent some potential which you have not fully developed? Dwarfs are traditionally hard-working people, often in mythology employed in mines, so there could be a reference to personal development.

dying See BIRTH, DEATH AND TRANSFORMATION (p. 76).

Dyeing If you were dyeing some material, the COLOURS (see p. 94–5) concerned may be significant. If you were tie-dyeing, think of any restrictions in your waking life which may be relevant. Such a dream could relate to a need for change; and remember the possibility of a pun: perhaps you are dying to do something?

e

eagle A strong symbol of power, a dream of an eagle could suggest your own threatening behaviour to others, your search for a prey (if the bird represented yourself); a sitting or perching eagle could suggest you're biding your time. Or were you the threatened one? And if so, who was the eagle? The bird as symbol of John the Evangelist may be a rare modern interpretation, but for Americans it can certainly be a symbol of their country, of patriotism, defence, independence. See FISH, FLESH AND FOWL (p. 88). Also *bird*.

ear Apart from any physical suggestion (ear-ache, deafness) there could be an encouragement to listen – or to stop listening! And see also *body*.

earth Above all, earth (the planet, and the substance) symbolizes the Great Mother, fecundity, creativity and substance; it also represents order and stability. Our sense of security may be under challenge when our dreams make use of earth symbolism. We know our roots are in earth – we spring from it and return to it, so self-confidence may be under scrutiny. Dreams of being buried alive may be trying to tell us we are being buried by certain problems, almost certainly material ones. If we are digging, we may be trying to reach their source, or attempting to bring to light something hidden – perhaps we are being instructed to be more open-minded. What kind of earth was involved – smooth and loose, hard and stony, dry or muddy? "Earth" dreams could well be telling us to face up to reality, encouraging us to take a more practical outlook on life. Perhaps we should also be less stubborn, less rigid, less concerned with mere material progress – and problems connected with the latter are almost always related to our need for security and the necessity to convince ourselves of it. The need for growth and development, the flowering of our personality, is good reason for the use of earth symbolism in dreams.

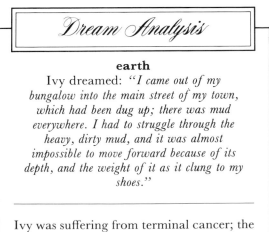

Dream Analysis

earth

Ivy dreamed: *"I came out of my bungalow into the main street of my town, which had been dug up; there was mud everywhere. I had to struggle through the heavy, dirty mud, and it was almost impossible to move forward because of its depth, and the weight of it as it clung to my shoes."*

Ivy was suffering from terminal cancer; the dream summed up her struggle against crippling illness.

earthquake The sensation of the earth moving, or giving way beneath your feet, suggests insecurity, psychological or material – try to relate the symbol to your waking life. Perhaps especially if cracks appear in the earth, there could be a serious warning; are you under tension, even about to "crack up"? Don't forget a possible physical cause: your partner's heavy breathing next to you, or some other noise might have prompted the dream. See *earth, cracks.*

eating If you went to bed hungry, wish-fulfilment is probably concerned, but eating may represent the intake of knowledge, or sensual pleasure. What were you eating – its texture, its shape? If it made you feel sick, the dream could be a warning – and not necessarily of overeating. Are you greedy, taking too much from others? See FOOD AND DRINK (p. 86–7).

echo What did the echo say? Could it represent a repeated warning? Or was it an echo from the past – a statement about past events or past behaviour? Were there mistakes you should not repeat?

egg A potent symbol. Freud, of course, found a sexual analogy, and certainly this could be a male sexual symbol; but the egg is perhaps more commonly a symbol of birth, a new beginning; perhaps there is a problem whose source is difficult to trace (a "chicken and egg" situation). Or there could be a pun: is the dream of someone who is a "good" or "bad egg"? Remember, too, the warnings against putting all your eggs in one basket; of the delicacy of eggs – are you dealing with a situation or a relationship which could easily crack and spill? There could be an allusion to male or female fertility.

elastic Should you be more flexible, stretch a point? If the elastic broke, and in the old context of supporting clothing, there could be an obvious comment on your sense of security, or lack of it. See also *embarrassment.*

election Obviously, the context of this dream is decisive. The winning or losing is important, the gaining of power or the abandoning of it to opponents. Clearly there could be a comment on almost any area of life. If you were standing for office, there could be a suggestion about your attitude to others: are you better than them, deserving of "election"? Are you accusing yourself, via your dreams, of showing off too much, bragging, exaggerating? Trying to bluff your way into a more important or powerful position? Or was your role a supportive one? If so, think

e

about the candidate and who he or she may represent. The decision – who to vote for – may refer to a problem in waking life (see *crossroad*). Should you consider your present course? What should your policy be? What line of action should you vote for?

electricity Were you being encouraged to increase your expenditure of energy, or conserve it? Do you lack power in some way? Were you "switching on" power, and should you do so in waking life? Do you need to "re-charge your batteries" in some way? If there were power cuts in your dream, what is frustrating your purposes in waking life? Did you receive a shock? The analogies are obvious. If the dream was of a particular power plug, switch or socket, it will be well worth checking it for safety.

elephant The association of the elephant with luck probably began with the Indian god Ganesha (see FLESH, p. 88–9). If you were riding, your dream may indicate that you are on top of your problems (material or financial, most probably). But the association with princely processions may suggest that you have been "lording it" over others, or showing off. Fear of the elephant may suggest fear of a large problem bearing down on you. Or if the elephant represented yourself, trampling down bushes and trees in its progress, you may be overbearingly pushing yourself or your ideas forward, not allowing new ideas and attitudes room to breath and influence you. See FISH, FLESH AND FOWL (p. 88).

elevator There is most likely a comment on your material progress in life, whether you were going up or down; or perhaps to your attitude to other people, getting off at floors below or above your own. Descending in an elevator may suggest

"coming down to reality"; being stuck in one may reflect the waking feeling that your progress in some way is impeded. Who was in the elevator with you, what might they represent, and what was their attitude in the dream? "Going up" or "down" may also have a sexual implication.

embarrassment This is an emotion that very frequently occurs in dream. Obviously the context is important, but embarrassment may often reflect lack of self-confidence. Perhaps you need more often to award yourself full marks for what you do well and to make the best of areas which you know you can develop. See CLOTHES AND NUDITY (p. 82–3).

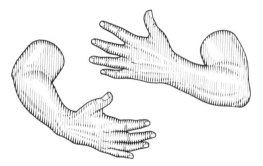

embrace Hopefully the embrace was a pleasant one. There was probably an assessment of the degree of your inner contentment, or an encouragement to love yourself more. But who/what was embracing you? If it was a nightmare creature, you should ask yourself whether you are in waking life embraced by some less than desirable idea or scheme, some negative personality trait, or even a cult, in which case a warning is involved. If you were embracing someone, there could be an indication that you are in need of love and affection; but there could be a similar warning, if what you are embracing is nauseous.

emigration Perhaps you are depressed or impatient with the present circumstances of your life, and long for a change; or you may need to make a fresh start, in some way, even to escape from your past or from negative elements of your personality. Should you face reality instead of turning your back on it? See *passport*.

emptiness/empty The chances are that there is something "empty" about your life. Consider the way in which you are expressing your emotions, and to whom; how are they received? Do you find it difficult to get a response from your partner, or is the dream symbolizing loneliness, an emotional desert? Opening a box or container and finding it empty suggests that your expectations (in whatever field) are greater than is warranted.

On the other hand, what is empty is capable of being filled, so optimism would suggest that you consider how to fill any void in your life.

endings The dream may reflect the end of some incident or passage in your waking life; if so, remember the ability of the unconscious to sum up shrewdly your real feelings on the matter. Look forward to the next phase, the next project, rather than fixing mind or emotions on the past.

enemy Is the enemy in your dream yourself, some element of your personality, some outside force or person? It is not always easy to decide; but there are usually clues. If you cannot fix on an answer, ask your dreams for further elucidation (see p. 47). The person indicated in your dream may not, of course, be an enemy in waking life, but possess characteristics which you find distasteful and want to eradicate in yourself. In that case, your dream may be a comment on your progress in that aim. Are you your own worst enemy? There could be a representation of sexual fear or fear of the sexual organs; consider your attitude to sex. Perhaps you need reassurance or counselling in this area. Some "old enemy" could be a problem you have had for years; your dreams may suggest that you should attack it more assertively.

engagement If you are unattached, this may be a wish-fulfilment dream like any other; or it could be making a statement about some commitment you have made (probably, but not necessarily, emotional). Your reaction to your dream engagement – apprehension, joy, horror – will be an important clue.

engine Remember that the body is an engine, so when engines appear in dreams there could well be a reference to your physical wellbeing, especially if the engine was running inefficiently, had broken down, or in some other way needed maintenance. The power of an engine could symbolize sexual energy or potency. If you were driving an engine, there could be an allusion to your capability to deal with life and its complexities, perhaps particularly where your physical life is concerned. Were you totally in control, or was the engine running away with you, or only pulling sluggishly? The answers will be relevant to your attitude and level of self-confidence (see *driving*). If you could not get the engine started, or in gear, ask yourself what is blocking your progress – maybe some inner reluctance? Or perhaps you do not yet feel yourself ready for a new commitment or project, whether making physical, intellectual or emotional demands.

enrolment A sign of commitment, perhaps? If you were "signing on" or taking an oath, your unconscious may be giving you the go-ahead for future development; you must also decide whether or not you really wanted to be involved in the organization to which you were pledging yourself. Your dream may have been suggesting that you should stretch your mind, especially if you were enrolling for some study course, or at college or university; or that you need more self-discipline, if you were joining the services. As always, the context of the symbol is vital.

entanglement If this was physical – if you were entangled in bushes or undergrowth – there is probably a reference to your being entangled by problems of some kind. The way in which you coped with this in your dream may sum up your current progress, or perhaps just your attitude to what is going on. If there was a personal reference, perhaps to a lover or prospective lover, there was perhaps a comment on a personal relationship; but remember that such a reference could also be to the masculine and feminine sides of your own nature.

entertainment This suggests display, perhaps "showing off"; or, if you were a member of the audience, perhaps has something to say about your view of the people performing: sometimes our dreams will place an employer, or someone we think "superior", in a ridiculous position – as comedian or clown – hinting that we take them perhaps too seriously. If you were the entertainer, the audience's response may suggest your friends' and acquaintances' attitude to your approach to them, which may perhaps be too ingratiating or showy.

envelope What are your present expectations in life? Do the contents of the envelope support your optimistic/pessimistic attitude to some communications you expect?

erection Erections always occur during REM or dreaming sleep, sexual or not, but a man dreaming of an erect penis will usually do so in the course of an overt sexual dream; otherwise, the allusion will generally be symbolic. There could be a reference to fears of impotence. With women, there may be an element of penis envy, though, of course, this too may simply be part of a sexual fantasy.

errand If you were rushing around on fruitless errands, your dreams may be hinting that you are wasting waking time on trivia, especially if in your dream you were making little progress. If

e

e

your errands were satisfying, then what is occupying your waking hours is probably rewarding, but do consider whether you are making the most of your potential – the associations of the word "errand" are not specially positive, and there could be the suggestion that you are playing a more subservient role than is either necessary or fulfilling. See also *messages* for the content of your errand will be very relevant. There might be a comment on the way your body communicates messages to your brain, so your physical well-being may be worth thinking about.

escape Researchers have shown that dreams of trying to escape are among the commonest of all. The idea suggests your dream may have been a frightening one, though one can need to escape from something ostensibly pleasant (on moral grounds, for instance). Physical flight, of course, suggests psychological flight, so the main question to ask is from what you were hoping to escape – and how wholeheartedly you made the effort. Then, *did* you escape, or were you caught? And what happened then? See PURSUIT (p. 66).

evening Evening, sunset, the death of the day, can be a regretful image of loss (see *ending*). Who or what was involved? But the evening is also a time of relaxation and the enjoyment of leisure, so there may be a suggestion that you need more leisure enjoyment. Is there a reference to "the evening of life" – to what you should do with your time after retirement? There could be a reference to the degree of self-fulfilment so far achieved.

evil The term "evil" is a strong one, meaning more than mere misgiving or suspicion. Sometimes we can have a general feeling of evil in a dream (occasionally this happens in waking life, with reference to a place or a person). It should not be ignored. Face up to the symbols in the dream, consider what they may represent, and make a special effort to discover what they are trying to tell you, for it is fairly obvious that you are worried about some problem, perhaps a deep-rooted psychological one, and are convinced that, unresolved, it could harm you. It is worth considering whether in waking life you are feeling guilty about your behaviour or attitude to someone else; this could have the effect of casting you as an "evil-doer". See *fear*.

examination In some way, you are probably being "put to the test"; you yourself may be the examiner! Your fear or nervousness or confidence in the dream will reflect your waking feelings about the real subject of your dream – which will more than likely be yourself, even if you are examining others. If this is so, try to think what area of your life the examination candidates may represent (though there is the possibility that you may be being over-critical of someone else). A physical examination by a doctor may reflect a conscious or unconscious worry about some health problem.

excavation You are probably into an interesting period of personal development and self-realization, finding out truths about yourself and new aspects of your personality. What did you discover? What may it symbolize for you? Remember, it was there, buried, all the time – so it may represent some aspect of your personality, some potential, you are uncovering for yourself – and now you must decide what to do with it. If you uncover something that frightens or disgusts you, try to be rational; remember, your dreams are your own – whatever you find is part of you, whether you like it or not, and it is for you to come to terms with it. See *archaeology, digging*.

exchange If you were exchanging gifts or ideas the dream may be commenting on your ability to contribute to, or be part of, the life of others or the community in general – your capacity to take from it, and to give something back. Was what you gave equal in value to what you received? Is there a personal characteristic you would be glad to exchange for another?

excitement What kind of excitement? It probably related to some area of your waking life which excites you, or perhaps which *should* excite you, but of which you are taking too little account. What you felt on waking is probably a good yardstick: if you were elated, then the dream is a positive one – but if you felt let down, that all the excitement of the dream was empty, your unconscious may be suggesting that you are perhaps whipping up too much expectation about some waking matter.

execution This is, of course, a very violent symbol, and therefore probably refers to a strong waking emotion. Who was being executed, and what did they represent? If you were watching an execution, remember that you could still be represented by the victim. The significance of the dream may be simple – perhaps there is something or someone you feel must be ruthlessly cut out of your life. Maybe you were "finishing off" a problem. If you were the victim, this may be symbolic of a deep guilt or inner disgust: only you can decide the source of such a feeling. This is one case in which it might be well to ask your dreams for further elucidation (see p. 47).

exercise Were you exercising your mind, your rights, your prerogative, your self-control, your body? There is perhaps a hint that you need to strengthen some area of your personality or means of self-expression, and your dream was goading you into action. Or, of course, just suggesting that you need more physical exercise!

exhibition Perhaps your dream was suggesting that you should take a look at the various aspects of your life, and examine your reactions to them? The kind of exhibition you were visiting, and of course the exhibits, are likely to represent the strikingly contrasted areas of your personality, and perhaps your main concerns and interests. But have you been "making an exhibition of yourself" lately? If you have been feeling depressed, neglected or unloved, you may in some way be attempting to attract attention. If so, it may be worth recalling and reconsidering recent actions and behaviour patterns, and perhaps moderating future ones. If your dream exhibition was an uplifting or culturally pleasing experience, the dream was probably a reassuring and strengthening one.

exile If you were the exile in your dream, perhaps this is somehow a reflection of an aspect of waking life: are you a "stranger" – starting work in a new job, away from familiar people and places? Your dream attitudes and emotions will be a comment on this, perhaps marking your progress of assimilation. If the exile was appealing to you for comfort, perhaps there is some emotion or intellectual concept you are denying yourself? Or are you rejecting someone, refusing to allow them to be part of your life?

expedition Think of an expedition and you think of challenge, of bravely setting forth into the unknown. You may be starting a journey of some sort (not, of course, necessarily physical), and the dream may be reassuring you. If not, is an expedition being suggested to you? You may be stagnating in some way, needing to push on to new frontiers of thought or opinion or behaviour. Or could your lifestyle be claustrophobic? Look for new avenues of interest, perhaps for a new relationship; be more adventurous and questing. If you were optimistically setting out in your dreams, you may be readier for waking adventure than you realize. See *exploration*.

expense Financial and emotional generosity are often linked, so your dream may be commenting on your ability to give love and affection. Perhaps you were confronted with some enormous expense, and felt you could not cope . . .

Similarly, you may be under emotional pressure, or have the waking notion that you cannot cope with the emotional demands being made on you. Or there may be a straightforward comment on your attitude to money. Should you be less extravagant – or less frugal? But think first about "loving and giving".

experiment If in the dream you were concerned with some kind of experiment, the dream is probably encouraging you to be more experimental and adventurous in some area of your life. The kind of experiment may be a clue to which area is under investigation – your self-image, sex life, or sparetime interests spring readily to mind. Perhaps you should take an analytical look at waking situations and examine them in a cool, rational, even clinical way?

expiation You may be nursing a guilt complex about someone or something, and should clear your conscience by putting things right.

exploration Very likely a reference to your own readiness to explore new areas of your personality and psyche. Your need to know more about yourself and your motivations are probably in focus. The dream, if it was optimistic and forward-looking, will be encouraging you to take action, or reassuring you if you have started your quest for more self-knowledge. Don't be apprehensive about what occurs in your dream: it might indeed be warning you that you are pressing ahead too quickly, or even that you may not be entirely happy about what you find. Consider the kind of landscape you are exploring. See LANDSCAPE (p. 68), *excavation*, *expedition*.

explosion Such a dream may well be suggesting that you are being too careful in holding back your emotions: explode, if you must – with anger, or maybe with love (look at the context and symbolism of the dream). Bottling up any kind of emotion for too long can lead to an explosion, and it had best be a controlled one. But the context of the dream is all-important. Concern with nuclear disarmament suggests a different setting altogether; the dream may then be a straight-forward expression of your overt fear. But, more likely, it will be a strong statement about your own psychological condition. Your deep concern for international peace and safety is no doubt admirable, but it might be replacing a concern with more personal matters, a diversion from family or emotional problems. See *bomb*.

eyes Eyes have traditionally been called the "mirrors of the soul", and represent a deeply personal and emotional symbol. Are you soul-searching at the moment? If your eyes were cloudy perhaps you are not seeing others, or yourself, or some circumstance, clearly. If there was something in your eye, then the inference is obvious. But there could well be a physical connotation: do your eyes need testing?

Dream Analysis

eyes

Kate dreamed: *"Someone I did not know told me that I had a film over my eyes. We went to a mirror in which I could see it — a kind of jelly, like uncooked egg white. He removed it."*

This dream occurred just as Kate, knowing she had to come to terms with some problems, had made arrangements to begin therapy. The unknown person, apparently a stranger, was the analyst. The dream reassured her that much could be done to help her, and was a constructive pun: she would see life in a new, clearer way.

eyes *Anima with eyes*, Peter Birkhauser

f

face The dream imagery could be encouraging you to face up to problems, or to reality. The face in your dream – kindly, beautiful, stern or ugly – may reflect them, as will your attitude to it. But if you were looking at your own face, whether you liked or disliked what you saw could offer a clue to your opinion of yourself. Was the dream suggesting that you are self-effacing, or even two-faced? If you were applying make-up, or wearing a face pack or a mask, you should ask yourself whether you need to change in some way, or are attempting to be what you are not. Washing your face might suggest that you are attempting to "come clean". Meeting an enemy "face to face", suggests a comment about the inner strength with which you can cope with rivals or opponents. See *body*.

factory Working in a factory suggests drudgery, maybe, but also activity, energy, power, leading eventually to a result – to production. Your dream may have suggested that, like Chaplin in *Modern Times*, you are being used by others, or are a mere cog in a wheel. Consider whether or not you are being imposed on in waking life. More positively, the dream could hint that you are a very busy, active person working systematically through everything you have to do, and getting the necessary results: though this seems reassuring, if there is a flaw in this plan, something in the dream may have suggested it. Especially if you were in charge of the factory or production line, the whole of your personality as well as various facets of it seems in focus here. See *buildings*, ENVIRONMENT (p. 92–3).

failure Perhaps you are unconsciously reaching the conclusion that, whatever your material success, you are in some way "a failure" in some area of your waking life – emotional, perhaps, or intellectual. If someone, a parent or an authority figure, was scolding you for failing, or for not trying harder to succeed, try to associate that person with some element of your own personality, linking directly with your whole attitude. It is an "inner parent" or boss that is rebuking you; you should be able to decide for what. Try to face the problem, and rebuild your self-confidence, perhaps (if the "failure" seems inevitable and irreducible) by referring to the more successful and rewarding areas of your life, those in which you have succeeded in the past, and will continue to do so.

fairground Whether this was a highly enjoyable dream, or a nightmarish one, many questions spring to mind. For instance, at the side shows, the shooting ranges and the coconut shies – who were you firing at? Who was "taking you for a ride" on the dodgems or roller-coaster? With whom did you enter the tunnel of love? Whose face and body was distorted in the hall of mirrors? What prizes did you win, and what do they represent? There is a rich selection of symbols to be considered, and one which will tax your interpretative ability. As with *buildings*, the fair could represent your whole self, and the various side shows part of your personality: try to look at every stall, every prize, from this point of view.

fairy Although this may relate, in now rather dated slang, to some gay friend, or to your own attitude to homosexuality, this dream may equally well be a wish-fulfilment about freedom and immortality, and indeed beauty. But fairies are also capable of being unpleasant, even evil.

fall, the See *autumn*.

falling A common dream, sometimes associated with Stage One sleep (falling asleep). But see also FLYING (p. 84–5).

falsehood Your attitude towards your dream falsehood is as critical as the form the lie took. In the context of the dream, were you blatant and uncaring, or guilty? Try to figure out to what incident in waking life the dream may relate. Of course it may be referring to your deception of someone else, but self-deceit may be concerned – you may be telling yourself that something about your life is "all right" when this is far from the truth. You may be trying to cover up or excuse yourself for a faulty decision, a deceptive action, and masking your guilt about it.

family As with every symbol, each reader will have his or her own reaction to the word "family". Does it suggest warmth, coming together, love, affection – or bitterness, antagonism, animosity, rivalry, jealousy, sheer incompatibility? There is also, of course, the family of man, with its deep wells of instinctive knowledge and emotion, Jung's "the collective unconscious". The complications are considerable. But think whether the accent, in your dream, was perhaps on your own personality – whether the individual family members, perhaps somewhat caricatured, may have been extensions of it, especially if you have very strong feelings about the people who appeared in the dream. Recognition of traits and characteristics

f

which seem as much a part of you as you are part of the family will help you to counter or change them; or by striving to understand them (in the guise perhaps of an admired older brother, sister or cousin with whom you may be able to build a tie of *friendship* quite separate from family feelings) you will be strengthening your own psychological wellbeing, becoming more whole, or (in the context of the dream) drawing the family together in true sympathy and understanding.

famine Dreaming of visiting a famine-stricken area (even if the dream related to an image seen on television or a newspaper photograph) may be a simple reflection of your sympathy, but it is more likely to refer to nourishment which you need – and by no means necessarily physical nourishment. We all see striking images of all sorts on television each day, and our unconscious choses one or the other, for its own purposes, and these are rarely overt. Your hunger is more probably for love and affection, for a richer emotional life. Ask yourself whether you are emotionally starved in some way, and thus a sort of "victim". Perhaps you should make an effort to enrich your life. You may need a new cultural or intellectual interest which will feed your emotional needs and bring spiritual satisfaction. If your dream persuades you that you should give not only money, but time and energy to raising funds for the victims of physical famine, you may be using the image to the best of ends.

farewell Was the parting glad or sad? Your dream could be marking the end of a phase (or a relationship) in your waking life. If not, is it suggesting that you should make such an end, say goodbye to someone or something – some objective in life, maybe?

fashion A "display" dream might suggest that you feel you are not making enough of an impression in your waking life, being "dowdy" in more than looks. Or perhaps you are depending too much on outward appearance and too little on real worth? There could be a pun on "fashioning" or making something. See CLOTHES AND NUDITY (p. 82–3).

father The interpretation of a dream which uses your father as its central image will depend to a great degree on your relationship with him in waking life. On the simplest level, this may be an offer of a "fatherly" piece of advice which you might regard just as you would regard real advice. Or there might be a reference to the masculine side of your personality, encouraging you to be more assertive. If your father was

ineffectual, the dream may refer to an unconscious search for a father figure. If there is a deep antagonism, your dream may be showing you the way to come to terms with a notoriously difficult and potentially crippling situation. If your father was over-strict, perhaps there is a warning that you are imitating him in the relationship with your own children – or that you are *too* self-disciplined: he is still living in you. Other dreams may illuminate the theme – and remember that other male figures, or certain symbols (a monumental building, a threatening mountain, some object which you associate with him) may appear in what seems to be a totally unrelated dream situation, revealing new twists in your relationship. If you dream that your father is unwell, or has had some misfortune, there is enough evidence to suggest it may be worth contacting him to check on his health and wellbeing.

fatigue A feeling of fatigue which is sufficiently strong to suggest itself as the main theme of a dream would seem to suggest that your physical vitality is low. You might also ask yourself whether you are fatigued by your present lifestyle, relationship or job. Americans whose dream found them doing 'fatigues" may have received a comment on some wrongdoing or possess a guilt complex in waking life.

fault No doubt a comment on some waking fault, mistake, error. How guilty did you feel, in your dream? Was the fault entirely yours? A dream of a geographical fault could be a punning comment on a flaw in your own nature, which might lead to an "earthquake" or shift in opinion or attitude. See *earthquake*.

fear A dream or nightmare in which fear is an overwhelming theme or mood will probably depress you, even fixing your mood for most of the day, and it is not always possible to be rational about it. Perhaps this is because it will almost certainly reflect some apprehension in your waking life. The way in which you faced up to the fear in your dream will give you a clue as to the level of your real, waking fear. If you cannot immediately match your dreaming apprehension to your waking life, think carefully, for the dream may be attempting to attract your attention to some very deep apprehension or even phobia, suggesting that it is time you get to work on it, perhaps with the aid of a therapist.

feast As with *famine*, a dream of a feast may be the result of a physical state; but it is perhaps more likely to refer to some other kind of need –

perhaps emotional or sexual. Consider where there is an imbalance in your life, and try to redress it. If you were simply enjoying your food (and consider its shape and texture), the dream may be summing up your present attitude, which is probably sane enough – the enjoyment of the fruits of your labours, and the inner contentment that follows. But if you were stuffing yourself, perhaps you are being over-indulgent and greedy, taking or expecting too much from others close to you (and not necessarily physically). See FOOD AND DRINK (p. 86–7).

feathers Fine feathers make fine birds: your dream could be suggesting you need more variety in your life. There is something intrinsically provocative about some feathers – peacock and ostrich, in particular. Could this reflect your recent behaviour? If you saw someone plucking a chicken, are you intent on revealing someone's true personality – or is someone trying to strip you of pretension or disguise? Feathers in a quilt or pillow offer comfort, warmth, security: if they were escaping, are you fearful of losing yours?

feed If you were feeding someone – a child or animal, perhaps – try to decide who, in your life, needs succour or additional emotional warmth and love. Are you neglecting yourself in some way, especially if the object of the operation is someone or something with whom you closely identify? See also *feast*, FOOD AND DRINK (p. 86).

feet Perhaps a comment on your present attitude to life: sensible and practical if your feet were on the ground. For a Christian, the washing of Christ's feet is a potent symbol of forgiveness, so having your feet treated or cared for may signify needing someone's compassion. See *body*.

fence If you were "fenced in", think about your present lifestyle, which could in some respects be claustrophobic; are you prevented from doing something you wish to do? Are you physically cramped, or caught in a cloying relationship? If you were fence-building, ask yourself what (who?) you are trying to shut out of your life. What was inside the fence, and what outside, is obviously important (see *gaol, prisoner*). If you were a criminal doing a deal with a "fence", are you trying to sell someone something – some aspect of yourself – which is counterfeit or "stolen", excusing yourself from some real-life misdemeanour, or trying to make the most of a bad job? If you were fencing with foils, or real swords, your intellectual brightness and agility may be in question, perhaps with reference to the other person concerned; some particular waking

argument may be indicated, and the agility and evasion of fencing suggests cunning, speed and cleverness.

festival Hopefully, a dream festival will reflect some waking celebration or happy mood. But your dream may simply be celebrating "you" – giving you a pat on the back for recent progress or achievement. A church festival may be commenting on the state of your religious faith, or lack of it. Unless the festival was spoiled or marred – and consider your mood on waking – this is almost certainly a positive and reassuring dream.

fetters A dream in which you are fettered probably reflects some heavy responsibility, problem or restriction in waking life, something "weighing you down". If you were released, or better still, released yourself, this is a hopeful symbol; you could be at a turning point in dealing with the problem concerned. See *chains, gaol, prisoner*.

feud We usually associate the word feud with long-lasting strife within a family, or between neighbours or former friends. Though the reasons may seem petty, rivalry in love, jealousy, or territorial rights are often the real cause. The warring factors in your dream may be contrasting areas of your own personality.

fiancé See *proposal*.

field See LANDSCAPE (p. 68–9).

fight A dream of aggression, or perhaps an encouragement to "put up a fight" for someone or something. Maybe you should be more assertive, even aggressive, in attitude and outlook.

figures If numbers are involved, all depends on your attitude to arithmetical problems in waking life: if they are part of your working day, this may simply be a "worry" dream, or suggest a difficulty in unwinding and relaxing; otherwise, certain obsessional problems may be suggested, or an over-concern with material matters. Are you, in waking life, summing up the pros and cons, the plusses and minuses, of a situation or problem? Perhaps you are concerned to "balance the books" in one particular area of your life.

film If your dream obviously refers to a film you saw the previous evening, it may still be a comment on some aspect of your life, otherwise why did your unconscious refer to it, rather than to anything else that happened during the day?

The details of the dream film will obviously be significant. But the reference may be an attempt to present this in a way which will enable you to see it more distantly, "up on a screen" rather than as part of your own experience. Often we find ourselves taking part in the action; again, this can offer the opportunity to see things more objectively – or can prompt us to make the effort to do so. Our problems are removed from the stalls to a place where they are in focus, but less tangible. See *camera*, *cinema*.

finance Your dream financial situation may be commenting on your real one, of course; but the relationship between money and the expression of emotion (see *expense*) suggests that there could be a reference to an emotional area of your life. An overdraft may mean that you have overspent on your emotional (or sexual) account; an overflowing bank balance that you are not giving out enough love and affection. But also consider whether your dream is offering a perfectly rational comment on your material financial circumstances.

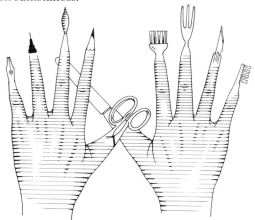

fingers Too many fingers in a pie? A finger pointing the way forward? A finger can obviously be a phallic symbol. And see *body*.

fire See FIRE (p. 78–9).

fishing You are unlikely to dream of fishing unless, in waking life, the activity means something to you, so first consider your attitude to it. Simple enjoyment of leisure in a peaceful LAND-SCAPE (see p. 68–9) may be a reassurance, or a hint that you need more relaxation. For fishing at sea, see *boat*, but add the ingredient that you are searching for something (in, perhaps, a stormy context). As WATER (see p. 80–1) is involved, there is very possibly a reference to your emotional life (are there calmer waters ahead?) Your catch, or lack of it, is significant. Fish taken from the sea, "the harvest of the deep", may suggest

experience of life, and the hint that you should make more of it. Something is perhaps being "brought to the surface"; maybe your dream is drawing attention to a psychological problem which you have been ignoring? If so, look to it. Or there may be a punning element: are you "fishing" for compliments? The fish is also a traditional Christian symbol.

fit The violent image of a fit, or convulsion, could focus on something very disturbing or distressing, so look at the context, which may give you a clue whether it is a psychological or material matter that is under discussion, and which has perhaps been more disturbing than you realize. Talk the problem over with a friend or counsellor, and if the reference seems purely physical, reassure yourself by consulting your doctor, especially if the dream recurs. There could be a pun: are you "fit for action", "fit for life", how fit are you, physically; were you being "fitted up" or for a garment? The waking parallels are clear.

flag If you were "flying the flag", ask whether the dream could be focusing on your sense of self-esteem. The symbol is probably positive, unless the flag was hanging limply at the top of the pole (on the face of it, a strong symbol of sexual insecurity, impotence or frigidity). Was the dream hinting that your energy is "flagging"? If your car was "flagged down", here is a possible hint that you stop some present course of action.

flames See FIRE (p. 78–9).

flash A blinding flash – of lightning? Something happening "in a flash"? This may be a lively reference to sudden self-realization or inspiration; perhaps you should follow up any new ideas you have had.

flesh Human or animal flesh? Enjoyable or horrifying? The fact that you have looked your dream up under "flesh" rather than *meat* suggests a perhaps unconscious feeling that the dream was sexual in nature; in which case either the pleasure or horror may refer to recent sexual proclivities or activities. Follow up any dream clues carefully, for there may be strong hints which could lead to more positive sexual experience, or a widening of interest and deepening of pleasure. One other suggestion: could the dream have been a simple reference to your being overweight, "fleshy" (see, possibly, *butcher*)?

flight A dream reference to "a flight" (i.e., an airline flight), may refer to a specific waking project, in which case the safety, exhilaration, apprehension, speed and comfort, or delay and late arrival, may reflect your view of it. But, of course, see FLYING (p. 84–5).

floating There are obvious associations with FLYING (p. 84–5) (effortlessness, freedom); but the connection with WATER (p. 80–1) suggests an emotional context. You are perhaps on top of emotional problems, enjoying what that area of your life is offering. But because the connection between you and the water is closer, more "embracing" than that between the flier and the air, it may be that you are not sufficiently distanced from any emotional problem that may be worrying you. If you start to sink, or are struggling, the inference is obvious; try to find your own way of staying afloat!

flood A dream of being involved in a flood is usually concerned with survival; what are you trying to survive in waking life? If you succeeded in keeping your head above water, clearly you are coping well; less well, if you were swept along by the flood – in which case examine your emotional reaction to some element in your life – someone or something may be making an overpoweringly strong impact on your emotions. Remember that *you* could be the flood, "in full flood" in some way in your waking life. There could be a warning that you are overwhelming others, swamping them by your actions and opinions. See *swimming*, WATER (p. 80–1).

floor Rather as with *earth*, the state of the floor is likely to be symbolically concerned with your feeling of security or lack of it, perhaps with a direct reference to your job (especially if you work indoors). If you were scrubbing the floor, perhaps there is a reference to your desire for a clean and tidy background or to drudgery in your work. But the context is important: if you were sitting comfortably on the floor, you are probably into a contented phase of your waking life. If you were laying a carpet, perhaps you are trying to lay plans, or make your life more comfortable. A rough, dirty floor or a beautiful one may equally be comments on your present situation. And remember *you* could be the floor: is anyone walking all over you at present?

flowers Because most people associate flowers with beauty and an enviably open, natural quality, there is a possible reference to your feeling about your own personality and developing consciousness (especially if the flowers were in bud, or opening). The COLOUR (p. 94–5) of the flowers may be significant, and it might be worthwhile referring to a good book on the traditional symbolic meaning of flowers (too complex to give here); you may not be conscious that you know about this, but you may unconsciously have assimilated the knowledge in childhood or through casual reading. The dream flowers could depict a developing love or sexual relationship, especially if you were picking or wanted to pick one in particular. The gathering of flowers is a potent symbol of fulfilment. If the flowers were withering or dead, or died when you picked them (one old tradition claims that "flowers fade on a flirt"!) there could be a comment on the end of an emotional relationship or commitment, a change in your feelings or allegiance. Perhaps in waking life you are passing through a period of sadness, in which case the symbol could in a sense be reassuring – the message that all things, even the most beautiful, pass away (dying lilies carved on the walls of the Taj Mahal confirm the death of the Princess buried there, as well as expressing sorrow at her death). Those especially impressed by dreams of this sort might like to consult C. G. Jung's *The Secret of the Golden Flower*. A dream that you caught a thrown wedding bouquet may be a wish-fulfilment.

fly The association of flies with *dirt* or *disease* could be a starting-point in your interpretation; but perhaps the symbol was a pun: you may be wanting to work out what someone else is planning, longing to be a "fly on the wall"; or caught up in a web of intrigue (was a *spider* on the scene?) A buzzing, worrisome fly may indicate a worrying, irritating person in your waking life. If you were consciously the fly, are you buzzing too busily around other people and their business? Beware the fly-spray!

flying See FLYING (p. 84–5).

fog An obvious hint that there is some waking situation or person you are not seeing too clearly; ask your dreams for further help (see p. 47) if the reference seems more oblique. See perhaps *blind*, WEATHER (p. 74–5).

food See FOOD AND DRINK (p. 86–7).

foot See *feet*.

football If you scored a goal, then it seems likely that the dream is a confirmation of some personal success, or an indication of extreme confidence. Further dreams may suggest you should continue to play a prominent part in the *game*! If you were a spectator and your team won the match, or a player who did not score but was on the winning side, this seems also a positive symbol, but one more connected with your part within a team of some sort than with your individual efforts. If you had the opportunity to score, but missed, the reference is perhaps to a missed opportunity, or one you may miss if you aren't careful. Are you simply "playing along" without sufficient involvement? And remember, you could be the *ball*: who's kicking you around?

ford A ford represents the easy way over a river: WATER (p. 80–1) is a strong symbol of emotional life – so are you seeking the easy way out of an emotional problem? Beware: fords can be deceptive, and can sometimes lead into deep water. The problem you face may seem deceptively simple. Perhaps you will find further clues in the LANDSCAPE (p. 68–9).

foreigner The appearance in a dream of a foreigner, speaking perhaps in an unknown tongue, suggests that there is some element in your waking life that is foreign to your nature, that you are maybe behaving uncharacteristically. But he or she might represent some strange situation within which you are trying to find your way. If so, what was the stranger's effect on you?

forest A "forest" suggests uncertainty and perhaps obstruction. Trying to find your way through it may reflect a search for some kind of breakthrough in your waking life – or a pun on not being able to see the wood for the trees. Trees, with their beauty and majesty and often great age might represent your unconscious itself, the depths of your psychological being, maturity and psychological growth. Cutting down a tree, if you are a man, has certain sexual connotations – a rebuke to over-expressed sexuality, perhaps? If you are a woman, there may be a reference to a particular man whom you wish to "cut down to size" sexually or otherwise. In fairy tales things were often found in forests: a Snow White figure, sleeping babes, a gingerbread house containing a witch . . . Think out the associations. See LANDSCAPE (p. 68–9).

forge The forging of links of friendship, bonds of love, springs to mind; consider whether you are ready to deepen an emotional relationship, or make some other commitment. Because of imminent actions you will probably achieve a greater sense of security and stability. The forging of documents or banknotes suggests deception.

fork Have you to "fork out" for anything – not necessarily financially, but perhaps emotionally? You could be "forking your way through" a

great number of problems, concerns or interests; consider the context of the dream – perhaps you are warned to be more selective. If you are musical, a tuning-fork may be involved – a symbol of "true" pitch, of being "in tune", perhaps psychologically. Are you using your intuition sufficiently? A fork is in some cultures a symbol of masculinity: the "poor forked creature" of Shakespeare, or the forked mandrake root of legend. Could that apply?

fort Your dreams may be telling you something about your emotional defences; or if the fort represents yourself, perhaps you are not taking enough care of your body, defending it sufficiently against attack from disease or illness. In each case, a fort under attack is significant. Perhaps you are mustering up psychological or physical strength to face some demanding situation.

fortune To dream of making your fortune is not, of course, predictive; but there may be a reference to inner riches, sources of yet unexpressed emotional depth. The loss of a fortune may refer to the loss of human love, or perhaps to an over-expenditure of emotional energy, draining your resources. A dream of having your fortune told may be one of wish-fulfilment – "if she tells me, it must be true". But not necessarily in waking life! You may be the gypsy, warning yourself of some coming difficulty; in which case take note of it – you are your own best fortune-teller.

fossil The fossil may represent knowledge gained a long time ago, or you may have been digging up the past. But perhaps you yourself (or someone else) may be "an old fossil" (however young you are in years). Consider whether you are moving with the times, or fossilized in some past attitude or opinion. See *archaeology*.

fountain Associated of course with WATER (See p. 80–1), and thus with emotion, fountains are usually considered beautiful – exuberant but controlled. There may be a comment on your sexual attitude to a lover; an overt reference to orgasm; but apart from this obvious analogy, the romantic overtones – a fountain is all decoration, all romantic expression – should not be overlooked, especially if the flow of water is blocked or perhaps frozen.

fox The fox's reputation for sly cunning may hint at some plotting in waking life; perhaps you are being particularly "foxy" at present. But foxes are said to be excellent parents; there may be an association there. Or the allusion may be to the fox as victim of cruel huntsmen. Are you hunted, or hunter, and if so, who does the other party represent? Are you in pursuit of something desirable, but only to be obtained at a certain price (the hunt ends in blood and pain).

frame Are you "framing up" for action? Or examining some situation with care, so as to confine it within careful bounds? If you were framing a photograph or picture, the subject of it will be an important clue. Remember that a frame "shows off" a picture, but also confines it behind glass, untouchable and fixed forever; obviously there could be a comment on your waking view or treatment of a lover or a child. Perhaps you were "framing" someone, or being "framed" – accused of something of which you are innocent. Who was the other person?

fraud Participation in a fraud could hint that in waking life you are either deceiving someone or taking the easy way out of a difficult situation. Perhaps you are taking advantage of others by using their difficulties to your own advantage. Or perhaps you unconsciously suspect someone is using or cheating you – in which case the dream may be a useful warning.

friend You may of course simply be dreaming of a friend in the same way as you would think of him or her in waking life; a pleasant and relaxing experience. But a friend, like a *family* member, can represent an aspect of one's own personality – perhaps a trait which in the first place attracted you. What your friend said or did in the dream is obviously important, and may underline your own reactions in a certain waking situation; or there may be a focus on something you deeply desire.

frost Perhaps a comment on an aspect of your life which you are unable fully to express: a frost holds back growth, and can even destroy. It seems most likely that the reference is to your emotions – perhaps you are behaving "coldly", or perhaps someone has this attitude to you. The beauty of frost patterns may represent a beautiful but unattainable person. You could ask your dreams (see p. 47) how best to make the sun melt the frost (see *cold*).

f

fountain *Fountain architecture*, H. Vredeman de Vries

fruit Ripe fruit sometimes suggests sensuality, pleasure. Certain fruits have particularly sexual connotations (see FOOD AND DRINK, p. 86–7). Do not ignore a possible reference to the fruits of your labours – material possessions or money.

fuel The reference probably refers in some way to your domestic life; if you were running short of fuel, consider whether you may be deficient in warmth – emotional warmth – or your body deficient in vitamins or protein.

funeral A dream funeral can refer to the death of something in us – a desire or an objective, perhaps, or the end of a material project. In any case it is likely to presage change. It can be a very positive symbol, for you are ready for new commitments, new experiences; you may be "burying the hatchet" and changing your attitude to someone. If you were watching your own funeral, there is no need for distress: question yourself – you were perhaps burying "the old you"; now you are ready for rebirth – so see BIRTH, DEATH AND TRANSFORMATION (p. 76–7), *coffin, corpse.*

fur A very sensual image, conveying a sense of warmth and luxury, and perhaps of achievement, if the fur is that of a coat or stole. But perhaps you felt that wearing another animal's skin was abhorrent to you? Then it may be that beneath the surface of some reward, some status symbol, is the feeling that you have been less than fair in acquiring it, or that something or someone is not actually as beautiful and desirable as you thought. The type of fur involved may well be important: are you a wolf in sheep's clothing – or a sheep masquerading as a wolf? A mink can be a vicious little creature; a fox, cunning . . .

furniture The furniture of your home can represent the furniture of your character: so if you were buying something new, or renewing something, the same process may be going on in waking life – your personality or mind may be expanding, taking in new facts and attitudes. But the purchase of heavy, unwieldy furniture, difficult to move, may represent a burden or responsibility you could well do without. If you were breaking furniture, perhaps some of your attitudes need radical rethinking! Furniture giving way under you has the same connotation as an uncertain *floor*, or the *ground* becoming uncertain during an *earthquake*.

fury See *anger.*

future The examination of allegedly predictive dreams has produced a few cases of unexplained accuracy (see p. 58), but it would be unwise to rely on them uncritically. A great deal more research is needed, for instance, into the conviction we sometimes have that an incident dreamed, perhaps months ago, has just happened. On the other hand, do not completely ignore warnings which seem rationally based. The unconscious can store up observations which may accurately "predict" an event. But a dream of some personal or national disaster is often unlikely to be fulfilled, except by chance.

g

gag If you were gagged in a dream, the chances are that your unconscious is strongly suggesting that you should shut up and keep quiet! It may be that you are being restrained from making some kind of declaration which is important to you: if so, decide who or what is blocking you, and the real reason. Perhaps you are yourself unable to speak, in which case there may be a psychological or intuitive inhibition. If you wake up laughing, having dreamed a "gag" or joke, and it is still funny in the morning, you will have experienced a remarkably rare phenomenon. More often than not, as with poetry or the plot of a thriller, it will not bear the light of reason!

gale Are you in some way being blown off course? Consider the possibility (see also *storm*, or, if relevant, *sea*). Or perhaps you know someone called Gail.

gallows Consider who or what is threatening you in waking life, or causing you distress. The *death* of someone (perhaps yourself) on the gallows need not necessarily be a distressing or worrying symbol; it could indicate an important change of some sort in your life, or may be summing up your feelings about something – "Hang it all, what do I care?" Unless, of course, you are feeling so guilty about something that hanging really seems a proper punishment!

gambling Probably a statement about some kind of risk-taking in which you may be involved: think about winnings and losses, the size of the stake. Some people place great importance on dreaming of a "lucky" number or a horse's name before a big race, and occasionally there are rumours of big winnings obtained after such "predictive" dreams. Such things have been known to happen, but be cautious about relying too much on such signals from the unconscious.

games The sort of game you were playing is obviously important, and it is tempting for once to be Freudian and suggest that there is probably a sexual dimension to a dream to which the description "game" applies. Your opponent in a game may be your lover or a partner of some kind, but could also represent an aspect of yourself – perhaps an aspect of your sexuality which you doubt. See *cards, football, team.*

garden A dream of a garden is likely to be one of the most complex symbolic dreams you can have, and will probably take a very great deal of interpreting, for there are many possible avenues to follow, with other possible references to consult – LANDSCAPE (p. 68–9) and *flowers*, to mention only two of the most important. If the dream really seems to concentrate on the garden itself, it is possible to think of it as representing our own characters (as with a *building*), or as a representation of our potential, the possibilities that lie before us. First try to decide which area of your life the garden represents, then consider its nature: is it carefully planned, well laid-out, beautifully cared-for? Or is it choked with weeds, dry and arid, a tangle of luxuriant but indisciplined growth? If the dream is suggesting that you should look more closely at yourself, the parallels may be obvious (if uncomfortable). And what about the paths? In a garden dream one is often walking down a path, sometimes one which seems familiar, sometimes one which winds under dark trees and into threatening thickets. Are you being led "up the garden path" by someone, or following a false trail? A promising avenue can be blocked by a locked gate, a closed door or a blank wall. In waking life, you may be moving ahead confidently and comfortably – but try to see around the bend ahead. Within the garden, look of course for other symbols – *trees, fountains, streams* and so on, which may be secondary but important.

gas This could be a punning dream – what have you been gassing about? But check your house for physical gas leaks, too. See *fuel.*

gate In the dream, was it swinging, open, or shut? Perhaps it was keeping you away from some desirable walk or landscape, or inviting you through? Comparable to a *door*, a gate is less mysterious but at the same time somehow more strong and restrictive. If you had to climb over your gate, there may be a suggestion that additional energy and attack is needed to deal with a waking obstruction. How difficult was the climb, and how successful? The gate may have swung open of its own accord, a symbol perhaps of a welcoming of new opportunities.

gate-crashing Your dream may be suggesting that you are encroaching in some way on someone else's territory. So this is possibly a warning dream, especially if you were detected and thrown out! But if you enjoyed the experience, perhaps you should make the effort to enter a world (psychological or physical) which seems a little forbidding.

gay A dream about homosexuality or a homosexual is probably to be interpreted in terms of your own sexuality; it can be shocking for a dreamer who thinks of himself or herself as entirely heterosexual. But perhaps there is a suggestion that you should be more understanding, broad-minded, or may even in some way be repressing your true sexuality. The unconscious is particularly wise in this area of our lives, and close attention to the sexual symbol in our dreams can be extremely rewarding.

ghost Seeing your own ghost or *doppleganger* in waking life was always considered a sign of death. But your ghostly appearance in your own dream may suggest that in some way you are "a ghost of your former self", that you should take more care of yourself. Perhaps we should approach a dream ghost as we approach a "real" ghost (assuming that we believe in them): i.e., by trying to find out why it appeared, and what sort of help it needs. Which is just how we should approach our dreams themselves! See *double.*

giant Were you the giant, or intimidated by him? Could you be both David *and* Goliath? – in which case, what enormous obstacle have you to overcome within yourself? There could be a sexual reference (almost every giant in fiction is in some way connected with sex, and often depicted traditionally with enormous genitals). Was the giant threatening you with a large *club*? If you are

a man, perhaps your sexual needs are disproportionate, or you feel guilty about gratifying them;
if a woman, perhaps the thought of the male
body in arousal is repulsive or frightening to you,
or you feel your partner's sexual demands are
excessive. There is a possibility that a giant could
be an ogre of a father or a father figure. Your
dream may mean you have an inferiority complex or feel dominated by someone.

girl The context is obviously vital, but always
remember that any female figure in a dream
could represent the female side of one's
personality.

giving The act of giving anything in a dream is
probably related to the giving of emotional
energy, and how it is received, in waking life. But
what you give is a vitally important symbol.

giant *Nimrod*, Gustave Doré

girl

Ivy dreamed: *"I was a girl again, and all my friends were riding past me on bicycles. I so wanted to be with them, but my parents wouldn't let me have a bicycle – it was 'too dangerous'."*

The last of Ivy's dreams before she died of cancer, recalling her youth when she had longed for a bicycle; but it reflected an unconscious realization that life was passing her by, and referred obliquely to her incapacitating illness (see also p. 125).

glass Glass is brittle, and should be clear, sparkling, capable of being seen through (displaying rather than hiding); or if it is looking-glass, should reflect truly and without distortion. It can be broken accidentally, or ceremonially (the destruction of innocence). A dirty or distorting glass or mirror may suggest that you are not seeing clearly in waking life: something behind glass, unreachable, suggests "I know what I want – but I can't reach it!" Why not? The breaking of glass suggests a violent attempt to break through barriers which should not be there – though there can also be a suggestion of defloration, the ruining of innocence.

globe Have you "the whole world in your hands"? A global view of a problem or its solution? A *circle* is a potent symbol of wholeness, and has rather the same implication.

gloom Physical gloom in a dream suggests that you may lack direction in, or be uncertain about, your present waking life; why not ask your dreams to be more specific (see p. 47). But perhaps see *blind*.

glory Did you attain a state of glory? Be careful – you may be enjoying disproportionate admiration, be too pleased with yourself and your efforts. Consider a whole series of dreams and their symbols before supposing that you are a very special person.

glove Gloves, like shoes, have always been potent sexual symbols; a worn glove, a glove with a hole in it, a lost glove, a carefully dropped glove – all have obvious connotations either for women (whose unconscious will usually be sending out signals about their attitude to sexuality) or men (whose attitude to women may be under examination). But gloves also have connotations of comfort and security, as well as of secrecy.

goal Did you score, or miss? Is something in your life a hit-or-miss affair? Was the dream making a statement about your objectives in life, and the way you attain them? See *football*.

goat In addition to the religious antithesis of goats and sheep, goats can climb dexterously to the top of a rock, or remain tethered to a post. Which was the case in your dream, and what did such a symbol have to say about the present state of your waking life, your ambitions? Are you held back by responsibilities and commitments? If so, think again; they may be an excuse for your failure to break the rope and make off up the mountainside. Think of the symbol in a sexual context too; the great god Pan is half-goat, and highly sexually active men have for centuries been described as having "a goatish disposition".

God The appearance of God in a dream will be (like every other dream symbol) entirely subjective, and reveal your unconscious (true) view of the Creator or the creative impulse – whether you are atheist, agnostic, Christian, Buddhist or whatever. But the chances are that this will not necessarily be a "religious" dream, but have something to say about authority in the abstract, about your inner god's laws, opinions, restrictions. The repressive side of your nature (nurtured perhaps by a god-like father figure) may be making itself felt, or perhaps there will be a protest against it – in which case stormy conflicts may demand resolution. A series of similar dreams may confirm what such strong symbolism has to say about your problems or attitudes. Less profound could be a dream of someone else as God – a hint you are making "a tin god" of someone who may be less impressive than you think; or one in which you are "playing God" in some way – always a potentially dangerous occupation, especially where other people are concerned. Are you self-opinionated or vain?

gold Have you "struck gold" with an idea or concept? Gold is a potent symbol: there could be a comment on self-realization. Or perhaps you are gathering particularly rich experiences of life at present.

government If you were in Government, "in power", in your dream, there could be a suggestion that you are in excellent control of your life and current situation; on the other hand, be

g

g

careful not to be autocratic; take note of the opposition, which itself may find a place in your dreams shortly, if in an oblique way.

gown Did the gown fit well, and did you feel good in it? The chances are that your dream was making a statement about how you fit into your present lifestyle, or the sort of image you are projecting. If you were buying a gown, could this have been a comment on a tendency to show off? Or are you experiencing a period of change – in image, but perhaps also in personality? There are overtones of wish-fulfilment, maybe – especially if you are a single woman in need of a relationship, and dreamed of buying a wedding dress. See CLOTHES AND NUDITY (p. 82–3).

grandparents Grandparents may sometimes be more sympathetic figures in early memories than parents, and dreams involving them may be offering particularly sound advice. See *family*.

grapes There sometimes seems something sensual and affluent about grapes – an association no doubt with their juicy sweetness and succulence. But there is also an association with sickness and convalescence. You may be specially enjoying life at present; but taken with the grape symbolism, perhaps other areas of your dreams are issuing a health warning – or just a warning that your life is too sybaritic at present!

grass Did the COLOUR (p. 94–5) of the grass and its condition impress you (green and lush, brown and parched)? Were you cutting grass or sowing it? Romping on it, or playing some kind of *game*? There may be a comment on your present life, its richness or otherwise. Or, in thieves' slang, a pun: have you been telling tales, gossiping, "grassing" on someone? Did the grass seem greener on the other side of the hedge, and if so, should you be moving on in some way?

grave Dreaming of a grave may link up with *funeral* or perhaps DEATH (p. 76–7). You may find these entries reassuring. The grave itself has associations perhaps with *digging*; there may be a pun on a "grave" man or situation as opposed to the symbolism of an ending or rebirth. There may be a hint that you should take some situation in your waking life more gravely or seriously than you are at present.

greed There may be the suggestion here that you are being greedy in some way or another in your waking life – too demanding of your partner, perhaps, or of your children; maybe they need more love, consideration, time. Greedily swal-

lowing food which you do not really care for might suggest you are a "glutton for punishment"; or you may simply be eating too much at present, so that your liver is complaining!

green Though one of God's favourite colours (the colour of creation), green is also the colour of *jealousy* and *envy* – if also of innocence. See COLOUR (p. 94–5).

grief An overpowering feeling of a grief in a dream may suggest something in your waking life which is distressing you more than you consciously realize. If this is true, try to find a way of expressing your grief more openly; the hurt will be quicker to heal. But deep grief, in a dream, can also refer to the past – to lost innocence or lost ideals, for instance.

grinding Grinding what: spices, corn – or just grindingly hard work? Your dream may simply be interpreting the conditions of your present work, maybe boringly repetitive. Ask it (p. 47) to suggest new outlets and areas of interest.

ground See *earth*, *earthquake*.

guard Perhaps a pun: do you need to be more on your guard in some area? If you were on guard, what were you guarding? Something that may symbolize your honour, your virtue (maybe in the shape of some much-loved possession)? A guard in a train may perhaps symbolize some authority figure: who, and performing what duty, or giving what instruction?

guest Perhaps the dream is suggesting that you are an unwanted guest, drawing your attention to the fact that you are unduly interfering with other people's enjoyment or freedom. If you were receiving guests into your home, the dream may be saying that you are ready to accept new challenges and interests which will extend your personality.

guide You may be in need of guidance. Question your dreams (see p. 47) to discover in what area; you may be seeking a trail which will lead to greater fulfilment or personal development.

guillotine Decide whether you are about to be prevented, or "cut off" from doing something you really want to do; or whether you need to cut someone out of your life. See *execution*.

guitar The guitar has always been, because of its shape and perhaps the sensuality of its tone, a symbol of the female body. A man playing a guitar in a dream, or perhaps simply listening to it, may be engaging in a sexual fantasy, or expressing the desire for greater sexual fulfilment. A woman having the same dream may perhaps be neglecting the female side of her psyche. Incidentally, was the guitar sharp or flat, was its tone rich or meagre?

gun Perhaps the most famous, or notorious, of all phallic symbols. The questions that instantly suggest themselves include: did the gun fail to go off? Who were you shooting at? Who was shooting at you? Was it loaded with blanks? Did you hit the target? And so on.

gutter On the face of it, a rather sad dream symbol; perhaps you are feeling particularly "low" at present, either emotionally forlorn or financially "in the gutter".

gym Perhaps the dream is hinting about physical fitness; but dreams of a successful work-out seem likely to be very positive, work is going well. Unless of course, there is someone called Jim in your life!

h

hair A dream of hair may well be drawing our attention to the state of our self-esteem, for loss of hair, falling hair, baldness, often symbolize loss of self-respect, while beautiful, luxurious hair is a boost to our ego. But hair is also a symbol of the life force itself, its sexual appeal is an important factor, and for men there is a strong allusion to potency. Young boys' frequent dislike of going to the barber has been seen as a castration fear. Some women have a somewhat similar complex, connected to the inherent fear of having the head shaved for a misdemeanour, and perhaps too to the sacrifice of sexual life by nuns, some of whom symbolize this by having their heads shaved. Think around these possibilities and apply them to the context of the dream, which could be a statement of importance. See *baldness*.

hall See ENVIRONMENT (p. 92–3). Such a building suggests a communal attitude, but a large, empty hall could represent an important and under-exploited area of your personality. The objects and people *in* the hall could be critical in interpretation.

hammer A very "male" instrument, so think about possible sexual connotations. But are you trying to "hammer out" a deal, or a solution? Or have you "taken a hammering" lately? Perhaps you need to strike a blow at someone or something.

hand Hopefully your hand was not injured in any way; there may be an allusion to "a helping hand"; or you may have something important "on hand". See *body*.

hanging See *gallows*; if you were hanging someone or something, you must decide whether you need to eliminate some psychological characteristic – or simply to mature in some way, remembering that to hang game is to mature it for the table. Hanging in the sense of killing someone is most likely to refer to the need to eradicate some distasteful element from your life, perhaps as likely to be a personal failing as another person. See also, perhaps, *death, execution, guillotine*.

harbour Harbours are protective, and while your dreams could be focusing on some personal quality, what was inside the dream harbour may well be important. Ask yourself whether in waking life you are "harbouring" resentment – some old grudge. The dream may be reassuring you of emotional and material security; perhaps your ship has come in!

hare The hare is speedy, wily, occasionally (in March) mad; your dream could be suggesting that you are "haring off" – perhaps in the wrong direction; or outdistancing your competitors. But have you changed course recently, perhaps for no good reason? The dream may possibly be a pun on *hair*.

harmony Listening to beautiful music is an image of pure pleasure. There may be a comment on the harmony of your waking life, and the presence or absence of it in the dream will be relevant. It has been known for composers to benefit from their dreams.

harp This could possibly be a symbol of heaven. But perhaps you are "harping on" about something. Try to remember if you were the soloist, and the reactions of your audience.

harvest Hopefully your hard work has paid off, and you are now in a position to reap what you have sown – the benefit of work and experience. What you were harvesting is, of course, relevant; but the dream is likely to be focusing on increased security, knowledge or fulfilment – unless, of course, it is a warning dream, and your unconscious fears you are about to reap what you have sown in a less than pleasant sense. See *corn*.

hat Sometimes a hat can seem to change one's entire personality: are you attempting to do this at present? Freud insisted that both women's and men's hats could be interpreted "with certainty" (*sic*) as genital organs – significant perhaps if you hoped your hat would impress someone, or if you lost it, or threw it away.

hatchet Perhaps you are doing "a hatchet job" on someone, or some drastic action is called for. Or you may be ready to "bury the hatchet". But the hatchet is also another of Freud's favoured male phallic symbols (see *gun*): men especially should consider it in that light – who you were attacking, or whether you were just waving it aimlessly about . . .

hatred If you were overwhelmed with the emotion, in your dream, there may be a focus on some negative waking feeling, perhaps about an element of your own personality: the person or thing you were hating is, of course, very relevant, but you may well need considerable self-analysis to get to the root of the problem. Once you have identified the real object of your hatred, you are halfway to resolving the problem; but if your efforts leave you perplexed or distressed, it will be worth considering asking a counsellor or therapist for help.

hawk A bird of prey not unlike the *eagle*; but we think of the hawk, perhaps, as specially predatory and wild, tenacious in the chase and having a particularly sharp eye – so there may be a suggestion that you should imitate the bird before swooping on any victim you have in mind. If you were frightened by a hawk or bird of prey, your dream could be warning you about an attack apparently "out of the blue" from some unexpected assailant your unconscious has detected.

head See *body* if actual pain is involved. But perhaps you are simply keeping ahead in your work? Or maybe you should be taking the lead in some project or some aspect of your life. Things are perhaps coming to a head. Two heads (if you dream of them) may indeed be better than one. Maybe you should examine what is going on in your head at present: your private thoughts, psychological problems, or whatever.

headline Do your waking actions smack of the sensational, so that you are "making headline

news" (if only privately)? If you read a striking headline in your dream, it may be trying to punch home some important message, personal or psychological. There may be a suggestion that you should allow your head to rule your heart. It might just be worth remembering that the "head-line" in palmistry shows the way one thinks: whether one is original, factual, imaginative, grasping, open handed . . . (see also *messages*, perhaps).

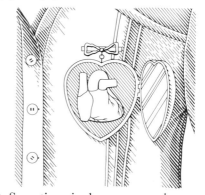

heart Sometimes in sleep we move into a position in which we are very conscious of the sound of our heart beat, and this may trigger off a dream; the very sound sometimes prompts us to symbolize the heart by dreaming of a hollow, empty wooden box, or some similar object. News of heart transplants, or open-heart surgery, could figure in dreams – especially if at the moment you are changing lovers – transplanting your heart, as it were, from one to the other. Ask yourself if you are putting enough "heart" into your work, or your relationship. Or should you follow your heart rather than your head when making some current decision? Such dreams really could focus on the core of your being, your deepest and most significant emotions and sentiments, for since time immemorial the symbol of the heart has represented man's spiritual centre, understanding and love.

hearth See FIRE (p. 78–9), but confinement to the domestic fireplace could also indicate a connection with the family, or perhaps with your start in life, your social origins. Comfort and security seem likely to be underlined, a close-knit *family* circle. Set the other symbols, and the action of the dream in that context, and see what it suggests. Perhaps there is a need for greater warmth, greater security or protection. Often our imagination is kindled by "pictures in the fire"; has this a significance?

heat Heat symbolizes energy, work, passion – sexual and emotional energy; but also sunshine, illuminating and producing life. Then there is the heat of the kitchen (if you don't like it, leave!). Your physical body temperature may trigger this kind of dream, but if that is not the cause, try to refer the heat in your dream to your present attitudes, feelings, opinions and needs. See *kitchen*, FIRE (p. 78–9).

heaven and hell Happiness or despair, the symbolic flavours of heaven or hell, may in a dream simply be reflections of your current feelings about your life. Our personal symbols of these "places" depend very much on our background, education, reading, cultural background . . . Your dream may be telling you something very important and very basic. Or, alternatively, a dream of your idea of heaven may be escapist: perhaps you simply need a holiday! A terrifying dream of hell may reflect your guilty feelings about some action.

hedge See *fence*; it could be either less restrictive (made not of iron but of earth and plants), or more difficult to get through (a tangle of brambles, maybe). Still, a restriction on your freedom, perhaps a barrier between you and something you seek. If you were clipping and shaping it, this may be a hint to make the best of things, through self-discipline and persuasion. Consider carefully what seemed to be on the other side of the hedge, and most important, your own reaction and attitude to it. See LANDSCAPE (p. 68–9), *grass*.

hell See *heaven and hell*.

helmet A protective article, so the dream may be saying you are about to do battle; or if the helmet was punctured, may be about to suffer a defeat, or be feeling defenceless. A helmet can be merely ceremonial, so there may be a reference to self-esteem – or a sexual symbol (see *hat*).

herd The dream could be rebuking you for going too much with the herd, failing to think and strike out a line for yourself. Or was it a pun, and have you just heard something that disturbs you?

hero/heroine Someone you admire, no doubt; but analyse your admiration, for it is the root of it which is probably in question in your dream – a quality you wish to encourage in yourself. Consider whether your dream seemed to be encouraging you, or putting you down: was your hero victorious, triumphant, but human – or so far beyond your admiration that you could never hope to emulate him? There could be a comment on your own achievements so far, as well as an encouragement to scale new heights. The Hero is an important Jungian archetype (see p. 25).

hide and seek Are you taking evasive action in waking life, or perhaps restless, continually changing your mind or your attitudes? Were you "found out", in your dream? Indecision could be coming under scrutiny – or coquettish behaviour.

hill You may in waking life be coping with an obstacle, or some difficulty; so whether you were toiling breathlessly up the hill or mounting it easily and with confidence may have something to say about your confidence about reaching an ultimate objective. There could be the inference that the problem may be more laborious than you suppose, or the hill may symbolize a heavy responsibility. See *earth*, LANDSCAPE (p. 68–9), *mountain*.

hit Scoring a hit (as with scoring a *goal* in *football*) seems likely to refer to some recent or approaching success; an encouraging dream, then. But "hitting out" is another matter; you may be harbouring anger or aggression. Consider whether you need in waking life to find some way of letting out that emotion as you do when you hit a ball – perhaps through exercise, or simply having a blazing row with someone. Think too of the pun "making a hit" with someone. See also *bat*, *ball*, *game*, *goal*.

hive If the hive represents your own personality or life-style, then intense activity – but also contentment – seem to be indicated. Bees are notoriously orderly and hard workers. Try to see anything which happened to the hive – a disturbance, its being moved, or whatever – in terms of your working, or perhaps domestic life. See *bees*, *honey*.

hole A hole in a garment may be drawing your attention to the fact that your visual image needs refurbishing! But a dream of a hole in the ground, or in some object, carries strong sexual implications. What was going into, or coming out of, the hole? Were you actually going into a hole yourself, as Alice did, to get to Wonderland (see *falling*)? If you were digging a hole, maybe you are in the planning stages of a new project, and preparing to lay the foundations (but also see *archaeology*). What were you putting into the hole, if anything? An empty hole seems to suggest that your life may be rather empty at present; turn your waking thoughts towards new interests, perhaps new relationships, to make it more fulfilling and worthwhile. The dream could be punning on "whole": perhaps psychological wholeness and its development.

holiday Perhaps you are simply ready for one. But a holiday indicates change, escape: are you trying to escape from reality at present? Dreams of places we have not visited, but which make a strong impression on us, are not only good entertainment value, but could reflect a need for challenge, especially intellectual challenge. You may need new horizons. See *expedition, journey*.

home Your dreams are probably focusing on your basic security; think about the dream in the context of your childhood and your relationship with your parents. Your dream could also be saying "come home" – not necessarily physically, but in the sense of getting your priorities right, returning to the basic values of life. Maybe at present you are thinking of starting a family, or home-making for the first time; if so, your dream should be specially important in its implications, telling you something of your true attitude to the future.

honey Sweet, very nutritional, and natural; a lot of hard work and energy go into its production. It is probably one of the foremost "comfort" foods. So dreaming of honey could relate to very natural, sweet, kind but productive actions, of your own or someone else's. But to many people honey is almost too sweet, and if this is your reaction, maybe the dream is referring to someone whose pleasant behaviour to you may be false or cloying (or to whom you behave in that way). Think of your emotional "riches"; is there perhaps a reference to your paternal or maternal instincts. See *bees, hive*.

honeymoon This could be a wish-fulfilment dream, if you have not experienced one; if your dream honeymoon was triumphantly successful or terrifyingly unsuccessful, there may be a comment on sexual apprehension or fear which perhaps you should analyse.

honour Your dreams could be encouraging you by referring to some honour you deserve; the kind of honour being bestowed may be significant. Try to decide what you admire in the person receiving the honour; or, if you were receiving it, what you feel about the person presenting it. See *badge, medal, investiture*.

horn A word with very ancient sexual connotations, so possibly a phallic symbol. But also ask who was blowing it. Perhaps you are trying to attract attention by "blowing your own horn". A car horn is, of course, a warning – another possible element?

horse The horse, a symbol of energy and strength, is often a sexual symbol in dreams, especially if one is riding it. See *animals*, FISH, FLESH AND FOWL (p. 88–9).

hospital Buildings in dreams often represent the dreamer. If the hospital building represents you yourself, the department in which your dream is set is obviously important, as is the illness being treated (if there is one). If you were playing doctor, there may be a reference to some sort of supportive role you are playing in your waking life. As a patient, you may be trying to recover from an injury done to you: or perhaps you have been cruel to yourself lately, or are just in need of comfort. See ENVIRONMENT (p. 92–3) and *invalid*.

hotel One significance of a hotel is that you pay to stay in it; so is someone offering in some way to buy you or your services – or are you seeking to purchase someone else's time or energy? Alternatively, the dream might refer to your need for a change of routine, or simply a rest. The staff of the hotel may give you a hint of its significance; but this seems likely to be a difficult symbol to interpret. You may have to ask your dream for elucidation. See *buildings*, ENVIRONMENT (p. 92).

hound As a hunting animal, a hound has perhaps less pleasant connotations than a *dog*; perhaps someone is "hounding" you. Or is this a terrifying symbol? See *dog, animals*, FLESH (p. 88).

house Numerous researchers have suggested that the most likely interpretation of a house appearing in a dream is that it represents the human body. Think of this possibility first (and see ENVIRONMENT (p. 92–3). But consider your dream house also as possibly a representation of your whole personality. Try to remember whether the rooms were full or empty, or if you found the furniture attractive. Were you thinking of moving out, or of making major renovations? The discovery of a set of rooms you never thought existed could suggest that you are starting out on an important new project, or making major new discoveries. A very complex symbol, and worth serious consideration.

housekeeper A great deal depends on your attitude to housekeeping: if you are happy in that role, your dreams may be reassuring you, but there may be a reference to your whole self (see *house*) rather than your domestic arrangements. If your dream housekeeper was a domineering person, perhaps there is some comment on an authority figure who may be dominating your life – or perhaps there is a reference to a repressive mother figure. Are your dreams suggesting that you should "put your house in order", referring perhaps to confused private emotions?

humour See *laughter*.

hunger There is always a possibility that the dream is reflecting the fact that you have gone to bed hungry, but dreams of hunger may refer to a need for greater love and affection in your life – or indeed, a need to give out more emotion. In one way or another, your emotions need feeding.

hunting See PURSUIT (p. 66). You may be trying to get the better of someone in waking life – to catch up with them or discover something about them; or your motives may be more sinister (hunts can end in pain and death). Question your motivation and emotions, especially if another person is involved. You may, on the other hand, be on some kind of "trail". What does the beast being hunted represent to you? Or perhaps you were being hunted. See *fox, killing*.

husband Dreams about husbands, wives or partners may actually be referring to the side of our personality reflected in that partner: so a woman who dreams of her husband may find that the dreams are referring to the masculine, assertive side of her nature, and his actions in the dream could be actions she herself might consider taking. But before trying to assess such dreams in detail you must consider your present relation-

hound *Woman and animal*, Paul Klee

ship with your husband. If the relationship is uneasy, your actions in the dream could be a kind of wish-fulfilment – or could symbolize an attitude which is too easy-going on your part. If a man dreams of someone else's husband, he should ask himself what that man represents – what are his feelings with regard to the dream husband's wife, for instance? One's relationship with a husband or wife is so personal and idiosyncratic that the symbol must be among the most complex and difficult to analyse (perhaps one reason why the unconscious seems only rarely to use it). Again, the context of the dream is all-important so try to remember your feelings. See *proposal*, *wife*.

i

ice The coldness of ice may be a reference to the state of your emotions; perhaps you are apprehensive about expressing them in a fulfilling and worthwhile manner. If the symbol is an iceberg, remember that most of it is below the water, so you may disguise your coolness under a surface amiability. But examine what was near the berg: fog, mist, storm, ships in difficulty? Ice cubes in a drink may symbolize your social life (perhaps it needs improving), or even inviting you to "cool it" where your drinking – or other – habits are concerned! Slipping on ice may be a strong hint of personal insecurity.

ice cream The coldness of ice cream is matched by a certain sensuality and sweetness; perhaps the dream is suggesting that you should savour the expression of your emotions more than at present. Was there a reference to your childhood? If so, might there be some allusion to a coolness between you and your parents? Or was the ice cream a treat? Maybe you are being advised to "cool it".

identity To lose one's identity in a dream – or to find it – can be very disturbing, but perhaps relates to your waking consciousness of your individuality; you may feel uncertain as to just who you are. The dream is more likely to be emotional rather than narrative (unless you have succeeded in relating a particular symbol – identity card, perhaps, driving-licence or even credit-card – to your personal identity). It will either be reassuring, underlining the fact that you are succeeding in the process of self-realiza-

tion, or it will leave you in doubt. At all events it should give you a broad hint as to the state of your search for your place in society. Your mood in the dream will be important.

idol A dream of a pagan idol, some representation of a god, seems to have a lighter significance than a dream of "God" in the sense of a paramount creator. Maybe you are in danger of seeing yourself as a "tin god", or treating someone else, or your work, or even a sport of

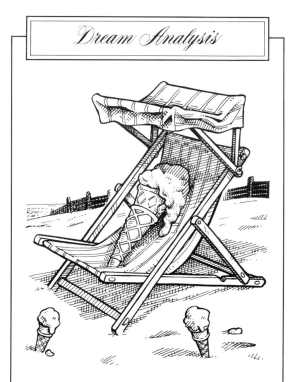

Dream Analysis

ice cream

Julia dreamed: *"I came across Joan Bakewell relaxing in a deck chair. She said, 'I love ice cream, and I just don't care, I'm going to sit here and eat as much of it as I can.' Later in the dream I walked past her again, and she was asleep, covered in melted ice cream."*

This was a funny, but very reassuring dream. Joan Bakewell is a well-known television interviewer whose work I much admire, and from whom I have learned a great deal. I had an appointment next day to fulfil an interesting but demanding television contract, and was apprehensive about it. Ms Bakewell's uninhibited enjoyment of the ice cream seemed to prompt me to "cool it", and enjoy the experience.

which you are passionately fond, as though it were the be-all and end-all of life. In that sense, such a dream may be a warning.

illness Physical illness in a dream – your own or someone else's, even that of an animal – can of course be a symbol of psychological illness; so carefully think about how the illness could relate to your state of mind. There can be some reference, however, to an illness yet undiagnosed (see p. 59). Also see *hospital, invalid.*

image To dream of your own image – that is, your personal appearance and "style" – perhaps seen in a mirror, might suggest that you should think about it, change it if it seems boring or outdated; but the context of the dream will probably suggest your approach. See CLOTHES (p. 82). For "graven image" or god, see *idol.*

incest A dream of incest with parents almost always seems to be a reflection of childishness, and sometimes very profoundly so – the dreamer expressing a longing to return to the security of a complete union with the mother or father. Sexual dreams about siblings, or your children, may be very disturbing indeed, but try to be rational if you are disturbed by the dream's sexuality – there is by no means necessarily an indication that you suffer from some psychological illness. If you are in doubt, ask your dreams for further elucidation (see p. 47); if you continue to be disturbed, by all means think about consulting a counsellor or therapist.

income Taking stock of your income in a dream, counting your money or possessions, is very likely to be a reflection of your waking concern with your spiritual or emotional assets; though, of course, you may simply be worried about money! It is often worthwhile to be self-critical when such a dream occurs, and consider whether you are being emotionally miserly or over-possessive.

incompetence Is the dream highlighting an area of your waking life, or emphasizing some unreadiness or insecurity in you? It may be hinting that you should search for greater background knowledge or for experience which will enable you to build up your confidence. Incompetence in others could reflect your own lack of confidence in the area in which they were concerned. Don't forget to consider the results of the dream incompetence!

incubation Are you, or should you be, incubating some idea? If you have the germ of a notion which you have been ignoring, cultivate it! If the

egg in your dream remained obstinately whole, your waking idea may not yet be ready to be born. If it broke open – what came out, and what particular aspect might the newly-born creature symbolize?

incubus To dream of being visited by an evil spirit suggests a warning of some kind, the expression of some deep-seated fear. If the spirit took a recognizable form, this may be a hint; and, of course, there may be an obvious waking difficulty encroaching on your life. Otherwise, ask your dreams (see p. 47) for further elucidation. The term has also been used to describe a male spirit which appears in a dream to rape the female dreamer. If it has only the vague form of an unknown man, there may be a reference to a need for more forthright expression of sexuality (the dream need not be wholly unpleasant) – or of a fear of sex (more likely, if the rape was unpleasantly realistic). The appearance of a known man as an incubus focuses the fear or the wish-fulfilment more clearly, but need not refer to a particular individual.

infant The infant could be just what it seems: a *child* known to you. But consider also whether its characteristics, and the way you think about it, suggest some part of your own personality, and try to interpret the dream in that sense. A generalized dream of a child seems to hint at something which is peculiarly "your baby" – an idea or project just getting under way. Was it healthy or sickly, in need of nourishment or growing too fast? A dream of the Infant Christ would seem to be reassuring – possibly a comment on your religious attitudes.

infidelity Wish-fulfilment? Or emotional or spiritual infidelity? Were you enjoying yourself? In that case, it may be that your partnership is too claustrophobic, and you need occasionally to escape your partner's influence (not, of course, necessarily physically).

injection A syringe could obviously be a phallic symbol, but there could be a suggestion that you need an injection of some sort, to pep up your physical or emotional state, or to relieve pain or heart ache. Could you in some way inject more fun, or determination, or vigour into your waking life? Of course the kind of injection you were receiving, and the person administering it, will be significant; if you were injecting yourself, then there is the implication that you should help yourself (though in the context of dangerous drugs, the opposite would obviously be true). See *innoculation.*

injury What sort of injury, and who inflicted it? Those are, of course, the main questions – but remember that a physical injury could symbolize a spiritual or emotional injury. If you did yourself an injury, is there some aspect of your personality you dislike and wish to eradicate or weaken?

innoculation See *injection*. But, in this case, the purpose is prophylactic, so the dream is almost certainly a warning of some event or action which is preventable – especially if the innoculation was in preparation for a journey to a dangerous or unknown country (it may then refer to your starting a new job, study course, emotional commitment).

inquest Perhaps in waking life you are much concerned with past actions or situations, reassessing them with hindsight, asking yourself whether you did the right thing; or the dream may be insisting that you should be doing so – perhaps in relation to a specific action or event (think of the person on whom the inquest was being held, and what he or she represents to you). Certainly the focus seems to be on something that is over and done with, perhaps irreparable. Is the dream guiding you about your future? Try not to dwell too much on the past; get it into a coherent perspective, and move on. Perhaps you need to assuage feelings of guilt?

insanity A dream of actually being mad, or encountering an insane person, may be a warning that some area of your waking life is getting out of control, or is at least bewildering and disturbing you. The resolution of the dream may hint at how to approach the problem. There is no need, of course, to think that you are going mad in your waking life!

insects Insects are often thought of as unpleasant, and as destroyers – of plants, perhaps, or even the structure of a house. So recurring dreams of insects may refer to a waking fear or feeling that you or something in your life is under attack. Think about the insects in the dream and what they are attacking. A scorpion may be a reference to a verbally stinging attack; a spider, to the desire to catch someone in a web of words or actions. Insects can sometimes transform themselves – a caterpillar can become a beautiful butterfly.

instrument What kind of instrument? In some cases a sexual element may exist (see *guitar*). And are you playing your own tune, or someone else's? Is the tune itself melodious or off key? See *harp, music*.

insult An insult, however ridiculous or vicious, can have a basis in truth, and there could be a suggestion about the moderation of future behaviour. But maybe the insult was meant to sting you into a better apprehension of your own merits, an increased self-esteem.

insurance An allusion to your sense of security, and your attitude towards the future? Perhaps you are being reminded that your present waking actions will have long-term implications. Or you may have to pay now for later security.

intelligence test Dreaming about an intelligence test, and how you performed, may reflect your feelings about your waking performance at work, or indeed within your partnership, or in some other area of your life (what was the context, the subject of the test?). How are you measuring up to your own standards?

interrogator Your dream interrogator may represent some authority figure (parent or boss), and your dream reaction may reflect your waking reaction to him or her. But equally the interrogator could be some aspect of yourself, some inner authority trying to extract the last ounce of energy, effort, or information for a particular purpose. We tend to think of an interrogator as antagonistic, so the dream may be warning you against straining too hard to satisfy some demand. If you are a student, or concerned in study, a dream interrogation may point up areas in which a greater effort is needed.

invalid See *illness*, but if the dream is focusing on the feeling of being attentively nursed, cared for, cosseted, there may be a hint that you should take things more easily. If the illness seems serious, there could be an allusion to a dying love affair, business, or interest! do you really wish to reanimate it? If the invalid in the dream seems fatally ill, the answer seems likely to be no. There is not necessarily any allusion to a real illness. Don't forget the possibility of a pun: in-valid. See *illness, hospital*.

investiture Surely your dream was congratulating you on something accomplished, something done? If you were simply looking on, perhaps you envy someone's else's accomplishment, with a hint that you should try harder, with increased determination. See *honour*.

invisibility Dreaming that you are invisible may be a wish-fulfilment: do you wish to vanish from some scene in your waking life? To be less noticed? Perhaps a comment on shyness? What happened to you in the dream is obviously important in deciding what you were being "told". This may well be an occasion for asking your dreams for further hints (see p. 47).

iron To dream of doing some ironing may refer, punningly, to your desire to "iron out" some difficulty or problem, and perhaps to your progress in doing so (bad ironing, lots of creases, a hole in a sheet, do not seem promising symbols). If you burned yourself, perhaps you should not be interfering – "cool it", in other words. Or may you be about to "burn your fingers", financially? The metal iron has traditionally been associated with endurance, strength, vitality, anger and aggression: there may be some allusion either to your lack of some of these qualities – or your possessing them too strongly! Anaemic people need more iron, and this too may be worth thinking about. See *metals*.

island Is the dream suggesting that you are in some way isolated – perhaps pleasantly, but perhaps dangerously so? If you were on a bare desert island waiting to be rescued, looking out for someone to reach you, there may be a hint that your emotional life is somewhat barren. Being stranded by someone on an island suggests rejection. The pleasure of life on a welcoming island, on the other hand, may suggest that you need a little more fruitful solitary relaxation; trying desperately to reach such an island has an obvious additional meaning – what are you searching for? Some kind of emotional nirvana? If there is a strong feeling of isolation, this may have been a warning dream.

j

jam Possibly a representation of the sweet things of life (see FOOD AND DRINK, p. 86). But are you "in a jam"? Some sticky mess or other? If the jam was bright red, are you seeing red about just such a situation? See COLOUR (p. 94).

jar The content of the jar is likely to be as important as what became of it; there could be a sexual implication (see *jug*). Or is it a pun – something jarring your nerves?

jaw Have you been talking rather a lot lately? But remember that Winston Churchill said that "jaw-jaw is better than war-war"!

jealousy If this negative emotion colours your dreams, it is probably affecting your waking life in some way. The dream person of whom you were jealous may suggest the waking source of the emotion, but need not necessarily be its subject. Try not to let jealousy fester too long; it can have very adverse longterm effects. Direct your energies into positive new outlets rather than wasting them in soul-destroying resentfulness. Future dreams may offer suggestions as to future conduct: perhaps a blazing row rather than a lingering slow anger.

jewels Dreams about being adorned with jewels could be wish-fulfilment. But jewels can represent immaterial riches too, and there may be an emphasis on your most valuable attributes (which you may undervalue in waking life, but others may admire). If you were grasping for riches which eluded you, or have an eye on obviously unattainable jewels – the Crown Jewels or the Tiffany diamond – the dream is perhaps suggesting that you are setting your sights too high when fixing standards for yourself to pursue in waking life.

Jew Racial prejudice apart – and dreams of the persecution of the Jews may be commenting on your own most secret feelings on the matter, just as they may hint that *you* have some personal attributes for which others might want to persecute *you* – the archetypal figure of The Wandering Jew, someone doomed to wander forever for a particular sin, might allude to a quality in yourself, or even an action, which you find unforgivable. Try to reconcile yourself to this, or even to correct it. Possibly, however, you wish you had more business acumen.

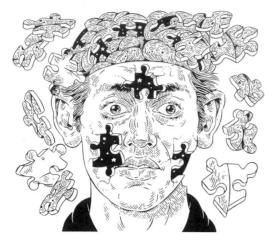

jigsaw Puzzles, in dreams, may reflect puzzles in waking life: so how did you deal with it in your dream? Was a particular piece missing – if so, are you searching for one special element in your own make-up which seems to be lacking? See *puzzle*.

journey A dream journey is most likely to refer to some emotional or intellectual journey or quest in your waking life. Ask yourself how the journey went, and what its circumstances were (see LANDSCAPE, p. 68). Your attitude in the dream may reflect, or be a comment on, your waking attitude – and perhaps suggest that you need more vigour, or caution, or adventurousness. If you were hesitant, there may be a hint that you are not yet ready for full involvement in the project you have in mind. Perhaps see *holiday*.

joy Just as you can experience the emotion of overwhelming grief in a dream, so you can experience great joy – often without any real object which seems to have inspired it. If it was related to any particular object, that is likely to represent an element which you very much need in your waking life. On the other hand, remember the punning possibility that you know a girl called Joy!

judge The judge is of course the authority figure *par excellence*. But should you be "judging for yourself" in some waking situation? Decide whether the judgment in the dream seemed fair or unfair, and relate it to whoever, in waking life, the dream judge seemed to represent. Perhaps your inner judge, your "real self", was passing judgment, in which case do not allow him to put you down too heavily: sometimes our dreams are harder on us than any waking judgment on ourselves or our peers. Maybe you should appeal to future dreams for further consideration, and a possible reduction of the sentence!

jug In art, many painters have used the symbol of a jug to indicate virginity – and a jug with a crack in it carried its own implication. This meaning can occur in dreams. See also *jar*, but a jug implies that the liquid in it can be poured out, that some part of you is perhaps ready to be given to someone else (and very possibly there is another sexual reference). The liquid itself may be important: milk perhaps refers to natural powers or to a maternal influence or instinct, water to emotions, wine perhaps to sensuality.

juggling Full marks if you succeeded in keeping all the balls in the air! The dream was very possibly commenting on how you manage to keep all the various elements of your personality – indeed, your life – in order and in play, perhaps how you manage to balance and counterbalance your relationships, your finances, your time. The articles with which you were juggling could reflect the areas of your life under scrutiny.

jumping For what? Hopefully for joy – but think carefully of the context: were you jumping a ditch or a hurdle? Did you succeed, or fall? This could be a reassuring dream, or one suggesting that the ambition or object you presently have in mind is at the moment beyond your power. Perhaps you need more training. As with *falling*, sometimes we "jump" when we are just going to sleep: this is a physiological trick of the body.

jungle If you had to hack your way through one, perhaps the dream referred to trying obstructive problems or concerns, personal or external, through which at present you have to make your way. Your progress may well have been reflected in the dream. If you were finding progress difficult, perhaps you need a "map" – consultation with a friend or colleague may help. See, perhaps, CROWDS (p. 96) a not dissimilar symbol.

jury Unlike judges, this symbol seems most likely to be concerned with your feelings about what others think of you. Do you feel you are constantly being judged by them? Was the jury hostile or friendly? Were you guilty or not guilty? It may be that a verdict of guilty is what you seek, if you are rather anti-establishment, or involved in a social protest of some kind.

k

kangaroo Carrying her young in a pouch, the kangaroo (remember A.A. Milne's Kanga and Roo) may be a maternal symbol. Perhaps you are being overprotective towards your children. Or are you making progress in leaps and bounds?

keeper Was the keeper in charge of a dangerous animal – perhaps under threat of attack? There may be a reference here to an area of your psyche which is only just under control: your temper, perhaps? Try to recall what happened to the keeper – and of course his charge. This is obviously an essential factor to be considered and interpreted in terms of yourself and your waking life.

key One of the most potent of phallic symbols, especially for the woman who feels incomplete without sexual experience: the images of "unlocking", "opening", "freeing" are clear, and have been used endlessly, for instance, in bawdy poetry. The man who unlocks a series of rooms, in a dream, is having a dream of polygamy, or perhaps of a brothel. The key could, however, have been one you need to resolve a waking problem; perhaps you have almost arrived at its solution. To lose the key could symbolize frustration or a blockage of your progress (though for men there is, of course, an obvious sexual symbolism). "The key to the heart" offers a more romantic possible connotation. And finally, of course, there is the religious symbol – most obviously seen in its connection with St Peter, offering the keys of heaven.

kick Are you, or should you be, "kicking up a fuss" about something at present? Are you "kicking against the pricks" – fighting the inevitable? Try to recall exactly whom you were kicking – or who was kicking you, for this is obviously important.

killing A dream of violence, but perhaps something in yourself needs to be killed. Consider the dream creature – did it represent perhaps a quality of yours, or even another person you need to clear out of your life? Try not to dwell too much on DEATH (see p. 76) as an ending, but as a new beginning. See *funeral*, for there may be a strong reference to change, and *hunting*.

king What did the king in your dream represent? Do you aspire to his qualities, whether he was an authoritarian monarch or the supreme master of his field, someone like Elvis, King of Rock? Are you placing someone you admire on a throne – perhaps a more resplendent one than they merit? Or are you showing off too much, or behaving too domineeringly? See *throne*.

kiss This may well be part of a wish-fulfilment dream. But there are other kinds of kiss: the kiss of peace, or the kiss of betrayal? A kiss is in some ways a more intense symbol of affection and love than a more overt sexual action, and places the person you kiss – or what he or she represents – in a very special and loving relationship. Even betrayal is therefore far more intense. Think carefully about this dream, and what it could mean in terms of "closeness" with its real subject.

kitchen The kitchen is a key symbol in dreams of a house which really relate to you and your body (see ENVIRONMENT, p. 92). The kitchen, with its source of heat and the preparation of food, can be the centre of your physical being; so difficulty

Dream Analysis

kitchen
Sarah dreamed: *"I was fitting a new, rather large kitchen into an aircraft. The work was completed and I was with someone who had paid for it, admiring the result."*

The dream related to Sarah's musical studies (see p. 163), which had given her some difficulty. But after a rewarding lesson with her teacher, she had been told that she now knew the basics of her subject, and was ready to use the technique in any way she wished. The dream made a lot of sense to her, for the kitchen represented all the hard work she had put in, and the reference to the aircraft was "making it plain (plane)" to her that she was ready to "take off".

with the fire or the cooker could be an oblique reference to your health. It is also the room where food is prepared – the so-called way to a man's (or a woman's?) heart: there could also be a reference to the way you are caring for your lover.

kite Freedom rather than restriction would seem to be indicated – though carefully considered and guided freedom; freedom to soar within the limits of wisdom. So what strings are attached to you at present? Are you trying to break them? Or do you rely on them to guide you? If someone is consciously pulling strings for you at present, is it really worth it? The kite is most likely to represent you yourself; but it might represent a lover, or a member of your family. There may be connotations with FLYING (p. 84).

knife According to Freud, a major phallic symbol, and significantly one often found in a context of violence; so think very carefully about what you were doing with the knife, who if anyone you were attacking, and who or what they may represent. On the other hand, there may be something you wish to cut out of your personality or someone you wish to cut out of your life. Might it be some specific habit or tendency you want to "cut out"? With many people this is smoking: so how are you progressing? Was the knife sharp, or blunt? There may also be an idea of danger here. The knife is an instrument of violence – but it can also cut you free.

knitting A complex symbol, possibly referring to mending or making, but also perhaps a tangle – in which case think of it as an analogy of life; *you* are supposed to be in control, shaping the garment! Dropped stitches meaning dropped opportunities?

knock There may be a punning reference to your having "knocked" someone – or to someone "knocking" you. But look at other symbols in the same dream, for we often knock on something to attract attention to ourselves or something we think important. This is also one of those dreams which obviously might be prompted by a real knocking noise coming within earshot of the dreamer.

knot Perhaps you have tied a symbolic knot recently, signifying some bond such as marriage or a permanent relationship. On the other hand, are you wrestling with some "knotty" problem? If so, and you unravelled your dream knot, be reassured. Or, yet another possibility, should you be telling someone to "get knotted"?

l

label A label which has come loose, or is incorrectly addressed, could be a symbol commenting on your own loss of direction; but think of the possibility of your being "labelled" for some personality trait or action, and whether this is desirable or not.

laboratory What are you trying to prove? It may be that you are putting yourself to the test in some way, or perhaps living through testing conditions in waking life. Should you experiment a little, or are you getting obsessed by the hows and whys of your current life? The kind of experiment conducted in your dream will obviously be important and may offer other symbols for interpretation.

labyrinth See *maze*.

lace Beautiful, transparent but very complicated, and often incorporated in sexually provocative garments. Did it remind you of anyone in the dream, or later?

ladder Another symbol Freud strongly associated with sexual intercourse. If so, whether you climb it successfully or fall off is obviously significant. But the ladder may symbolize other things – ambition for instance. We speak of "climbing another rung up the ladder". Consider its length, its angle, whether it reached the heights you desired; if not, perhaps you should modify your plans.

lady See *woman*.

lake A dream of water in any form is usually making a statement about our emotional level. A lake as a symbol seems very likely to be doing this. Try to recall whether it was deep or shallow, placid or troubled, for these factors will obviously be relevant. See WATER (p. 80).

lameness Do not be too distressed if you dream that you are lame, although this is the sort of dream symbol that could haunt you depressingly. What is suggested may just as well be referring to an area of your mind, or of your behaviour in waking life. Are you making a "lame" response to a situation? Or you may be crying out for a little assistance, support or reassurance in some area. On the other hand, perhaps it is someone else who needs your help.

lament Are you feeling particularly sorry for yourself at present? Maybe your dreams suggest that you take a really positive look at your life, that you stop grumbling at others, or simply, stop mourning about something that is over and done with. If you have experienced some recent bereavement or loss, the dream could simply be a further expression of your grief, preparing you for a return to ordinary life. See DEATH (p. 76).

lamp This seems likely to be a positive symbol, for dreams of light usually offer guidance, reassurance, hope. The COLOUR (see p. 94), and relative warmth of the lamp may offer a comment. If you knocked a lamp over, there may be a reference to disappointment; if it caught fire to other objects, try to recall the nature of these, for they could be important. And there could also be a warning here. A dream lamp which goes out could refer to disappointment, or to a loss of sense of direction in waking life – or maybe you are not seeing some areas of your life too clearly: other symbols in the dream should indicate what is being spoken of – but ask your dreams for more clues (see p. 47 if you fail to grasp their point). See *light*, FIRE (p. 78), perhaps COLOUR (p. 94).

land see LANDSCAPE (p. 68), *earth*, perhaps *island*; your sense of security could be under discussion, but the main symbol in the dream seems likely to be something other than "land" as a whole. Unless recently you "landed" something – a new job, perhaps.

landlord Someone in charge of the house, and therefore probably your governing conscience. Don't allow it to cramp your assertive spirit – it is there to give you a moral core, to back up your determination to attain what you most desire. If it starts demanding too much rent, it is up to you to decide whether the property is worth that much! Any demand in waking life – emotional, perhaps – may be in question.

landscape See p. 68.

language If you were learning a language with some difficulty, perhaps that difficulty applies in waking life to unfamiliar problems. Maybe you are not communicating as well as you might with those around you, and your dreams are mirroring a sense of isolation. Is your present lifestyle somewhat lonely?

1

landscape *Landscape with balloon*, Max Beckmann

laughter Laughter in a dream almost always wakes us up, though, alas, when we examine the dream it usually no longer seems very funny. Humorous dreams do not very often seem to have a great deal of waking significance.

launching The reference is probably to the launching of some new idea, project or relationship. If all went well in the dream, so much the better – though it could be wish fulfilment. But if not, some warning may be involved – so look for weaknesses or trouble spots.

law A dream of consulting or using the law seems likely to hint that you should be stricter with yourself in some way; maybe you have broken some self-imposed rule recently, and are chastising yourself for it? On the other hand it may have been someone else who was "laying down the law". See *judge, jury, trial*.

lead The metal lead is heavy and poisonous and was in antiquity associated with curses and the baleful divinity called Uranus. Could it relate in your dream to someone's attitude towards you, or to some commitment which may turn out to be a dreary burden, perhaps psychologically negative? Hopefully, the dream does not relate to your attitude to someone else. On another track, to dream of being on a lead or leash may hint that you are too easily led, or are too much under someone else's control. Perhaps someone is trying to guide you in a direction in which you do not really want to go. Or possibly the dream is an encouragement for you to take the lead in some way. Playing follow-my-leader suggests you may need to express your own individuality more forcefully. If you dream your dog's lead has broken, perhaps you have broken away from someone's influence – but perhaps your unconscious is inviting you to check whether the real dog's lead is ready for replacement.

leakage Has somebody been "leaking" information? Should you keep quiet about some confidence, or refrain from placing your confidence in someone else? If you have a hot-water bottle, check it for leaks though you may be too late!

leap The obvious inference is that you are about to take a leap of some kind in waking life. Did you clear the gap or hurdle? And over what were you jumping? That should give you a clue to the dream. See *jump*, FLYING (p. 84).

learning The dream may be suggesting that you should embark on a period of self-exploration. On the other hand, the act of learning in a dream

Dream Analysis

laughter
Derek dreamed: *"I was in a narrow, dark French street. In the distance I heard the noise of horses' hooves, and into view came a funeral procession with plumed horses and carriages. As the first coach passed, I saw that the passengers were* moules *(mussels), dressed in top hats and mourning bands. In the second carriage were chickens, similarly dressed. . . . The funeral was that of my dinner. I awoke laughing."*

This dream occurred a few hours after a splendid meal on the Côte d'Azur. It was that unusual thing, an overtly funny dream, but it also reflected some concern for the animals killed to feed the diner (Bernard Shaw, a vegetarian, always claimed that his funeral would be attended by the animals he had not eaten).

may be wish-fulfilment – perhaps you simply feel under-educated in some way, or that you long for deeper knowledge. It may be worth putting some time and energy aside for study.

leather This is a tough and durable substance, and the dream may be commenting on your powers of resistance or inner strength. Or have you been behaving in a thick-skinned manner recently?

leaves Perhaps a reference to the *seasons*. What was the conditions of the leaves: green and summery, or withered and autumnal? It is worth trying to recall the shape of the leaves, for some leaves may traditionally suggest a particular meaning – the fig-leaf, for instance, carries a sexual symbolism. Were the leaves accompanied by flowers or buds? On the whole, fresh spring leaves suggest new birth, or the realization of an ambition or a love or a new project. If you were arranging them, perhaps the time has come to show off that area of your interest, or to express your talents. Sweeping up dead leaves suggests the end of a project or episode (see DEATH, *funeral*), but may also involve knowledge and experience – especially if, for instance, the leaves were placed on a compost heap. Were your dreams suggesting that you should "leave something alone"? See also *garden, flowers*.

lecture Perhaps you have been "lecturing" someone recently; decide whether you have been going on too long about some matter! If you were listening to a lecture the dream may be suggesting that you should gather opinion about a project; or your dream reaction may hint at your real reaction to opinion.

legs A symbol of progress, perhaps: are you standing on your own legs? If you were concerned about them in your dream (see *lameness*) there was perhaps a reference to a lack of self-confidence. See *body, kick*.

letter See *messages*. Are you carrying out instructions "to the letter"?

library Probably a reference to the stored-up knowledge and experience you have acquired over the years. The dream could also be suggesting that at present you need to draw upon it. If you were looking for a book but could not find it, maybe there is a reference to an under-developed aspect of your personality.

lie See *falsehood*, but to dream of a lie may be a pun – should you "lie low" at present?

lifeboat If you seem to be drowning in problems at present, the dream may be a reassurance – or otherwise, of course. Try to remember if there was a reference to someone in particular who could help you. See WATER (p. 80).

light Almost always a reference to some spiritual or psychological illumination; the phrase "to see the light" obviously applies. But what kind of light was it, and what was its colour? A warm yellow glow seems likely to be positive; a red light, a warning; a green light, a "go-ahead" sign (though don't rely solely on the colours of traffic lights). So see COLOUR (p. 94). Are your burdens getting lighter? Or should you be trying to lighten someone else's burden?

lightning A symbol of sudden revelation or realization, or perhaps the sign of a really good idea. See if there is a clue in the dream to tell you to what the flash refers.

line A reference to a particular line of thought? But perhaps a punning reference to the "lines" which were a punishment at school? A suggestion that you should "drop someone a line"?

lion The king of beasts: friendly, or attacking? Have you been roaring, lately? Should you be lion-hearted? If you were intimidated, who did the lion represent, and what should be your attitude to this? If you identify with the qualities of the lion, are you being specially domineering at present? Lions are very regal, dignified: should you be more (or less) so?

liquor See *food and drink* (p. 86); possibly a warning to cut down your intake?

listening Is there something you *want* to hear? Should you be paying more attention to what others are saying? Or to your own inner desires? Take warning from any unpleasant fact you heard about yourself.

litter Your dream litter may be symbolizing worn-out ideas or projects or opinions for which you have no further use or respect. If you were collecting it up and dumping it, the comment is obvious (and positive). If you were raking through it regretfully, perhaps looking for something lost, there is another interpretation. Is your life littered with useless trivia, unnecessary problems, or even people who are unworthy of your time and energy? A litter of puppies has quite another meaning. See *animals, birth*.

loan The dream may be suggesting you are drawing too heavily on your emotional resources, or that you need greater support from those close to you. Decide where, if anywhere, in waking life you need help, and don't be apprehensive about asking for it. See *bank*.

lock Freud has suggested this is a female sexual symbol, and certainly see *key* for that aspect. But perhaps you are "locked into" or "locked out of" some area of your life. Consider carefully any psychological problem which may be inhibiting you from full and rewarding self-expression; to unlock this area, you need to find the right key (not necessarily sexual, of course). If your dream lock was on a canal, again there is a constriction – the water is confined, but only to allow for later expansion and progress; and in that case the focus seems to be on your emotional life. See WATER (p. 80).

loneliness There could be a parallel with a sense of loneliness in waking life, or a warning. But remember that the other elements in the dream should give you more clues for its interpretation, so see, perhaps, LANDSCAPE (p. 68), or *void*.

looking-glass See *mirror*.

lottery Risk-taking seems indicated here. So if you have recently taken a risk of some kind, the dream may be commenting on it. Your number may have come up in more ways than one, and you should certainly always think twice about making a bet because of a supposed hint in a dream! You may be paying a hefty price for your "stake" in real life – but ask yourself whether you are being over- or under-confident in your waking attitude to any gamble. If you lost everything in your dream, try to make an association with any risky situation in your present life.

love Firstly, of course, who was in love with you, or who was the subject of your love? This could be a simple wish-fulfilment dream, or a signpost to the future. Alternatively, the dream could be suggesting that you should love yourself a little more. If there are elements of your personality you dislike, how can you make them more acceptable? Other symbols in the dream should point to its real significance, which is unlikely to be as simple as you may think.

luggage A dream representation of your responsibilities, perhaps, or maybe a statement about your security. Do you feel insecure in waking life if not surrounded by possessions? A dream of lost luggage could then be particularly distressing. But if in your dream you were relieved of your luggage, handed it confidently over to a porter, and felt freer as a result, think about the possibility of delegation in your waking life. A particular piece of luggage could have a very personal meaning for you. What?

lumber Your dream probably referred to psychological "lumber" which is stored in the depths of your unconscious, and may be suggesting that you should rationalize or get rid of it and clear some extra space for action! Maybe you are into a period of self-analysis, finding out new things about yourself, some of which you think should be quickly disposed of! If this is so, your dream is probably supporting you, for the very word "lumber" suggests something no one needs.

m

machinery A piece of machinery in a dream is often a symbol for the human mind or body, and very possibly for yours. What state was it in? Well-oiled, or rusty? Active or inactive? Perhaps you or your mind need to go into action: or is your dream suggesting that your life and approach to life are too mechanical?

madness Have you experienced "a moment of madness" recently? If someone else has behaved in a mad fashion, did you rather envy them or what they stood for? Perhaps you have a yen for a slightly more reckless way of life. Are your dreams suggesting you are too madly in love?

madonna For a man, the Virgin Mary, the archetypal mother figure, appearing in a dream will probably be making a statement about his attitude to his own mother in the context of his ability to come to terms with mature relationships with women. There is a not infrequent psychological problem when a man at first regards a loved one as pure and virginal, then when the natural sexual relationship develops, rejects her as impure and unworthy. The dream will be worth very serious consideration, and could help you to clarify your feelings in this sometimes difficult area. The feminine area of the personality in women, as well as men, may also be highlighted.

magic Magic can be pure and beautiful (white) or tricky and dangerous (black). Have you been "up to tricks" recently? Is your dream warning you of someone who may be deceiving you? Or was something simply magic in the sense of wonderful?

malice A negative feeling which, like a general sense of *evil*, can permeate a dream, and might be a warning. At whom was it directed, by whom, why, and how?

mandala This circular symbol of psychological wholeness, which we can often construct unconsciously in waking life (when doodling, arranging flowers or fruit, for instance) can, as C.G. Jung pointed out, help us literally to "centre ourselves". A dream of creating a mandala, or even looking at one, is likely to indicate that your unconscious is focusing on the very depths of your personality, and that you are entering a stage of considerable personal development and an unfolding of spiritual truths.

maniac Perhaps a warning that you should restrain extremes of action or behaviour: have you been behaving like a maniac lately? We often seem to use the term to describe bad drivers. Should your driving technique be improved? See *madness*.

mansion See *house*, of course, and ENVIRONMENT (p. 92). However, the sense of a "great house" seems perhaps to indicate undue self-regard; with its slightly old-fashioned ring, it may refer to extreme conservatism in your approach to life. If it was dilapidated and run-down, maybe you need to look to your physical or mental agility. Also think of the Biblical quotation: "In my Father's house are many mansions". Could there be a reference to one particular aspect of your personality?

map This symbol would seem to suggest you may be "looking for the way". Do you feel you have lost your direction, in some sense? Or maybe you are making careful plans for some new important project. Were you reading the map carefully, or just glancing at it?

market Buying, selling, communication between people – a dream perhaps about what you have to offer in life (in whatever sphere) and how you are "marketing" it, presenting it to others. Did you strike a good bargain, or did no-one want your goods. If you were buying, what were you after? And what sort of market was it? An antique market might suggest the acquiring of knowledge or be a reference to your past, or to inherited personality traits; a cattle market would of course have different associations.

marriage In some circumstances this will be a wish-fulfilment dream, of course. But perhaps the dream marriage represents a linkage, a marriage, of two areas of your personality. Or are you setting the seal on a business project, or about to sign a contract with someone? There could be a comment on your sense of security, emotional or material.

martyrdom Who was the martyr, and what did he or she represent? Perhaps you were the martyr. Are you defending a particular standpoint to the end? Or in some way martyring yourself? Or is someone taking advantage of you? It may make you feel virtuous, but is that what life is about?

mask Were you putting one on, or taking it off? Should you face up to reality rather than hide behind a dream? Are you masking some aspect of your personality from the world, or from someone in particular? How successful were you in concealing your face – and were you happy about it? Do you want to unmask someone?

massage This is restorative and extremely enjoyable, helping to tone the body, and often an erotic experience. Your dream may be suggesting that you need additional physical warmth, or perhaps some therapeutic treatment; but it may also be a simple sensual experience.

master Perhaps a punning dream: are you attempting to, or must you, "master" a situation? There may be a focus on an authority figure – a teacher, perhaps; if he was stern, your dream could be suggesting you should be more disciplined in your waking life; but he might also be reassuring. See, perhaps, *father, god, teacher*.

mat Are people wiping their feet on you?

match Is there perhaps a suggestion that you should "light up" in some way? But maybe you were burned by your dream match, in which case there could be a warning ("burning your fingers"), and you must search for the waking situation to which to apply it. Perhaps you should illuminate your whole personality? If you were trying to match some articles, there may be a pun on "match-making". If you were watching a competitive sport or match, see *game*.

mattress Were you well supported by your mattress, or uncomfortable? Perhaps a reference to the support given you in waking life, maybe by partner or family (a mattress is a very domestic symbol). Perhaps see *bed*.

maypole A highly phallic symbol (suppressed by the Puritans for that reason), but connected with holidays, dancing, sport – simple enjoyment. So, if you were attracted by the fun, and joining in, the dream is probably making a comment on your free-and-easy attitude to sex, or a suggestion that you should enjoy it more.

maze Your waking life may be specially complicated at present, the bewildered attempts to find your way out may simply mirror that. If you were leading others to freedom out of a maze, you are probably well in control, and the dream is a reassuring one.

meal Everything depends on what the meal consisted of (see FOOD AND DRINK, p. 86) and the circumstances in which it was eaten. A comment perhaps on your sensual needs or expression.

measurement You could be "sizing up" some aspect of a waking situation. Try to recall whether, in your dream, your measurements were faulty or correct.

medal If you were receiving a medal, you are probably simply being praised for some recent action or piece of personal development. If you watched someone else receiving one, what does he or she represent to you? Could it be something to which you aspire? See *investiture, honour*.

medicine Are you about to receive a taste of your own medicine? You can probably decide on the size of the dose!

melting The dream may be a representation of the melting of your emotions, perhaps, but try to remember what was melting – this will provide the clue. Your dream may be saying that you are "thawing out" in some way – or perhaps that someone else is (in which case wish-fulfilment may be involved).

menu The contents may in some way summarize your own attitudes, desires, plans; were the items "on" or "off" the menu? Were they expensive or cheap? See FOOD AND DRINK (p. 86).

mermaid Mermaids are of course sea-creatures (see WATER, p. 80). Though enticing, they are virgins: if you are a woman, could this be a comment on your attitude to sex? Men lured by mermaids always come to a bad, usually watery end (remember water symbolizes the emotions!). So perhaps this is a warning dream. Try to identify the mermaid with someone in your waking life.

mess You may, of course, be in one. Did you clear it up, or leave it? Were other people involved? Did they help or hinder, were they offended, or had they perhaps made the mess? Dreaming of dining in an officers' mess seems to indicate a lofty, superior or formal view of FOOD AND DRINK (p. 86).

messages Our dreams are always telling us *something*, so in a sense they are all in essence messages. But among the most frequent dreams are those in which we receive messages, which take a variety of forms. Sometimes they are intensely dramatic, sometimes prophetic, though (rather like dreams of disasters) they seldom come true, or are important and world-shattering when we recall them on waking! It occasionally happens that a dream is conveying literal news of an accident or illness – such dreams have been recorded – but it is much more likely that it is a symbolic message, since, as we know, dreams work in symbols. How was the message conveyed? By telephone? By someone bursting into your room? The method could comment on the meaning. And who was conveying the message? While the real message is from your own unconscious, the dream messenger may represent the area of your personality most deeply concerned. Some people see themselves on television, or hear themselves on the radio, reading the text of the message; such a dream is more than likely focusing on a deep-rooted psychological problem, or on your psychological development.

metals The type of metal involved should provide a clue. Look specially at puns – an iron will, a golden opportunity, a leaden aspect, a mercurial personality, perhaps even a plutonic (platonic) relationship! Were you buying metal, forging it, melting it down, breaking it up, or making something from it? See also *gold, iron, lead, steel* and *tin*.

mice If you were frightened of your dream mice, is there a hint that you are unduly afraid of the small issues or problems of your waking life; are they getting out of proportion? But mice are also shy, so maybe the dream is commenting on your social life, or your image. Mice caught in a trap could represent a waking concern that insignificant trifling things in your life are being criticized or seized on by others. Mice busily eating at food in your larder may suggest that other people are nibbling away at your self-confidence or other resources.

microphone So have you something to say? Or (if the dream microphone was faulty) are you being prevented from saying it?

microscope A concern with minutiae seems indicated. Perhaps you are into a period of minute self-examination or analysis. Did you like what you saw? Try not to enlarge small problems until they fill the entire eye!

milk A reference perhaps to the maternal instinct. If you were giving milk to someone, perhaps this is a suggestion about your ability to strengthen and support other people (or a particular person). Drinking milk yourself may suggest that you feel in need of sustenance – not of course necessarily physical. Is someone in need of kindness at present? Or is someone "milking" you in some way (even financially)? A woman may dream that her milk has dried up, which may be a fairly strong indication that she is withdrawing sympathy or support, perhaps from children but perhaps from someone to whom she feels "motherly" (even a partner). Or there could be a suggestion that she *should* withdraw such support and sympathy. The contented feeding of a baby is immensely reassuring, though of course it could be a painful wish-fulfilment if you are reluctantly childless.

mill A reference to hard, "grinding" work, or to the refining of thought perhaps. Alternatively, you could be "going through the mill" in some respect. The context will be important: whether the mill was working well or inefficiently, what was being ground, and so on.

mime If you were miming because you had been prevented from speaking, perhaps the dream is suggesting that you should watch your tongue. Mime is imitative, but is also to do with "showing"; perhaps your actions at present should be so clear that they speak louder than words? Mime is an aspect of *theatre*, so consider if you maybe have hidden talents.

mimicry Are you trying too hard (or not hard enough) to emulate someone you respect or admire? Or are they displaying some of your characteristics, likable or unlikable? Are you unwisely poking fun at someone in waking life?

miracles Fascinating and exciting, but – for ordinary mortals anyway – impossible to perform. Are you being invited to stop trying to work miracles, slow down, not to try so hard? A dream of something miraculous occurring may simply mirror an extraordinary waking event.

mirror What did you see in your dream mirror? Whatever it was, it probably represented you yourself, so consider this first of all – and what you felt about it. Were you trying to use a magic mirror to get a clearer view of yourself, or someone else? Remember, mirror-images reverse reality, and sometimes distort it. Is the dream making a reference to wishful thinking? There may be a suggestion of vanity, or lack of self-esteem. If the mirror was broken, have you recently been shattered by some event or realization? Or should you prepare for a long period of struggle? See also *crack*, *glass*.

miscarriage If you are pregnant, do not let the dream distress you, but by all means check with your gynaecologist. The dream could refer to some miscarried plan in waking life, or to something which has miscarried in the post, perhaps. There might be a reference to some responsibility you are carrying – perhaps one of which you should, or wish to, rid yourself, but to which you feel bound.

misery Another abstract emotion which could colour your day if you wake up under its influence. There may be a reference to some factor in your waking life, but decide first of all whether you are being a misery to yourself. Ask your dreams (see p. 47) how you can improve your attitude to life, express yourself more rewardingly.

mistake This dream could carry a warning: check the areas of your life to which the dream may be referring. There may be a reference to some mistake you made in the past, and which you may be about to repeat.

mockery If you were being mocked, maybe you take your waking self too seriously; or are secretly afraid of being mocked; or are over-concerned with what people say. If you were mocking someone else, he or she may represent an aspect of yourself of which you are scornful – or perhaps someone you take seriously, but who deserves a more sceptical look.

model To dream you belong to the glamorous world of fashion models may be a wish-fulfilment. But perhaps it is a hint that you are not attaining your view of a model citizen, wife, lover. Or is vanity striking home? Alternatively, you may be modelling yourself too much on someone else. If you were making a model (of what?) perhaps you are trying to reduce some problem to manageable proportions, or your dream may be suggesting that you express yourself through some kind of creative work.

money In waking life our attitudes to money and to love are often strikingly similar, so the first thing to do is attempt to draw that parallel: were you being generous, mean, covetous, possessive, spending too freely, or saving too carefully? There could of course be mundane financial parallels; but more than likely it will be your emotional or sexual life under scrutiny.

monastery Was this a peaceful place, in which you felt relaxed and at ease, or was it restrictive and tightly disciplined? This, and your reaction, will be clues as to whether you are being advised to be more contemplative and introverted, or in need of discipline. Monasteries are entirely masculine, so for either sex will probably relate to the masculine side of the nature, perhaps to aggression or assertion – a plea for greater sensitivity, maybe, or a more caring attitude. As with a dream of a nunnery, the reference to restrictions on sexuality (or a restriction to a single sex, probably your own) may be significant.

monkey See *animals*.

monster Dream monsters come in a greater variety of size and shape than in any science fiction novel or film. If the same monster keeps appearing in your dreams, get to know him as completely as possible, even if he is fearsome; ask your dreams questions about him (see p. 47), and try to come to terms with him – even cultivate sympathy with him. For, remember, your dreams are you, and you are they, so the monster may very well represent some part of you. With acceptance, he should be prepared to work for you instead of against you (he is probably strong and forceful, if maybe a trifle stupid – think of Caliban in *The Tempest*, in a sense Prospero's *alter ego*). He could represent any one of many aspects of your life: a parent, employer, perhaps, a partner. He could represent sex, or marriage, or old age, or death . . . But you must learn to control him, and as you make the attempt you will find that no matter how disturbing your dream at first was, you may begin to enjoy it. See also *fear*.

monument To what? Past glory, a dead love? Put flowers on it if you must, but it may well be that your dreams will soon be encouraging you to move on and look to the future. See also *statue*.

Moon, the The age-old symbol of woman, the intuitive, *yin* side of psyche. Perhaps your dream is encouraging you to allow this area greater freedom of expression (whether you are male or female). But are you crying or reaching for the Moon at present? If so, what comment did your dream seem to make? The Moon sometimes seems to relate to our past, to what we inherit. It can also represent our changing moods (moon and mind are closely associated). Was the moon full or new, waxing or waning? Were there clues suggesting the reference of the dream? If not, invite them (see p. 47).

mother The relationship between mother and child is extremely complex, whatever the circumstances; but there is inevitably a strong tie and an equally strong *desire* to love, irrespective of intervening tensions and differences. When we dream of our mother we are focusing on the feminine side of our nature, and much of what we really are. Our dream mother will warn, chastise, encourage us, and it is vitally important that we come to terms with her if we are to function as self-contained, psychologically whole entities. This applies to both men and women. With men we have the added complication of their needing to come to terms with women sexually, so that

m

they can express themselves maturely within a relationship (see *madonna*). Dreams of your mother are usually aligned to these complex areas; you should try particularly hard to interpret them really fully, and if in doubt or unhappy because of your dreams, you should perhaps seek therapeutic guidance. You may be searching for a mother figure in waking life, especially if your real mother died when you were young.

mountain If you were at the top of it the dream may be saying that you have little to worry about in waking life! If it loomed above you, on the other hand, your dream may be warning you of coming responsibilities or of your attitude towards your eventual goal or aspirations. If you were confidently climbing it, this will be a positive symbol – but see also LANDSCAPE (p. 68) and perhaps *earth*; what kind of ground was beneath your feet?

mourning When we suffer loss of any kind, whether of a loved one or even of a beloved object, it is right for us to mourn; it is a way of adjusting to the loss, to our changed circumstances; thus we re-gather psychological and emotional strength. If you are unhappy or in some way feeling the loss of something – an enjoyable job, perhaps, or a partnership – your dream may be showing you the way to compensate. Allow yourself time to grieve, to go through the necessary emotions. Your dreams will tell you when you are ready to become more assertive again. If you were dreaming of mourning clothes, could you be putting on an act, pretending to mourn? But see COLOUR (p. 94).

moving Your dream may be reflecting restlessness in waking life – saying that it is time to move on. But there could be a pun on something that has moved you. Or are you "moving heaven and earth" to get what you want? Or someone close to you may not be movable!

murder Whether you were being murdered, or murdering someone, the chances are that you are killing off something in waking life. It may be a relationship, or (perhaps more likely) a personal characteristic you dislike in yourself. The person you were murdering, or who was murdering you, may offer a clue as to what you need to kill. But as always when *death* emerges as a dream symbol, the accent will be on change. See DEATH (p. 76).

museum Your dream museum probably represented your personality, and contained symbols of the inherited psychological characteristics of your own nature, which you are perhaps regarding objectively at present. Your reaction to the contents is crucial: were you clearing out the fustier exhibits, re-arranging others, adding new ones? If bewildered, ask your dreams (see p. 47) for more explanation; this could be a complex but very important and revealing dream.

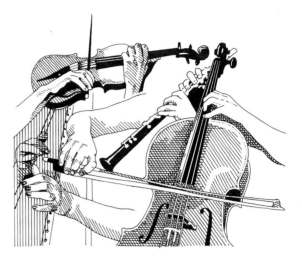

music Were you making it, or listening to it? The dream was referring perhaps to how you fit in with other people, or what you contribute to your group. Have you heard news recently that was music to your ears? Are you totally in control of your own life, in tune with yourself? The sound of the music may reflect the overall atmosphere of your life – harmonious, discordant, rhythmic, even unpredictable or unduly raucous.

n

nag A dream of an old horse or nag may be a pun on nagging; and if you dreamed of being nagged, perhaps your dream is insisting that it is time you made some sort of a change in your waking lifestyle or attitude to others.

nail Perhaps a simple phallic symbol (as the *horseshoe* is a female one); but the dream could be suggesting in an encouraging way that you are hitting some nail on the head. If you dreamed of a nail being hammered through your hands or feet, see *stigmata*. A dream of a broken fingernail could be making a statement about your image, especially if you were over-concerned about it.

nakedness see CLOTHES AND NUDITY (p. 82).

navigation A suggestion that you are steering your way through difficulties or problems in waking life. Were you on or off course, or entirely lost? If someone was navigating on your behalf, did this person represent an authority figure?

neighbours Think of your dream neighbours not just as people, but as representing some aspect of your life. On the other hand, your dream may be commenting on some waking-life situation particularly close to you.

nest Most likely a reference to your home, or your home-making instincts. Perhaps finance is involved (were you feathering your nest?), or was there a reference to eggs or to birds flying the nest – a symbol of your children? The dream could certainly be making a comment on your overall attitude to your family. Also perhaps see ENVIRONMENT (p. 92).

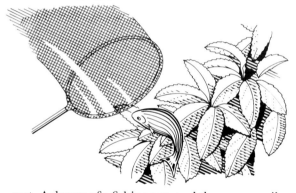

net A dream of a fishing net, and thus necessarily of WATER (see p. 80), would seem to suggest that your dream is referring to a search for some emotional prize, or perhaps a reference to one harvested from past experience. If you were peering through net curtains, see *lace*; a mosquito net suggests you are guarding yourself from some kind of adversity, but still able to move freely about your business. If you were caught in a net, there may be an allusion to some waking concern or problem, and you should try to recall your feelings, whether someone had trapped you, whether or not you escaped – and if so, how.

newspaper Consider what you were reading – the headlines and your reaction to them. If you were wrapping something in newspaper, the relationship between the content of the newspaper and the contents of the parcel would be very revealing.

night If it was really dark and you were lost, perhaps you should question your present direction in life (see *blindness*). A beautiful starry night, or a full moon, suggests a reflection of your

Michael was reassured by this dream, since at the time it occured he was coming to terms with a variety of problems; the fact that in his dream he was unconcerned by the messiness of his task was particularly interesting, since he knew he was at a point where he was well able to concentrate on really important matters, and would not be put off by any petty unpleasantness that his actions might provoke.

present psychological mood – dreamy, romantic, even starry-eyed. If a long night was ending, perhaps you are coming out of a depression, or some waking problem.

noise Perhaps the dream is suggesting you should make a noise about something in your waking life; should speak out, attract attention. Noise can also be confusing: are you trying to listen to, or do, too many things at once? But make sure the dream was not triggered by some real noise in the vicinity.

note If you were reading a note, see *messages*; your dream could be suggesting you keep certain things at the front of your mind – to make a careful note of what is going on. A musical note is a very different matter: whether it was sharp or flat or beautifully in tune is relevant, and could well relate to the present theme of your life. But such a dream will possibly only occur to someone to whom music is important and meaningful.

numbers A dream preoccupation with numbers seems most likely to be concerned with material things in your waking life: are you perhaps preoccupied with possessions? But what were you counting? The dream could be suggesting that your number is up, in some way. If you dreamed of a "lucky" number, do *not* immediately make a massive bet on that basis! An actual number which appears in a dream is almost inevitably one which means something to us – an old telephone number, the number of a childhood house – so think about that, too.

n

nun A reference perhaps to some aspect of sexuality: do you aspire to a spectacular degree of purity? Are you preoccupied with the conception of virginity? Men, especially, should see *madonna*. Women who dream of taking the veil could be seeking peace and security, or expressing a need to cut themselves off in some way from everyday affairs and perhaps from their family: this may only mean they need a rest!

nursery A reference, perhaps, to the maternal instinct; but a dream of your own childhood nursery may hint that you are living in the past, and need to be more aware of the present and the future.

nut A simple punning dream? Are you behaving in a "nutty" manner? Are you a hard nut to crack? If cracking innumerable nuts, perhaps you are seeking the resolution of a problem, or trying to get to its core – to the kernel.

O

objective Whether you reached your dream objective or not is of course crucial, for the dream no doubt refers to waking objectives and ambitions, though if the word itself was emphasized it may be encouraging you to be more objective in considering some problem.

obscenity A potentially worrying dream if you are repelled by and avoid obscenity in waking life. There may be a comment on a restricted sexuality, if you were casually uttering the obscenities yourself: if there was a strong feeling of revulsion, perhaps you have recently done something from which your inner self is recoiling. Perhaps you should ask your dreams (see p. 47) for additional help.

obstacle What was the obstacle, and did you successfully surmount it? You may well be encountering obstacles in your waking life, and here may be a hint about overcoming them. The kind of obstacle could suggest you think more carefully about waking plans.

obedience Depending on the dream and your attitude in it, there may be a suggestion that you rebel a little, or that you are not allowing yourself sufficient self-expression.

offence Your dream could be comment on some recent waking offence, suggesting that you are over- or under-reacting to it. If someone was offensive to you in your dream, you may need to reassess your opinion of, or attitude to, that person.

office A dream of the office in which you work may well refer to your own personality, and be making a statement about the way you conduct your affairs, your practicality (see ENVIRONMENT p. 92). If the office was a strange one, perhaps you are in waking life concerned to compare your way of life with other people's, your attitudes and ideals with theirs. Perhaps you are ready to assimilate some new characteristics.

officer If you were the officer, the dream was commenting on your powers of leadership, so decide whether you are too authoritarian (or not authoritarian enough). There could be a comment on some authority figure and your attitude to him or her.

officialdom Usually associated with boredom and frustration, so perhaps summing up some area of your present waking life. Ask your dreams (see p. 47) to show you ways around the difficulties, or you may be submerged by tedious problems.

oil Generally associated with the idea of riches, but also fuel which keeps us warm. Perhaps you need some psychological oil to get you moving? Have you been pouring oil on troubled waters lately? Or are your own waters troubled – have you emotional problems that need calming? Who could supply the oil for the purpose? Oils are used for massage and in perfumes, to nourish and improve the tone of the skin; so perhaps there is a reference to sensuality.

ointment A reference to healing, perhaps – maybe of an old wound. Unless there was a fly in the ointment, or it was smelly and unpleasant – in which case you may have been the fly – or of course the ointment!

old age see *age*.

opening Were you attending some kind of opening – of a play or an exhibition? Such occasions are usually celebratory, so perhaps you feel particularly confident: or of course there is the sexual innuendo. Dreaming of opening a package is probably a reference to self-discovery, and what you found inside the package should be illuminating.

O

operation As with *opening*, above, this could refer to self-discovery, with looking into yourself. But a medical operation suggests repairs or the extraction of something harmful, so you should consider whether you have to make amends to someone, or what psychological problem needs resolution. As usual, do not be concerned that there is necessarily an allusion to a physical ailment; check with your doctor if you are nervous. Any other kind of operation – military, for instance – could be a reference to practical planning, or to some aspect of your working life.

opponent The most important thing is to decide what waking opponent is referred to – perhaps an aspect of yourself (see *duel*). So there could be an inner conflict that needs resolution.

orchestra A reference perhaps to mass opinion: if your dream orchestra moved you, are you paying too much attention to following the crowd? Dreaming of playing in an orchestra could refer to your need to fit into society, or your attitude to that need.

organ It takes a lot of wind to make an organ sound, and if you were tremendously impressed by the sound of a dream organ you might consider whether you are something of a windbag in waking life! The shape of organ pipes, and the very name itself, could suggest the sexual organs; look for clues elsewhere in the dream, if this seems likely.

orgy A wish-fulfilment dream, perhaps; or a dream running counter to your normal sexual tastes, but suggesting that they are perhaps too conservative, that you should relax a little in this area of your life.

ornament Think carefully: you could have been the ornament. Were you smashed? Out of fashion, or simply decorative and little else?

orphan A comment perhaps on loneliness, lack of security. Are you in need of greater love and affection? Perhaps (especially if you came across an orphan in your dream) you have more affection to express to others than you realize.

outcast Perhaps a reflection of your waking emotions; or maybe the outcast represents a characteristic of which you have rid yourself.

oven See *heat*, *kitchen*. Are you cooking something up for someone? Was the dream suggesting that you are pregnant, as in the expression "a bun in the oven"?

p

pain The dream was probably triggered by some minor body ache or pain – cramp, perhaps, or a muscle spasm brought on by lying in a strange position. Dreams have been known to signal symptoms of illness, however, before they have been medically diagnosed, so if you dream of a pain in a specific part of your body, and especially if the dream recurs, it may be worth having a medical check-up. However, there could be another sort of warning: are you being a pain in the neck?

paint/painting If you dreamed of painting a picture, and this is not one of your usual occupations, the dream may be hinting that you should try it (painting, apart from anything else, offers a further means of recording your dreams which can be more successful and psychologically rewarding than writing them down – see p. 47). But perhaps you were daubing paint on a wall or writing some slogan: the content will be very revealing (see *messages*). Were you re-painting something? – if so, is there a hint of some

painting
John dreamed: "*I had a huge picture to paint, on a vast, broad canvas which was set up on the sea front. I was about to start, and trying to decide which parts of it I could actually reach. Some of it was very close to the rocks, and to steps going down to the sea. I was saying to myself, 'I can reach that area, but I must be careful, because I might step back and fall into the sea.' I also realized that parts of the canvas would be totally inaccessible.*"

This dream was important because John was planning to write a wide-ranging book for which he had a lot of material to organize on his "canvas". He realized there were some areas of the book which were outside his range, where he could easily get out of depth, and the dream was warning him about the possible difficulty. The sea symbol referred to the fact that John's book was going to deal with aspects of the unconscious and the human psyche.

kind of cover-up, or a whitewash job? Or are you restoring something – your self-respect, for instance? COLOUR (see p. 94) will be an important clue. If you are mixing paint, perhaps you are stirring things up in waking life.

paper Clean white sheets of paper; a muddle of official papers; wall-paper – all will say something individual. If the paper is white and clean, you could be about to make a fresh start in some area of your life. Official forms may suggest problems concerning authority – wall-paper, some kind of cover-up. Or your dream could have made a statement about something ephemeral: if it was of, say, a paper bird or aeroplane or a paper hat, there could be a reference perhaps to a fleeting love affair. A dream of a manuscript or a daily journal might be referring to the past.

parachute Hopefully a safe and happy landing; but if the parachute didn't open, the chances are that this was a simple *falling* dream. See also FLYING (p. 84).

parade A commemoration or celebration may simply be asserting your own importance or achievement, especially if you were at the centre of it. Or were you watching a menacing parade of armaments? If so, the dream may possibly represent some rivalry in your life, which could mean sexual rivals if you are a man.

paradise It is unlikely you are about to go there on a permanent basis! Hopefully the dream was beautiful, placid and peaceful, perhaps romantic, so there may be an element of wish-fulfilment. Perhaps you simply need more peace and quiet in your waking life. Or maybe the dream was saying that you are at present in paradise on earth, in which case you are very fortunate. A dream of being cast out of paradise may refer to the end of something enjoyable, or even (if you are biblically minded) to a sense of sin.

paralysis The dream may be suggestive of some form of psychological paralysis which is blocking your progress, or the inability to do anything at all about some worrying waking situation. In the former case, try to work out what is cramping you; eventual resolution could come through self- and dream-analysis, though you may need counselling.

parapet A reference to your sense of security, perhaps; you could be at a crucial point in decision-making, deciding whether or not to jump, making your mind up rationally and objectively, guarded from the drop. "Look before you leap" may be the relevant motto.

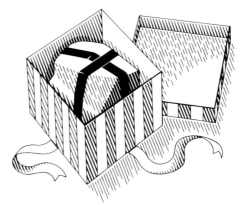

parcel A dream of wrapping a parcel may refer to your having "wrapped up" some project or plan. Was it neatly and securely wrapped, or did the string fail to hold it together? If the latter, maybe you are not so much in control of the waking situation as you think. Unpacking a parcel could suggest that you are into a period of self-discovery; it will be interesting to work out how you identify with the contents of the parcel. Think of the legend of Pandora's box; it might be interesting to re-read that myth and refer it to your dream.

park/parking If you were simply enjoying walking in a park see LANDSCAPE (p. 68), ENVIRONMENT (p. 92); if you were trespassing, perhaps you are encroaching on someone's life. Could the dream be referring to some illicit affair? If you parked your car illegally, or forgot where you parked it, remember that a car is almost always a dream symbol for oneself – for men, often one's sexual self. Are you trespassing on someone's property – even psychologically?

parents see *mother, father, family.*

parliament If you were a member, perhaps your dream is urging that you speak out about some public matter that concerns you; perhaps

p

you need to attract more attention to yourself. The dream may be a comment on your powers of leadership or your need for power. Were you shouted down, or did you get the enthusiastic approval of the House?

partner Perhaps a reference to your other self; if you are a woman, to the more masculine, assertive side of your nature, if a man, to your intuitive, feminine side. The dream could be commenting on your attitude to your partner, or to your sexuality. Most often, our partners are simply present in our dreams, and if they become the focal point of a dream it is likely to be an important one. Wish-fulfilment may be involved; if so, what can you do to make your waking partnership as good as your dream one?

party If your dream was of an enjoyable, frivolous party, could it be a hint that you are making light of your life at present? If there were many people at the party, and especially if you found them difficult, when organizing the party, see *crowds*. A dream of a political party is perhaps a reference to your opinions and emotions regarding important impersonal matters.

passage see *tunnel*, ENVIRONMENT (p. 92).

passport A reference to your identity. Are you suffering from some sort of identity crisis? Having your passport examined and stamped may signify approval of some new move or project. See, perhaps, *journey*, *crossroads*, *identity*.

past, the A great many symbols in dreams can of course refer to the past. If you dream continually of returning to old environments or situations, you should ask yourself why: it is perhaps a signal that you need the reassurance of the known rather than the insecurity of the unknown (the present, the future). There may be a suggestion that you use experience gained in the past to help you with waking life; you are unlikely to make the same mistake twice, let alone three times . . . If you still feel uncertain or apprehensive, ask your dreams (see p. 47) for more information, and try to avoid living in the past; develop a more assertive, forward-looking outlook.

paste Paste is used to repair things, patch them up, perhaps to make the best of a bad job. Your dream paste could well be reflecting some waking situation which is simply "sticky", or the fact that you are making amends, or making the best of things. But perhaps you were the paste; in which case your involvement is considerable. The dream may then be commenting on your

tenacity, or the fact that you are clinging on to old ideas, or perhaps people. We sometimes refer to costume or mock jewellery as "paste": if this symbol appears in the dream, see *jewellery*, but ask yourself whether you are perhaps behaving in a way which is untrue to your real personality.

path A reference perhaps to your progress, both psychological and material; relate it if you can to your present progress and future plans. See LANDSCAPE (p. 68) of course; consider whether the path was up- or down-hill, stony or smooth or slippery. See also ENVIRONMENT (p. 92).

patient There may have been a punning comment on your patience (or lack of it). But see *invalid*, *illness*, *hospital*. If you were playing patience in your dream, perhaps you are playing some kind of waiting game in real life.

pattern A great deal depends on the type of pattern and your attitude towards it. Perhaps you were trying to piece together various aspects of your life, or there may have been a comment on your sexuality or sensuality if the pattern had voluptuous curves, pleasing and beautiful. If you were working with a dress pattern, perhaps you are trying to copy someone you admire.

pavement See *path*; but if you were preoccupied with the pavement itself, consider whether it seemed to offer more security, or whether it was giving way beneath you. Was there a suggestion that you need more security, or perhaps less?

pen/pencil Sometimes a phallic symbol, especially if you were sharpening it or filling it with ink, or indeed if it was leaking. If you were more conscious of what you were writing than of the instrument, see *message*. The pen or pencil could represent someone you are manipulating; if your pen or pencil was borrowed by someone else, perhaps they are manipulating you.

penetration More than likely a dream with sexual connotations. A fear of penetration or an aggressive determination to penetrate tells its own story, whatever varieties of *tool* may have been employed.

penis The actual appearance of a penis in a dream seems rare; much more often it appears disguised in *phallic* form (see the Glossary). The overt appearance of a penis is so strongly sexual a statement that, if it gives rise to peculiar fear or horror, it should perhaps prompt the dreamer to consider his or her whole attitude to sexuality, and possibly consult a therapist.

pepper A reference perhaps to someone who is "hot stuff", or very spicy?

perfume Whether or not a dream can convey the actual odour of a perfume, dreams of it may relate to nostalgic memories such a perfume calls up; if you were choosing a perfume, perhaps you are faced with decisions in your waking life, or are ready for a change of image, since perfume can play an important part in the presentation of an individual image.

period For a woman, a dream of her period may coincide with its coming on; but the dream could also relate to some regular event in her life. There may be a suggestion that you should visit your doctor, if you have difficult periods.

perversion A dream of sexual perversion can be very disturbing. Try to view it objectively. What you regard as a perversion may in fact be common sexual preference for others; so there may be a hint to be less puritanical in your attitudes, or even that you should relax into your own sexuality more than you have previously been able to do. There may be a reference to unconscious sexual preferences of which you are not aware. Try if you can to come to terms with them. If you are really confused or in doubt, consult your doctor.

petrol A dream that may relate to your physical energy level, especially perhaps if you were filling your *car* at a petrol station (a dream of one's car is very often related to oneself). Petrol is expensive and explosive: could that have a reference to your present life?

phallus See *penis*, and definition in the Glossary.

photograph If you were taking a photograph, there is perhaps something in your recent waking life that you are particularly eager to remember:

the subject of your photograph should offer a clue. If you were tearing up an old photograph there could be a reference to your determination to live in the present, escape from your past. See *camera*; perhaps *message*.

piano There may be a reference to the past if you were unwillingly put to the instrument as a child. But are you playing someone else's tune in waking life? Or there could be wish-fulfilment involved. Moving a heavy piano may refer to a large, unwieldy problem.

picnic Consider the individual symbols: FOOD (see p. 86), the other people involved, the LANDSCAPE (see p. 68). Usually a picnic party is a small, select one, sometimes upset by *insects*, *wasps*, *bees*. All these symbols will be inter-related.

picture See *artist*, *painting*, COLOUR (p. 94), LANDSCAPE (p. 68). If your concentration was on constructing your picture, perhaps the emphasis was on something in waking life of which you want to get a clearer picture. It could be telling you something very specific, and one would expect the subject to be the strongest clue. If it changed, or refused to be captured, the reference may be to changing opinions or attitudes. Buying or selling a picture suggests the passing on of something very much your own – experience, perhaps, or affection.

pie see FOOD AND DRINK (p. 86); but you should consider the contents (remember the blackbird "when the pie was opened"), and try to recall your feelings.

pig Maybe a warning that you have recently been behaving like one; or a reference to someone else who has been selfish or chauvinistic.

pigeon See FISH, FLESH AND FOWL (p. 88) but there could be a reference to your love-life – pigeons and doves are faithful creatures.

pilgrim Probably a reference to some kind of waking pilgrimage or quest, maybe after truth or psychological or spiritual development. Consider whether you are making, or should make, sacrifices for such things.

pillow See *cushion*; but the pillow is usually associated with the head. Maybe you are attempting to soften some blow, or your dream is suggesting that you should relax your mind.

pill Perhaps a pun on some bitter pill you have had to swallow. If you are a woman and dream that you forgot to take your contraceptive pill – count them carefully! The dream may suggest you should go on the pill; ask your dreams for reassurance if you need it (see p. 47).

pin This may be a phallic symbol (see *penetration*), or have a more personal allusion if you commonly use pins in your waking life. If you pricked your finger in your dream, could this be a reference to a wish (perhaps unconscious) for a less chaste life?

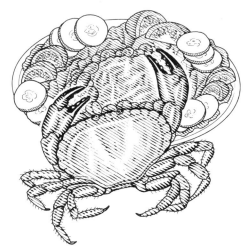

pincers You may be trying hard to grab at something in your waking life; your dreams will either be reassuring you or otherwise, depending on what happened and your own feelings. A time, perhaps, to reassess your present situation. If the pincers or claws belonged to a crab, consider whether there is anything grasping or covetous in your waking behaviour pattern.

pipe A symbol of comfort, associated (like the cigarette) with sucking at the breast, and so probably a symbol of insecurity. There may be a longing too for the peace and contentment offered in the tobacco advertisements. But the almost universal disapproval of smoking may have turned this into a suggestion that you have something to be ashamed of. Also important,

perhaps, is the punning aspect: are you indulging in pipe dreams in waking life? A drain pipe is of course another matter! Climbing down one suggests a strongly felt desire to escape from someone or something.

pirate Have you pirated something in waking life? Seized someone else's partner? Pirates may be romantic, but they are also violent and dangerous and often end up on the gibbet; so a wish-fulfilment interpretation may not be the whole story. But "pirating" could be the keyword, so consider whether someone is mercilessly taking advantage of you – or you of them – in the way of stealing their material.

plains see LANDSCAPE (p. 68).

plane see FLYING (p. 84), TRAVEL (p. 70); but consider also the possibility of a pun – making something plain to someone.

planet There is an enormous popular interest in astrology; if you dream of a particular planet, look up the relevant astrological significance, and indeed the myths associated with it (the Greek and Roman gods after whom the planets are named, for instance). You could be feeling specially at one with the universe at present, perhaps having taken strides, psychologically. Don't allow yourself to be swept too far out into space; you could loose touch with reality.

plants A dream of the growth of plants probably refers to your own growth and development. If the plants were sending out shoots or bursting into flower, it seems likely that new developments are occurring in your life. Drooping or withered plants suggest the opposite; your dreams may suggest, if asked (see p. 47) ways in which you can renew yourself, your self-confidence and self-esteem. There could be a reference too to your sexuality, your libido being either powerful or low.

plaster A plaster cast is a copy, but never precisely the same as the original, so there may be a reference to your attempting to replicate past circumstances, perhaps to try to make a new love conform to the pattern of an old one. If you have to wear a plaster cast, your movement may be inhibited, but in the end there will be strengthening and a mending, so the allusion seems to be to discipline, strength through restraint. If you were mixing plaster, perhaps you are making preparations to settle some matter (did the plaster set too quickly?) If plastering a room, remember that a house

p

probably represents yourself, so maybe you are paying special attention to one particular area of your image, repairing it or "putting a good face" on it. The application of sticking plaster (to what part of your *body*?) suggests you may have been hurt recently and are trying to cover up or heal yourself. Such wounds need air: are you sure it is not a case of "out of sight, out of mind"?

plate See, perhaps, FOOD AND DRINK (p. 86); but your dream could be suggesting that you have too much on your plate at present. If you were throwing plates, maybe the dream was simply reflecting inner tension.

platform Usually connected with meetings, or of course with stations. Waiting for a train suggests anticipation of expected events: are they late, or overdue? If sitting on a platform at a meeting, are you in waking life in some elevated position, "on display" in some way?

playing see *games*, *music*.

plot A plot or conspiracy in a dream may be a warning, whether you are plotting or plotted against. The other people involved in the dream will be significant.

plough For men especially, a sexual symbol used throughout the ages, but likely to refer to your own sexual desires rather than to their subject (though there is the suggestion of preparing for fecundity, sowing new life, so perhaps a dream about a desire for children). The meticulous ploughing of a field may suggest the pattern of your life, steady routine, a need for security. Perhaps it hints that you are in a rut, just "ploughing on". See *earth*, LANDSCAPE (p. 68).

poacher A hint of illicit action of some kind in waking life: are you poaching someone else's preserves, or is someone else poaching yours?

pocket Possibly a sexual symbol, but maybe a suggestion of undue secrecy, or a reference to the cunning, protective or even possessive areas of your personality. Was there a hole in your pocket through which your resources were draining away? See *money*, *container*.

poet This could be a wish-fulfilment dream, perhaps, or image projection. Alternatively, your dream may be telling you that you are neglecting the spiritual side of your personality, are too concerned with material things.

poison What could be poisoning you in waking life? Someone, or something – or you yourself? If you were poisoning someone else, consider what they may represent to you. See *murder*, DEATH (p. 76).

pole A phallic symbol, of course (see *maypole*), unless of course there is a punning reference to someone Polish.

police Your dream was probably referring to an inner authority figure, or to your conscience. If you know that your behaviour has been less than perfect recently, you may now be trying to arrest yourself: "arrest" in the sense, perhaps, of "stop". You may need help if you are to cease the behaviour which is (perhaps unconsciously) distressing you. The police are also a support, protection and help; maybe it is this that you need at present, especially if you are being unjustly treated.

politician We have placed politicians in power, so they are authority figures to us. But they talk a lot, can bend the truth, are often mistrusted, sometimes abuse their positions. So this may be a suggestion that you should view your inner conscience with some scepticism: is it being misled? The dream reference may be to someone you know, who seeks authority over you, or is misusing his or her position.

polygamy Unless this is an overt sexual dream (see *orgy*) some reference to your attitude to sex seems likely; you may not fully have resolved this.

pool Almost certainly a reference to your emotions (see WATER, p. 80). How deep, clear, cloudy, beautiful or menacing was the pool? Alternatively, there may be a pun on the football pools, or a pool game.

porter Usually trustworthy, helpful; is this your role in life, or is there a reference to someone you know, a carrier of others' burdens?

portrait Was it a portrait of yourself? If so, was it beautiful, or a caricature? Maybe the dream was referring to your view of yourself, or how you hope others see you. Oscar Wilde's *Picture of Dorian Gray* bore the sins of its subject . . .

pose Perhaps you have a conscious or unconscious need to conceal your real self by "posing" as something you are not. But remember who the artist was: yourself, or someone you love?

postcard See *messages*: but remember, a postcard is open and can be read by the postman, or anyone else.

postman A bringer of *messages*. Are you the bearer of news at present, or a message of some kind? Can you identify the postman with anyone else? Remember that the bringer of bad tidings was often slaughtered for his pains.

pot See *jar*, *container*. But there could be a reference to the drug. Or did you find a pot of gold, representing some important self-realization?

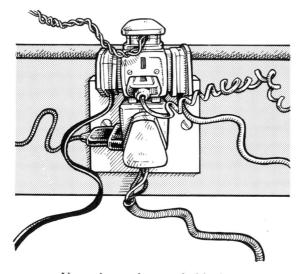

power Your dream has probably been telling you whether you have too much – or insufficient – power over yourself and your emotions, or warning you not to abuse your power over others. If no one was recognizing your power, or you felt drained of power, it may be that you lack stamina at present, and need a course of vitamins.

prayer Consider very carefully to whom you were praying: you may be seeking emotional support from someone close to you, perhaps from some authority figure. On the other hand, the dream may be suggesting you should stop praying for something, and go and get it for yourself.

preacher If the preacher in your dream was making you feel guilty about your transgressions, was the dream trying to point out that you should face up to reality and take positive, assertive action? Or even just stop feeling sorry for yourself? But perhaps you *should* make amends, or even change your ways. The preacher was very probably your own conscience, and the congregation could have represented a multitude of your problems, or reflected facets of your personality.

precipice see *cliff*.

pregnancy Possibly a wish-fulfilment dream; perhaps a hint that you are indeed pregnant (before medical tests have confirmed the fact). But the symbol can suggest the development of an idea not yet ready to be openly expressed. If you were happy about your pregnancy, and it was normal, then the idea is developing in your unconscious, and you should for the while let it be. If you were unwell, the dream could have suggested that you should re-think the idea, or even perhaps abort it.

present The dream could possibly be a pun on "here and now"; but giving a present may suggest that you should make an offer of some kind to someone (the gift you were giving will be significant). Receiving one may reflect present help and support from friends, or an unsolicited, unexpected development in your waking life.

price The dream may be questioning you about the price you have to pay for some commitment or responsibility; a warning seems likely. An unexpectedly low price may suggest you are undervaluing yourself – or someone else.

prick Probably a sexual symbol, either a pun or a suggestion that you are afraid of being sexually hurt. Another pun is possible: should you prick up your ears?

priest A father figure or symbol of authority. But see *confession*, *blessing*. There could be a focus on your purer, higher, more moral self. Whether warning or reassuring, such a dream is likely to be important in proportion to your veneration for the priesthood, but may be meaningful even if you are a sceptic.

prince/princess See *royalty*.

print Since for most people seeing something in print suggests it has additional authority, the dream will be emphasizing the *message* being

prick

Julia dreamed: "*I was watching someone (I did not know whether the person was male or female) having acupuncture needles lightly stuck into the side of a finger to relieve symptoms from which I knew they were suffering. They said the needles stuck into the finger hurt, too. I felt sympathy for them.*"

At the time of the dream I was helping a man come to terms with physical ailments which I suspected were directly related to sexual problems (the sexual ambiguity of the dream character seemed to emphasize the fact). I associated the acupuncture treatment, in which I am interested, with my own involvement in the case, and the fact that the treatment was given to the phallic finger indicated I was on the right lines.

procession of elephants

Julia dreamed: "*I dreamed I was looking out of the window of my apartment on the top floor of the house, and looking down on a procession of elephants passing along the street below.*"

Julia failed to remember this dream on waking, but while working on the proofs of this book was reminded of it by the entry under "elephant". The elephants were related to her feelings about Ganesha, the Indian elephant god of prosperity – and publishing! The fact that she was looking at the elephants from her window seemed to refer to the fact that the apartment below hers was on the market, and she was considering it as an investment; but the dream may have referred to this book. In any event, an encouraging, not to say amusing, symbol.

conveyed. Dreaming of having something printed, or actually printing it yourself, suggests you should publish some message which at the moment you may be keeping to yourself. Developing a photographic print may suggest you are cultivating or wish to possess the person photographed. See also *headline*, *photograph*.

prism A reference perhaps to the many facets of a problem or situation of which you are trying to see the light. See, perhaps, *crystal*, *rainbow*.

prison Apart from the possibility of imprisonment as a symbol of self-condemnation, a dream of being imprisoned, or visiting a person, may be focusing on some element of your personality which you are unable to release. You may be feeling claustrophobic, "shut in", at present; or perhaps your life lacks challenge. Take practical action to redress the balance. If you are unable to come to terms with your waking prison – practical or psychological – you could consider therapy, or attempt to unlock the gates by confiding in a reliable, close friend. Who was the governor, who the warders, in your dream?

prize Your unconscious is probably encouraging you to feel pleased with yourself – unless of course your dream prize slipped through your fingers. Consider why you get the prize. If you are a gambler, do not take your dream as a promise of success in that field! See *honour*, *medal*.

procession The nature of the procession is obviously important (see above, and the example under *laughter*, p. 156). Processions are usually formal, celebratory or mourning, so consider what waking event could have prompted this one – and just how successful your dream procession was. See *parade*.

proclamation Surely you have something you want to tell the world?

professor Was the dream professor authoritative or eccentric, even "mad"? Were there characteristics with which you can identify? What was the *message* conveyed? See perhaps *lecture*, *learning*, *teacher*.

promise Probably a dream reference to a waking commitment. Did you keep or break your dream promise? Perhaps there is a focus on a promise you made to yourself.

property A reference to your whole being is likely – there are analogies with *house*, but this is a wider symbol, likely to represent your emotional, physical and intellectual self. Were you buying property (at what price?) giving it away, securing it for your future?

prosecution A reference to waking guilt, perhaps, or to some situation in which you have acted against your better judgment. Perhaps you now have to pay for it, in some way. See *trial*: if you were acquitted, or the prosecution was dropped, this could be a reassuring dream.

prostitute Consider any sexual implications: for men there could be an important statement about their attitude to women. But of course the dream could be suggesting that you are prostituting yourself in some other way – at work, for instance, emotionally or morally. Any feeling of excitement or distaste may mirror your waking feeling about the true subject of the dream.

protest The chances are that you are feeling the need to speak up about something in your life, to externalize some emotion or commitment. It may be that your waking reaction to the real subject of the dream is weaker than is justified; the dream is focusing on it to prompt you to stronger action or reaction. If necessary, ask your dreams for more help (see p. 47), but if the protest or *demonstration* was an urgent one, try to get the basic problem sorted out quickly.

publicity Perhaps you feel that some action of yours, or some virtue, needs publicity; but you could be nursing feelings of guilt over deceptive behaviour which you fear may be made public. On the premise that all publicity is good publicity, maybe you should try to clear up misunderstanding *now*, or even show off a little. Unless you have been showing off too much lately.

pudding Are you feeling like one – overweight, physically stodgy? Or perhaps you are in the late stages of pregnancy, and not enjoying it! Were

Dream Analysis

protest

Beverley dreamed: *"I was combing and parting my hair. It had turned black at the roots. The hairdresser said she'd see what she could do about it."*

Beverley, a natural blonde, had this dream and the SMOKE and TATTOO dreams quoted on pp. 189 and 198 on three consecutive nights, soon after she had been made very angry and upset by a friend who had behaved unkindly and rather cruelly to her. She was mystified by the vivid appearance of black in her first dream, but took it to be a protest against her friend's attitude.

you stirring a pudding (and in waking life, "stirring it" in some way)? Finding money in a pudding suggests good things in an unlikely but festive context.

pulse If you were taking a pulse, are you sounding out some situation in waking life?

puncture Perhaps a sexual reference (to contraception, perhaps?) But have you been "let down" by someone, or let someone else down? Should you repair some situation? For a possible sexual association, see *penetration*.

punishment Threatened punishment may reflect a bad conscience; or perhaps you are punishing yourself too hard for some imagined misdemeanour. Set in the context of the past, the dream could be a comment on your relationship with parents or teachers, and perhaps through this to longterm psychological problems with which you have yet to come to terms.

puppet A dream warning seems likely. You may in real life be some kind of puppet. The crucial factor is, who was pulling the strings? If in the final analysis it was you yourself, perhaps you are simply behaving like a doll, reacting only to preconditioned opinions and attitudes.

purse See *pocket*; the Englishwoman's purse – a small container for cash – is often a female sexual symbol – have you been spending too freely from it recently? Are your emotions drained, your purse empty? Or are you guarding it obsessively? The American purse (or British handbag) may have been full of clutter: perhaps you were tidying it – in this case, perhaps you are reorganizing some area of your waking life, clearing up a muddle.

puzzle Of course this could be a reference to waking puzzles or problems; if you resolved the dream puzzle, fine! If not, ask your dream for more information (see p. 47).

q

r

quarantine A period of isolation to prevent disease spreading, quarantine in a dream seems likely to be warning you to stop some course of action before it hurts you or someone else. A possible warning to keep away from someone or something dangerous?

quarrel A dream quarrel can be almost as disturbing as a waking one; but it can also boost your confidence. Your waking reaction to your dream will be important. You may be goaded into externalizing your negative feelings about someone else, in which case the advice is probably sensible – you'll clear the air. But equally your dream quarrel could represent an inner psychological conflict (see *duel*). In that case there may be strain and tension; try to rationalize the conflict and then resolve it, with outside help if necessary.

quarry A quarry is usually a hole in a LAND-SCAPE (see p. 68), from which something has been taken; it may be the focus is on something which has left a gap in your life, and the gap may be as important as what made it. Has a relationship ended recently? If you were yourself quarrying, however, you may be using waking resources of emotional or physical energy to constructive ends. Or was the quarry some creature (or person) you were pursuing? Perhaps you yourself were the quarry. See PURSUIT (p. 66).

queen See *royalty*.

question The kind of question asked, and the person of whom it was asked, are obviously important factors. Was it a dream of being interrogated, or was the questioning friendly? It may be about knowledge, whether you possess it (knowing the answer) or do not, and may be suggesting that you increase your store – perhaps of understanding of others, or the dream may be encouraging you to study your own personal motivations more deeply.

quilt A quilt protects us, keeps us warm, can have complex, intriguing patterns; it may be the dream was encouraging you to relax and enjoy the complexities rather than worrying about them. Or did you throw the quilt off? In any event, if your dream ended in your waking cold and quilt-less, with the bedclothes on the floor, you can probably ignore it!

rabbit See *animals*, FISH, FLESH AND FOWL (p. 88); if your dream rabbit was a pet, think of it in the same context as a dog or cat. But remember, too, that perhaps the thing we most associate with rabbits is their intensive breeding activity!

racing The important questions to ask here are: were you a winner or loser; satisfied, elated, disappointed or frustrated? There may have been a comment on your recent progress, or lack of it. If you were at the races, see perhaps *gamble, bet, horse, dog*. Question your waking attitudes: you could be running risks, taking too many chances, expending too much energy in the hope that it will get you past the post first in an emotional or career situation. Incidentally, was there a starting *gun*? And if so, who fired it?

rack If you were being racked – tortured, to reveal some secret – this is an extreme form of *question*; and indeed, being racked was known as being "put to the question". Were you being stretched? If so, perhaps you are stretching yourself too far in some sense. Who was torturing you: your boss, a lover, a parent? Are you racking your brains for some kind of solution to a problem? That may be true especially if you were choosing items from a supermarket rack.

racket A comment on some form of devious waking plan or action? If you are not actually behaving in a criminal way, ask yourself whether you are perhaps taking too much from a lover or other innocent person, maybe emotionally.

racquet See *game*. Sexual symbolism seems likely: did the strings break? Did you serve several aces? Did it help you to win? Possibly, however, a pun on *racket*.

radio Probably see *message*. But we not only hear what is on the radio, we often overhear it, or fail to take it in; so consider whether your dream is trying to force you to listen to something important being said to you at the moment, which you are for some reason ignoring.

rags A dream suggestion, perhaps, that you should smarten yourself up; or that if you carry on as you are going you will soon be reduced to rags! Are you lacking in self-esteem? Or feeling too sorry for yourself? Remember you may be anyone in your dream, so if you saw a poor

r

Cinderella-like figure sorting through rags, it may be a hint that you should salvage the remnants of some aspect of your waking life. Ask yourself whether it would not be worthwhile. Remember, rags were once fine clothes! See CLOTHES AND NUDITY (p. 82), *image*.

raid A raid is unannounced and usually comes as a shock, so your dreams could be suggesting that some private and interior facet of your waking life is susceptible to sudden discovery. How did you react? Were you arrested, or ignored; innocent or guilty? How would you feel if what you are concealing was suddenly revealed?

railway Speed, but speed controlled and ordered, "on the rails". Perhaps you were being complimented on your sense of discipline – unless you went off the rails in your dream, and are likely to do so in waking life. Were the signals for or against you? Were there delays, frustrations and disorder? Were you on the right rails? Were you the station master, directing the traffic and organizing it, or the driver forced to stick to the track and subject to absolute control? But perhaps you were a passenger (first or second class or travelling without a ticket). From such a dream, with the possibility of complications, you can learn much; but it is idle to pretend it will be easy to interpret. Go for the main symbol and then relate it to the surrounding ones. Remember too that railways (especially steam railways) evoke nostalgia, so the dream could relate to the past. Trains entering tunnels are notorious symbols of sex and coitus.

rain See WEATHER (p. 74). Rain can wash away, and also refresh (see WATER p. 80). But your dream may have been a pun on "reign", in which case are you about to assume or resign power?

rainbow Hopes and aspirations could be in focus, spiritual or psychological development, or some deep-rooted desire, especially if you were hunting for the gold at the end of the rainbow, or if your rainbow came after a dream storm. See also COLOUR (p. 94), WEATHER (p. 74).

ransom Are you being made to pay heavily for something you treasure? Is someone taking advantage of you? Check your physical and emotional energy, and make sure you have enough for the tasks you want to complete.

rape Women who have been raped often find themselves undergoing the traumatic experience again in their dreams, possibly (but not certainly) as part of some natural therapeutic healing experience. If this is the case, describing the attack in great detail to some trusted friend may help, however embarrassing or frightening you may find it. It is of course important to come to terms with the experience in order to free yourself for a future enjoyable sexual life. If the rape was only a dream experience, a metaphor, ask yourself if anyone is taking advantage of you in waking life.

rat Who is the real-life rat? Or perhaps it is you who are behaving like a dirty rat? If you were aggressive towards the rat in your dream, it was reassuring you that you have the power to deal with the situation. See *animals*, FISH, FLESH AND FOWL (p. 88).

ration Rationing tends not only to mean shortage, but also an organized effort to make sure everyone has fair shares. Are you having to ration your love, perhaps between husband and children? Or do you feel you are not getting your proper share of affection at present? Or is there a reference to finance?

razor If you were sharpening an old-fashioned razor, perhaps you are preparing for some "cut-throat" activity in waking life – perhaps in business; or is someone "carving you up"? There may have been a sexual allusion: the act of shaving for men is sometimes a sexual metaphor (see *beards*). The process of shaving may refer to your personal image, suggesting you pay it more attention. Alternatively, you may be in some very tricky, uncertain situation, or balanced on the razor's edge.

reading See *messages*, *book*. You may be trying hard, in waking life, to organize your ideas, emotions and opinions into a cohesive whole and get them across to others.

rebel Rebellion may be called for in some aspect of your waking life, in which case your dream was probably encouraging it – unless you were being executed for rebellion, of course. See also *revolution, riot*.

recipe The *kitchen* is a symbol strongly connected with love and affection, as is *cooking*; so perhaps it refers to plans you are making for loved ones. Was the recipe successful, or faulty? If it was imperfect, reconsider your plans! There may have been a comment on study.

recitation There may be a reference here to some childhood experience, in which case the focus will probably be on self-confidence, especially perhaps in the context of your parents or teachers, and therefore to some authority figure, perhaps at work. Were you forgetting your lines, or being prompted, or told to speak up? All instructions may apply in your present waking life (other dream symbols should suggest the context). There may have been a reference to your experience and knowledge, and the good or indifferent use to which you are putting it.

recklessness A dream of recklessness will either mirror recent reckless behaviour, or encourage you to be a little less cautious. What was the context? There will be other symbols to which you may be able to refer.

recognition The recognition of someone in a dream may reflect your waking recognition of some personal characteristic, newly acquired self-knowledge, positive or otherwise. So does the person you recognized symbolize some trait in your own character? Sometimes such a dream draws our attention to our feeling for another person, a recognition of love or dislike.

reconcilation An allusion seems likely to some waking fact to which you must reconcile yourself: perhaps a facet of your character about which you feel unsure or worried. The dream is likely to be helping you to get used to a changed view or situation, to make peace with your new view of yourself. Or there could be a direct allusion to the patching-up of a quarrel.

record Perhaps a pun: a record referring to some personal target, a record you want to equal or beat; or you may be gathering facts "for the record". If you were making a record, see *message*. Alternatively this could be a straight wish-fulfilment dream.

red See COLOUR (p. 94).

reeds Struggling through reeds, presumably in a swamp, seems to reflect difficult progress in waking life (see ENVIRONMENT, p. 92). Thatching or basket-making is more positive, but what sort of progress did you make? Organ reeds seem likely to refer to sexuality.

refrigerator If you were storing things in a refrigerator, perhaps the dream is suggesting that you should restrain yourself in some way, "cool it", not get overheated. Taking things out of a refrigerator, on the other hand, seems likely to refer to your being ready to express yourself more warmly – the food is ready to serve! If your refrigerator had broken down, perhaps you are definitely thawing out or melting! But if the food had gone bad, perhaps you did so too soon. See perhaps, *ice*, FOOD AND DRINK (p. 86).

refugee A reference to your security; you could be at a loss what to do, running away from a problem, needing reassurance. But perhaps you *should* move on to safer areas. Were you supported by friends in your dream predicament? Perhaps a case in which you should ask your dreams (see p. 47) for further enlightenment.

refusal The context in which the refusal occurred is all-important: childhood, work or personal relationships. The refusal may parallel some denial in waking life, whether of you or by you; there may be a warning that you should think again about some action you are contemplating.

regret Regret in a dream is often connected with some symbol of the past, and there may be a suggestion that you are about to repeat a mistake you once made. This is an emotion that can spill over into your day when you wake, and if it persists you should ask your dream (see p. 47) for further elucidation.

rehearsal Your dream seems to be saying: "Make quite sure you know precisely what it is you have to do." Whether you were word-perfect, knew your part, is important – so is the personality of the director, who may possibly be you yourself. The other members of the cast may give you a hint of the waking context to which it refers. And see *acting*.

reincarnation A dream of reincarnation is probably a dream about change (see also BIRTH, DEATH, AND CHANGE, p. 76). Return as a dog or cat may have much the same meaning as dreaming you are a cat or dog: i.e., a reference to "cattiness" or faithfulness or whatever – but rather more intense. Since reincarnationists believe that reward or punishment is involved in such transformations, the dream could well be a warning. A dream about being some past, perhaps historical figure, may carry the suggestion that you have (or should have) recently changed in personality. Do you identify in some way with that person?

rejection A dream rather similar in nature to one of *refusal*; but in this case carrying a perhaps more personal connotation. Perhaps you have rejected, or should reject, some particular emotional attitude or line of thought; you may be readier to do so than you think.

rejuvenation Possibly a wish-fulfilment dream, of course; but as likely to be a reassuring dream – you are younger and stronger than your age, or not as old as you feel.

relatives See *family*; but perhaps a gathering of less intimate relatives – whole group of people with whom you may not feel entirely at ease, possibly met for a *wedding* or a *funeral*. Relatives often represent facets of ourselves, characteristics of which we may or may not be proud. Were your relatives conflicting with your friends? Might they represent day-to-day problems? See also, perhaps, CROWDS (p. 96), *party*.

release The dream is obviously placing an accent on freedom. Have you recently been released, or do you seek release, from a waking situation? If not, the dream could focus on a possible resolution of a particular problem or situation, or the desire to be free of it. If you know what you must do – do it; if not, ask your dreams (see p. 47) for further help. And see *prison*?

religion This could be a comment on your present spiritual state – or perhaps on some waking objective, or even person, that you are religiously pursuing. Alternatively, it could reflect an unconscious but devout wish for a more religious focus to your life – or the wish to be free of such a thing.

rent "Take what you want, and pay for it," said the ancient proverb. This dream no doubt emphasizes the price you have to pay for something in your life. Are you reluctant to accept the price (emotional, perhaps) of a relationship?

repetition Dull repetition seems to suggest something similarly boring in waking life. This may be you yourself – are you being particularly boring at present? But perhaps the dream was prompted by some repetitive noise in your vicinity – dripping tap, or something similar.

report A dream of a school report, with the anxiety and perhaps rebuke that it attracted, is surprisingly common. Are you over-anxious about someone's opinion of you? But if you were writing a report, perhaps this is a hint that you should rationalize your behaviour, or consider your past actions in a severely practical way; or perhaps that you should make better use of accumulated knowledge, or assess your problems in a cool, detached fashion, measuring them against set standards.

repression Such a dream must surely be related to some repression in waking life. Obviously it is important to relate your dream to the reality; a dream of childhood repression should prompt you to examine your present lifestyle, and whether it is still affected by the past.

reptile See *animals*, FISH, FLESH AND FOWL (p. 88).

repulsion It depends entirely on what repelled you: look up that symbol, and consider it carefully; often such a strong emotion is sex-orientated, but it could relate to another area of your life – your work, for instance.

reputation Most people care deeply about their reputation in one way or another, so this dream is probably a comment on your most basic feelings about yourself. Did it reflect pride or guilt? Or suggest that you care too much about what others think of you and your actions?

rescue The situation from which you were being rescued, or rescuing someone else, and the relative success of the attempt, is likely to be crucial. The dream may reflect a cry for help from your waking self; or there may be a warning to be more or less involved in some difficult situation.

responsibility A dream hint about a waking burden or commitment. In the dream, was the responsibility accepted or shirked?

rest Perhaps you need one.

restaurant See FOOD AND DRINK (p. 86).

retirement A wish-fulfilment dream, perhaps. Alternatively, you may simply be overburdened with work and responsibility, and long to retire from the situation. Try to remember if your dream suggested that your involvement with the situation was unnecessary or even unhelpful.

revelation The dream may suggest that you have seen the light, that something has finally dawned on you, that your way ahead is clear. But see, if necessary, *religion*.

revenge A less negative emotion than modern society perhaps suggests; the desire to get even is a deep one, and in dream may suggest your desire to balance one unproductive emotion with a more productive one, to punish an ill deed by doing a good one. The circumstances of the dream may point to an area of your inner life where there is imbalance.

revolution The dream image of psychological turbulence, suggesting that drastic action should be taken to change your attitudes or emotional balance. Maybe your whole personality is in revolt, and you are at a point where you should work drastically and deeply on conflicts or basic emotional problems. Subsequent dreams may support this theme; but in any event do not dismiss this one lightly – look closely on the regime against which you were revolting.

rest *Sleep*, Anon.

rhythm If you longed for it, a wish-fulfilment dream of more regularity and a steadier beat in your waking life. A jazzy rhythm suggests a frenetic pace in your waking life: perhaps it needs some adjusting.

riches Material riches in a dream often refer to spiritual riches: think of the parable of the talents – have you buried yours, or are you using them? A dream of simply counting your riches, or regarding them in a miserly way, may reflect too much pride and self-confidence in waking life. Are you covetous or grasping – not necessarily materially, but emotionally?

riddle A riddle in a dream almost certainly involves a pun; but the dream is probably asking you a complex and tricky question, the answer to which could be rewarding. Ask for elucidation (see p. 47) if you don't understand.

riding High, perhaps? In which case the dream is obviously as reassuring as a dream of riding a runaway horse may be a warning: for you may then be riding for a fall. What you are riding is of course important (there may be a sexual implication). If you were consciously riding away from something, the dream may suggest you need to distance yourself from a problem.

ring A strong focus, possibly, on a sexual commitment, marriage or engagement; or (see *mandala*) on emotional wholeness. A dream of losing your wedding or engagement ring may have something to say about your emotional commitment: are you losing interest in it, or lacking security? Disregard the dream if you wake to the sound of a telephone ringing!

riot Perhaps you need to attract attention in waking life. If so, are you going about it in the right way? Your recent behaviour may have been too disruptive; or maybe your dreams are encouraging you to make a fuss about what is bothering you – only you will know.

ritual The dream may possibly be making a reference to repetitive behaviour patterns. The nature of ritual itself is symbolic, so there is a kind of double-focus here: the dream symbol represents a waking symbol, which seems to indicate that it is important to you. Think about what the dream symbol means to you: ask (see p. 47) for further information if necessary.

rival A picture of what you would like to be, perhaps, in waking life. If you are shy and introverted, an encouragement to be more asser-tive and positive, to express your feelings more openly to your lover (your rival may also be you yourself – see *duel*). This is in any case likely to be a pretty strong and impressive dream, maybe involving an unpleasant truth.

river WATER (p. 80) is a strong emotional symbol, and rivers move through a LANDSCAPE (p. 68), watering and enhancing it; an allusion then to your emotional life and expression. Was it in flood, flowing placidly, frozen? If you were swimming in it, there may be an allusion to another person, or perhaps to how you are coping with emotional problems.

road Your future, past, and sense of direction may be in question. Note the condition of the road, whether it is straight or twisted, whether hedges obscured the view. What sort of LANDSCAPE (p. 68) did it pass through? This is an excellent symbol for testing skill at dream interpretation, for it should be fairly straightforward in its meaning, and the conclusions should be revealing as regards your present emotional and psychological state: are you on the right or the wrong road?

robber We think of a robber as pouncing on us on the open road, so the assault seems likely to be on your way of life or your progress through it. What do you make of that symbol? Was the robber recognizable.

robot Whether you were a robot, or were manipulating one, the dream was probably a warning! Are you being a mere robot, at work or in your relationship? Is the pattern of your life so automatic that you are finding little or no time for self-expression? Decide whether your lifestyle is fully under your own control, or whether you are being manipulated by someone else. And see also *puppet*.

rock A comment perhaps on your sense of security. If you were throwing rocks, perhaps you need to release tension or anger. Obviously your target is significant. Was there a pun on rock *music*?

rocket Probably a phallic symbol, especially if it was a firework; if a space vehicle, your dream could also be encouraging you to "take off".

romance This seems likely to be a comment on the way in which you show your affection, whether it is encouraging you to be more, or less, romantic – the context of the dream should tell you which. There may be a strong element of wish fulfilment, of course. It may be necessary to re-think this sphere of your life.

roof A comment perhaps on your paternal or maternal instincts, and the way in which you protect loved ones. The state of repair of the roof, or whether you were mending it, will be significant. Have you "hit the roof" lately? Perhaps your dreams are suggesting you have "a slate loose"! There may be an allusion to your head (a house is often a symbol for the *body*). If you are a man, are you worried about incipient baldness? Thatch can often be a reference to hair.

rooms Freud suggested strongly that, in men's dreams, rooms were almost always symbols for women ("If the ways in and out of them are represented, this interpretation is scarcely open to doubt.") If you accept this, whether you were trying to get in, whether the room was locked (see *key*) is clearly important. But exploring unknown rooms in a house can represent a seeking to extend your knowledge, to break out into new experiences. See ENVIRONMENT (p. 92).

roots You may be considering pulling up roots and moving on; or perhaps have been working on your family tree! Grass-root opinion may have been preoccupying you. Think too about your basic security. Cutting your way through tangled roots may hint at difficulties or complications you are presently coping with.

rope A symbol of attachment, of love, but are you giving yourself enough rope at present? Or perhaps you are tied up by problems; maybe there is something ropy about your life at present. Many puns are possible. Try to remember what was being done with the rope, and whether it was secure or threadbare.

rotting First consider whether your dream is saying something about some aspect of your life which may be disintegrating or rotting away.

Try to recall how you coped with the mess – by cleaning it up, or simply turning away from it. See *rubbish*.

royalty Many people dream of royalty, or of a ceremonial head of state; often the dreams involve personal meetings, and are sometimes very funny. They may reflect a keen waking interest in the affairs or kings, queens, princes or princesses, and frequently involve their descending to our level – dropping in for tea, or inviting us to dance. Freud believed that as a rule the king and queen represented the dreamer's parents, while a prince or princess represented the dreamer himself or herself. But it will be worth deciding whether you identify with any particular element or characteristic of the royal personality in your dream, or are preoccupied with the idea of reigning, ruling over others, being dominant. If you are basically rather shy and introverted, the dream may be encouraging you to work on your character and self-esteem. In Jungian terms, royal figures – especially kings and queens – may well be archetypal figures (see p. 26) representing *animus* (male principle) and *anima* (female principle).

rubbish A dream of clearing up rubbish often refers to a process of psychological spring-cleaning, rejection of out-worn ideas or attitudes, or may strongly suggest that it is time you did so. If you come across something valuable amid the rubbish, this may be a significant hint that, amid the clutter in your mind at present, there lies a useful idea or nugget of information.

ruin A dream of exploring a ruin seems likely to refer to the examination of your past, or perhaps to the deterioration of some element of your past attitudes or lifestyle. Your attitude to the ruin may involve nostalgia, relief that you have not to live there, admiration of a past beauty. Try to apply this to your waking feelings about your past in general, or some particular event if a symbol suggests it. See also ENVIRONMENT (p. 92).

running All depends on why you were running: to escape (from what?) or to reach some goal, or simply for pleasure or exercise? Should you turn and face your pursuer? See PURSUIT (p. 66).

rut Perhaps a dream suggestion that you are stuck in one (see *ploughing*), that you need more freedom, more adventure.

S

sack A reference, perhaps, to some burden you are carrying or coping with at present. What the sack contained will of course be very important, but is it a pun on the fact that you have had, or are fearful of getting, "the sack"?

sacrament A wish, perhaps, for a fresh start, or a feeling that you are ready for some new commitment; but there could be a statement about your beliefs and attitude towards religion.

sacrifice Have you made one, or should you be making one at present? You might like to consider whether you are sacrificing yourself and how worthwhile (or otherwise) this actually is. If distressingly violent symbols are involved – blood sacrifice, for instance – try to distance yourself from them, and look for connecting links with possibly violent waking emotions.

safe A comment on security, perhaps a pun on how safe you feel, or are. If you were hiding things in a safe, what were they symbols of? If your safe was being robbed, in which waking area do you feel insecure?

sail Your dream may be suggesting that you are sailing into – or out of – calm or stormy waters, or that you have to trim your sails in some way. Does this reflect on your financial situation?

saints A particular saint in a dream could represent some ideal and/or a very impressive authority figure in your waking life. Maybe you need greater support, for some practical or spiritual reason. You may be trying to emulate saintly behaviour.

sale If you were buying at a sale, did you find some bargains? These will in themselves be important symbols, perhaps of attributes which

you are conscious are in some way devalued. Is there a possibility that you have sold yourself short, that you underestimate yourself?

salt An important and very basic commodity – perhaps the phrase "the salt of the earth" has some relevance. Your dream could suggest that you are aggravating some situation in an attempt to heal it – rubbing salt into the wound.

salute A gesture of respect, and one which acknowledges status in life: there could be a suggestion that you should know your place (whether it is authoritative or subordinate), depending on whether you were saluting or receiving the salute.

sanctuary You may simply be in need of peace, quiet and seclusion, of cutting out for a while from your usual routine and commitments. Or perhaps you feel someone is intruding unnecessarily into your life, if your sanctuary was disturbed. Perhaps you are unhappy, and feel you need to be restored by faith, spiritual advice and consolation.

sand If in a desert or on a beach see LANDSCAPE (p. 68); but perhaps the dream was suggesting that the sands of time are running out? If the sand was gritty, and was making its way into some part of your life where it was unwelcome, perhaps there is some irritating and trying, sprawling and uncontrollable problem worrying you at the moment.

savage Dreams of a wild, primitive man or woman may well allude your sexuality; fear of the savage in the dream may suggest that you are not getting as much sexual pleasure or fulfilment as you should. If *you* were the savage, your dreams may be commenting on recent activities, in bed or out, which have lacked delicacy or tact.

saw Perhaps a male sexual symbol (think of the repetitive pumping motion of the act of sawing). So consider who, if anyone, was with you, and what you were sawing. On a non-sexual level there could be a simple allusion to repetitive, physical hard work, or even a punning reference to something you saw.

scales You may be at the point of making a decision, weighing the merits and demerits of a particular case; the balance of the scales will of course be important. Or there may be a comment about your weight, if you were weighing yourself. If your dream was about fish scales, remember that however beautiful they are, one has to get rid of them before eating the fish, so they may refer to something in your waking life which is lovely but ultimately useless or even unpleasant.

scandal If in the dream you were worried that someone was talking scandal about you, it may be that you are rather too concerned in waking life about what others think of you. Perhaps you should consider whether you are paying too much attention to trivia, and not enough to important issues. Or, if you were talking scandal, you may be using someone else's misfortunes for your own aggrandisement.

school It is not uncommon to dream that we are back at school, and there is often an allusion to lack of self-confidence – the feeling that we have not learned the lessons of life sufficiently well. There may be an allusion to some childhood trauma which has a bearing on some present waking situation. On the other hand, occasionally we get the better of some teacher we hated, which can be reassuring and pleasant, a hint that we are on top of some personality trait, maybe, which that person represented. The other people in the dream will, as usual, afford a clue as to what the dream is really about, as will the contents, appearance and general atmosphere of the schoolroom – see also ENVIRONMENT (p. 92) if this made an impact on you.

schoolmaster/mistress See *school*, above; in general, an authority figure, perhaps representing a parent or employer – hopefully guiding but perhaps chastising you. If the latter, how did you react – with anger or resignation? If you stood up to the teacher, the suggestion is that your self-confidence is in fine working order; if you were cowering and afraid, there could be a hint that you should stand up for yourself.

science/scientists A vague term: a dream of being involved in scientific experiment will involve more concrete symbols to which you should look for an explanation. But in general the dream may suggest a more rational approach to current problems than you are at present employing, that you should be more detached.

score See *goal, game, ball*, &c. For a man, the term "score" often has a specific sexual meaning, and the obvious inference may be drawn. But there may be a simple allusion to recent successes, the suggestion that you should make more of them.

scream We can wake up screaming after a frightening dream; in that case, it is of course the dream that matters. To dream of someone

screaming is perhaps an allusion to someone desperately crying for help – and don't forget that that someone may be yourself, so consider whether some waking predicament may in fact be more oppressive or worrying than you think. Was there perhaps an allusion to the necessity for a "screaming row" with someone?

screen If you were being medically screened, it may be just worthwhile considering a check-up, though the hint may be that you should examine yourself and your motives more closely. If you were appearing on screen, see *cinema, television*; there is probably a reflection of your recent behaviour, or to some character-change. You should try to look objectively at your present situation: the symbol is not unlike that in a *message* dream. But a screen is also a means of concealment.

screw A very old slang word for coitus, so your dream may well be sexual in nature; but there could be a suggestion that you are "screwing" someone financially, or making a mess of some situation – "screwing the whole thing up".

sea The sea is an important symbol (see WATER, p. 80), and when it occurs in dreams it is often conveying a message from the deep unconscious. Our relationship with our mothers, or our own maternal instinct, is very likely to be in question, as are the emotional, intuitive and instinctive levels of our personality. Consider especially the state of your dream sea: smooth and warm, stormy, icy: this will be the beginning of your interpretation.

search Unless you dream of something you have, in waking life, just lost, the dream probably refers to some quality which you feel has vanished from your life; or perhaps you are searching for a psychological pattern, "soul-searching". Spiritual development and psychological wholeness, or love, could be the outcome of your search, and your dream may well be pointing the way, indicating the direction in which you should search. This is a case in which you could ask your dreams (see p. 47) for more help.

seasons, the A dream about the seasons as such – and not just the climate of your dream – seems likely to indicate the state of your present outlook on life – spring suggests hope, summer contentment, autumn awareness and consolidation, winter resignation. If you do not find those key words sufficiently suggestive, you can work out your own. Especially if the seasons were changing, your dream may be commenting on, or suggesting, some form of change, perhaps related to your spiritual development or the unfolding of your personality: winter may be turning into spring, for instance. Such dreams are often memorably beautiful, and can be important. See WEATHER (p. 74).

seat Maybe you should sit on some problem for a while. Or perhaps your dream is suggesting that you need to relax and put your feet up? Whether your seat was comfortable and secure is an important factor. If you were in the driving seat, perhaps you have recently assumed great power, or control of your life.

secret Are you being secretive in waking life? Or is the dream hinting that you should shut up and keep quiet? Sometimes we dream that we have discovered the secret of life: alas, when we wake, it generally proves to be meaningless!

secretary An emphasis, perhaps, on help, support, making order out of chaos. Maybe this is your present role in life! Your dreams may be suggesting that you should be a little more ambitious, if you were conscious that your position was too menial. A person's dreams of his or her secretary could carry a sexual implication – but so could dreams of your boss, of whatever sex! Wish-fulfilment of course might be involved.

seed The symbol may refer to your need to conceive, but if this does not apply, then there may be the suggestion that you should be putting your ideas to someone – "planting" them, in fact. What happened to the seed in your dream – whether it germinated and grew into a healthy plant – will reflect the state of your confidence in your idea, and of course the kind of seed is also important. There might be a hint that you are in search of spiritual or intellectual development. See also *plants*.

seesaw The dream could very well be a punning one: now you *see* something, then you *saw* it. Perhaps there is a suggestion, in a dream of childhood play, that the way in which you now see your past is in need of considerable rethinking, readjustment. How did you react to seasaws when a child? Were you afraid of them? Is there something in your childhood which you fear to recognize? The dream may refer to indecision or self-confidence, or mood swings (first up, then down).

self-control Ask yourself whether you have enough, or too much, self-control in your waking life and relationships.

selling What? Yourself? And at what a price? Too cheaply, perhaps. But you could in some way have been "selling" someone else. How does the object you were selling in your dream relate to yourself or another person? There could be a reference to your self-confidence or the need to compromise in waking life.

separation The fact that you are looking under this heading suggests that you experienced a strong feeling of separation in your dream, but it is more important to ask: from what? A partner, or a pet, or your family in general? There is no reason to suppose such a dream is prophetic, but it may hint at some perhaps psychological separation between you and the other person concerned. Or there could be a suggestion that you should try to distance yourself from some problems associated with them, to be more objective. In your waking life you may have to try more determinedly to separate your emotions from whatever you have to do – perhaps an uncharacteristically hard line you have to take.

servant If you were the servant, perhaps the dream is suggesting you are too subservient in waking life. If you were giving orders to a servant, maybe you are attempting to discipline yourself in waking life, or scolding yourself for lack of efficiency.

sewing If you were repairing clothing, the dream may suggest you should make amends for some action. But perhaps you should simply become more creative, or remember that a stitch in time saves nine.

sex See p. 90–1.

shadow Some on-going problem, or some person, may be casting a long shadow over your waking life at present, and the dream may be suggesting a way of approaching this, or getting rid of it altogether (significant reassurance if you have lost your shadow!) There may be the suggestion that you are not the person you once were ("a shadow of your former self"); if this seems likely, think about any changes that may have taken place, and perhaps have a medical check-up. For Jung's coinage of the psychological significance of "shadow" see the Glossary; dreams with such significance often point to means of self-improvement or the enhancement of one's life, by underlining qualities which are basically incompatible with our real nature. Like most of Jung's dream theories, this one is well worth following up – though be warned: it can sometimes take a very long time to decide who one's shadow really is!

shame The abstract feeling of shame may have followed you into your dreams from waking life: or the dream may be hinting that you *should* feel it, in respect of some recent action. Take notice. Dreams often know best. A pun – "What a shame" – suggests a disappointment.

sharing The dream may possibly be suggesting that you should be more generous, perhaps in emotion, perhaps in a financial sense (the two, in dreams, are often allied). Remember, a problem shared is a problem halved – a motto of which your dream may be reminding you.

sheep A suggestion perhaps that you are not exercising due individuality at present; or that you are, or should be, feeling "sheepish" about something. But see *animals*, *herd*.

shells Beautiful structures, protecting the creatures within them; and through them, we hear the sound of the sea. So it seems likely there is a relation to your maternal instinct, or to the fact that you should listen more to your intuition, and follow up any suggested course of action. Unless, of course, you are spending too much time inside your own particular shell.

shelter Were you sheltering from a storm, or an attacker? Perhaps you seek greater protection from the rat-race, perhaps more emotional security. Or, if you were in charge of the shelter, you may need to express more fully your own protective instinct.

shepherd The crucial factor seems to be whether you were or were not successfully in charge of your flock – and thus, perhaps, of waking problems, difficulties or responsibilities. Or were you being shepherded along?

shield You no doubt feel the need to protect yourself in some sense, in waking life. Further details of your dream may suggest against what, and how. If the shield was shattered, look for some new means of warding off unpleasantness.

ship Dreaming of a ship may lead you on to refer to other symbols, perhaps, so see WATER (p. 80), WEATHER (p. 74), possibly *river* and *sea*. But consider how secure you felt. There could be a reference to your "dream ship". If you were launching a ship, the reference will no doubt be to some important new project or sphere of life. Or has your ship come home?

shipwreck You may be feeling hopeless, at present, about the wreck of some scheme, some personal relationship – that "all is lost" – especially if the ship sank with all hands. However, presumably you survived. Ask your dreams (see p. 47) to suggest ways of beginning to rebuild.

shirt If you were without one, there may have been a comment on your financial state – or if you had lost one, on some risk you are about to take! So think twice. Alternatively, this may have been a comment on your image or appearance in public. See CLOTHES (p. 82).

shoes You may be feeling down at heel (see CLOTHES, p. 82). Female shoes can be, for males, a sexual symbol; if you were buying new ones, maybe there was a reference to a developing relationship.

shoot/shooting You may well have a waking desire to be right on target, in some area of your life, and the dream may be reassuring or warning you about your accuracy. Any dream in which *guns* appear is likely to contain a sexual element: if you were a man, shooting birds, there may be a reference to your attitude to women in general; a dream of shooting a beloved is not necessarily antagonistic (unless in the dream real antagonism was felt) – you may simply be expressing a desire to capture her – there is often a degree of violence in sexuality, after all.

shop Whether you were buying or selling in the dream, and what goods were involved, will be crucial to interpretation. Are you shopping around in waking life – for a possible partner, a job, a house? Think about the shop, how well-stocked it was, whether it was big or small. There might be a reference there to yourself and your inner resources. See, if necessary, *buying*, *selling*.

shore The seashore would seem to be either the place from which you set out to sea, or a hopeful landing-place: so you may be about to start a period of self-examination (see *sea*), or have reached land after such a voyage. If you were scanning the horizon for a *ship*, you may be concerned at the non-achievement of some aspiration or desire. You could be hunting for *shells* or for things hidden in the sand: a comment perhaps on a desire to enlarge your inner resources. There should be plenty of symbols in the dream to enable you to interpret it in the context of some kind of self-exploration, perhaps. See, perhaps, WATER (p. 80), LANDSCAPE (p. 68).

shout Perhaps you have something to shout about, and your dream was encouraging you to do so – unless the shout was a cry for help.

Dream Analysis

sickness and release

Julia dreamed: "*Derek and I went to visit Andrew, a man who was very dear to us, and who had had a massive heart attack and stroke, and had been confined to a wheelchair. We went into his sitting room, but there was no sign of the wheelchair, medicines, walking aids or anything connected with his illness. He was sitting in an ordinary arm-chair, and as we entered stood up and said: 'Julia, I'm cured – I'm really better!' I wept for joy.*"

Next morning I heard that our friend had died. The reassuring prophetic dream had said, quite rightly, that he was free from his suffering, though I was deeply unhappy about the death of a marvellous person.

shower Of blessings, perhaps. Or did it precede a storm? Perhaps a representation of a minor quarrel, soon over; it may even have been welcome and refreshing. And see *rain*, WEATHER (p. 74), perhaps WATER (p. 80).

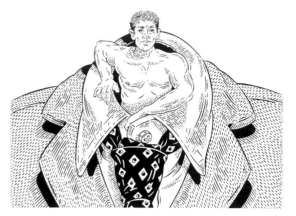

shrinking Refer, perhaps, to CHANGE (p. 76). There may be a warning that you are in some way less than lifesize at present, or that you are on the contrary too "big", showing off, perhaps. You may be shrinking from unpalatable facts; if male, your dream may be referring perhaps to your potency or fears about it. Other symbols in the dream should offer clues; but maybe this is a case for asking the dream (see p. 47) for further hints and explanations.

shyness Dream shyness may echo the real thing, simply drawing attention to your condition. But there may, in the dream, have been some curative hint. Certainly, since your dreams have brought the subject up, you could ask them (see p. 47) how the problem can best be tackled. Try to think positively about the things you know you are good at, for instance – there is bound to be something of which you can feel proud, and which you can use to build your self-confidence.

sickness As we have often suggested, a dream of a particular illness could be hinting at a real medical condition, and it might be as well to check with your doctor (some practitioners might recognize the possibility that your dreams are predating their prognosis). But your dream malady may be a comment on other areas of your waking life. A dream of a weak heart may be a symbol of your attachment to someone, for instance; you might then be heart-sick, or home-sick, or just sick to the teeth with someone or something.

siege You could be laying in psychological supplies and building inner strength for a siege – strengthening your defences for a long argument or contest. Fine, as long as you are not also building inner tension, so examine your dream for any symbols of trouble inside the walls! If you are actually under siege, firing off arrows, pouring boiling oil on your enemies, recollect that in the end your provisions may run out.

signalling See *message*. But what sort of signals, and to whom? In waking life, they may have been subconscious – but your dreams will have recognized them, and may be encouraging or discouraging you (were your signals received?) Of course it may be you who are ignoring signals sent to you in your waking hours; your dreams may be prompting recognition and suggesting reaction. Take note of distress signals, whether from yourself or someone else; they may be a pointer to some problem you have not yet consciously recognized.

signature Have you signed away something important – perhaps even yourself? Were you forging someone else's signature (stealing their good name)? If you were puzzled by an illegible signature, perhaps someone's waking actions are indecipherable at present; did your dream suggest a possible reaction?

silence A dream of deep and restful silence is most probably a cry for just such a respite in waking life.

silver There is something quiet and reassuring about silver: it seems to reflect a gentle and confident wealth, wealth allied with beauty – and there are allusions to the Moon. A dream of silver could relate (as "financial" dreams often do) to your emotional resources and expression, especially if you were giving, or indeed if you were receiving it. See *money*.

sin Whether it is you or some other person in the dream who is seen as the sinner, it will almost inevitably be some misdemeanour of yours to which it is referring (accusing another person of some sin in the dream, you should consider whether it is not yourself that is really guilty of it). However free you may feel of guilt when awake, your subconscious accuses you, and you should try to face the problem, which is unlikely to go away of its own accord. The relation between sin and religion suggests a traditional, old-fashioned, note.

singing Were you singing your own praises (if not, why not)? Singing out of tune, in a choir, suggests you may not fit well into some waking environment. Wish-fulfilment may be involved.

single Not necessarily a comment on your present state, or even a piece of wish-fulfilment! Perhaps a suggestion that you should go it alone in some way, in which case you must decide whether you feel strong enough to do so, and ask for more help if you need it. Dreaming of making a pop single on the record scene may be saying much the same thing, in a pun.

sister Your feelings towards your sister in waking life – love, jealousy, admiration, whatever – is obviously a key factor; a display of these qualities, or even a notable lack of them, in your dream, may well point up your feelings about your own character and disposition. If you are a woman, there may be a punning reference to womanhood as a whole, and a suggestion that you wish to join with the aspirations of the feminist movement. See, also, *family*.

skating The freedom of movement and the attractive motion of successful skating, not unlike FLYING (see p. 84) suggests that we may be skating over our problems, and therefore not giving them enough attention. Or perhaps we are skating on thin ice – taking risks in our waking life? The proximity of *ice* (frozen water) suggests that your emotions may be involved, and that they may in some way be too cool and remote – but that you are enjoying the detachment which enables you to move freely and gracefully about on your own terms. If the ice was cracking and melting, perhaps your emotions are breaking through; if you fell through it, however, or got wet and cold, or even started to *drown*, a warning is obviously involved.

skeleton The immediate question is, was it in a cupboard (or hidden in some other way)? The reference to a guilty secret would then seem unmistakable! However, perhaps you have been getting down to the *bones* of some important problem; or if *archaeology* was involved, there may be a reference to someone you knew many years ago. There are other possibilities: your pun-loving dreams may be referring to your having been on too strict a diet (hopefully not to the extent of anorexia), or warning you against overspending (lean times are ahead!).

skin So much a part of our outward image, the self we present to others, that a dream of a blemished skin would seem to suggest that we are fearful of giving the wrong impression, or even have something shameful which we had hoped to conceal. A skin rash may punningly suggest a rash action. Think too of all the popular allusions: are you too thick- or thin-skinned?

skirt See CLOTHES (p. 82); but remember the derogatory chauvinist reference to a woman as "a bit of skirt" – could that have an application? A man's dream of wearing a skirt may refer to an ambivalent feeling about having to do "woman's work", or to the female elements in his personality, perhaps too firmly suppressed (should he show his feelings more openly?).

sky, the Fine, open, cloudless skies seem to suggest that indeed the sky is the limit for some project in which you are engaged; there may be a reference to the opening-out of your personality (especially, perhaps, if you are conscious of an open sky while dreaming of FLYING, p. 84). Heavy, lowering skies, thick grey clouds, suggest claustrophobia, an overcast personality, possibly a gathering *storm*. And see WEATHER (p. 74).

skull The most famous skull in fiction, Yorick's in *Hamlet*, suggests introspection, a longing to get to the root of life, to know the meaning of life and death. This need not be a frightening dream, but one which should encourage the dreamer to follow his instinct, which is possibly encouraging him or her to live life at a deeper level than hitherto, to get at the real facts.

skyscraper A symbol of ambition and material progress; if you are king of your own skyscraper, a reassuring and encouraging dream. If, as is often the case, the building is really a metaphor for yourself, you should be in good shape! See ENVIRONMENT (p. 92).

slander A dream warning to curb your tongue? Or a suggestion of fear that someone is bad-mouthing you? You may be your own worst enemy at present.

slaughter If you were slaughtering an animal, much will depend on what that animal was, and what it means to you, symbolically, in waking life. A lamb, for instance, is generally the symbol of innocence, so if you were killing one (or watching it being killed) there may be a comment on the loss of your own innocence. The slaughter of an ox may relate to a loss of power; that of a ram, to a loss of sexual energy (for a man), and so on. Because warm-blooded living creatures are involved, the reference may well be a sexual one. See, perhaps, *killing, murder*.

slavery You may be a slave to some activity, or some individual – perhaps in a sexual sense (there may even be an element of wish-fulfilment involved). But consider the more serious implications if, as may be possible, you are a slave to some habit or tendency, some obsessive activity – or even to your family.

sleep It is only slightly less odd to dream you are asleep than to dream that you are dreaming; but it can happen, and one possibility is that your dream is hinting that you need more sleep, or perhaps simply need to relax and achieve a higher degree of inner calm.

sliding Backsliding? Feeling insecure? Perhaps a comment on your present feeling about security. If you were sliding or skidding in a *car*, then perhaps the dream is suggesting that you are out of control, and maybe in sexual context.

slimming It may not only be physically that you need to lose weight: perhaps you should cut back on your work, your spare time activities.

slippers See *shoes*; but the symbol is a more relaxed, comfortable, easy-going one, and the dream would seem to suggest that you should take things more easily.

slums First see *buildings*, ENVIRONMENT (p. 92); then consider whether you are perhaps feeling rather sorry for yourself at present. Was the dream suggesting that you should try to be more positive in outlook? Or are you in a poor physical state, and in need of revitalizing your system, perhaps through exercise.

smash The article you were smashing is of course important, but obviously you have aggressive feelings which need release. Or there may be something in your outer or inner life which you need to destroy.

smell A real smell may make its way into your nostrils while you are asleep, and stimulate a dream: Freud recalls a man who, when eau de cologne was held under his nose, dreamed he was

S

in a perfume shop in Cairo! Usually, smells seem to evoke places and people associated with them, and because of the direct stimulus, such dreams may not always be important. If you dream of smelling gas, however, do check your gas supply for leaks.

smile A symbol of approval; you are probably making good progress, especially if the smile was on the face of some authority figure. Did it please or surprise you?

smoke Perhaps you are not seeing certain aspects of your waking life as clearly as you might; you may need to ask your dreams (see p. 47) for help. Consider the colour and density of smoke, and the fact that "there's no smoke without fire" – there may be an oblique reference to FIRE (see p. 78) as a symbol which you have yet to recognize.

Dream Analysis

smoke
Beverley dreamed: *"I was on a canal bank, and a huge, filthy cargo boat came by letting out a lot of black smoke which hung over the canal, blotting out my view of the other bank."*

This was the second of three consecutive dreams (see pp. 174 and 198) Beverley had after a friend had behaved hurtfully towards her. She was considering whether or not to sever her relationship with the friend, but was perplexed and didn't know what to do. The black smoke (and black had appeared in the first dream) prevented her from seeing the whole landscape of her dream, just as she could not see clearly her waking situation. The dirty, cumbersome cargo boat seemed to represent her hurt feelings.

smoking If you are a smoker it is to be hoped that the dream was telling you just what is going to happen to you if you don't stop! There may be encouragement, if you are in the process of giving up, and perhaps some helpful suggestions.

snake The snake symbol appears worldwide in most mythologies: in the west, the strongest reference is perhaps to the serpent in the Garden

Dream Analysis

snakes
Krishna dreamed: *Krishna had recurring and horrific dreams of snakes which so terrified her that if, on waking, she went for a glass of milk, she would be afraid to open the refrigerator for fear that a snake would be lurking inside it. For a while the dreams ceased, but then recurred even more distressingly.*

Krishna grew up in a rather restrictive society in which sex before marriage was out of the question. For five years she shared a loving but asexual relationship with a boy friend, during which she was haunted by her dream snakes. When the relationship ended, the dreams ceased; but later, in England, when she fell in love with another young man and began a mature relationship, she found herself to be sexually inhibited, and the snakes reappeared, even more forbiddingly. Therapy related the snakes, as phallus symbols, to her difficulty in enjoying full sexual activity after the inhibitions of her youth. She began to face her private monster, and work her way towards a fulfilling relationship.

After some weeks, during which she worked on her dreams, confronting the snakes in the knowledge of their symbolic meaning, Krishna became a changed woman; she looked well, and was extremely happy. The dream, instead of recurring several times a night, occurred with decreasing frequency, and when it did occur she was unafraid and concentrated on analysing its significance. Her relationship with her lover became fulfilled, and she was able to set a date for her wedding.

Her story potently illustrates the way in which we can defeat our dream monsters as heroes and heroines of mythology did, by understanding their significance.

S

of Eden, which introduced Adam and Eve to sin (often believed by Christians to involve sex). Many other cultures also make a connection between a snake and the penis, although psychic and spiritual, as well as sexual, energy is symbolized by the snake. If the snakes in your dream frighted you, you should perhaps consider your attitude to sex, for your dream may be making a definite and important statement about your reaction to it. But there could also be a reference to some deep-rooted psychological problem. You must face up to the snake and tackle it (see *monster*). If you cannot reduce the element of fear to manageable proportions you may need counselling of some sort, especially if the dream recurs; your sex-life may well be not as fulfilling and

snake *Sinbad and the Serpent*, Edmund Dulac

rewarding as it could (and should) be. Remember, however, that a serpent creature has often been a symbol of wisdom and knowledge (the famous Oracle at Delphi was a snake-goddess). See also *fear*, *animals*, perhaps *sin*, FISH, FLESH AND FOWL (p. 88).

snow Perhaps a symbol of purity, if it was untrodden and unstained. If the snow was churned up or dirty, are you considering some action in waking life which may in retrospect prey on your conscience or sully your reputation? If the whole LANDSCAPE (see p. 68) is covered with snow, perhaps there is a suggestion that your own concern for purity is blinding and inhibiting. See WEATHER (p. 74), COLOUR (p. 94).

soldiers A dream of violence, perhaps, but the dream may be suggesting that you should conform or be more disciplined. Soldiers are usually masculine, so there may be a reference to the masculine side of your nature (whether you are male or female). You may be preparing to do battle in some way, in your waking life, or to protect yourself from some onslaught; you may need to be more on the defensive. If you dream that soldiers arrested or confined you in some way (see *prison, fence*) you should decide whether someone has not undue power over you in waking life, and enjoys exercising it. See, perhaps, *battle, war*.

song You obviously have something to sing about! But if you were singing in your dream, did you forget your words, or the tune, or were you failing to be a good member of the *choir*? – then there may be a warning that you are underestimating the difficulty of a task you are about to perform in waking life, or failing to be a good member of a team. What you were singing will be significant, of course; if it was a song from your childhood, your dream may be focusing on some longstanding problem or inhibition. See also *singing, recitation*.

sorrow This was probably a prevailing mood in your dream, and can depress you on waking. The reference may be to a particular area of your life which has elements that you have not yet come to terms with, perhaps just because you cannot face the sorrow it might bring you or someone else. You perhaps should seek more help from your dreams (see p. 47).

soul A reference to spiritual development seems likely. Or perhaps you are getting to the essence of some waking problem. If your soul was leaving your body, leaving you soul-less, are you contem-

plating some particularly hard-hearted course of action? Dreaming of soul music can be a pun, with the same reference as the above.

sowing You may have been sowing *seeds* of some kind, in which case there may either be a reference to procreation or to some new idea you are about to try to sell: did the seeds fall on rich or stony ground? Is there a possible pun on *sewing*, especially if you have been doing some recently?

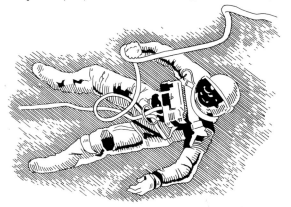

space You may simply need more space in your waking life (actually or psychologically, perhaps within a relationship). If you were alone in space, and frightened, maybe you are lonely at present, or have lost your sense of direction in life.

spear A Freudian phallic symbol; also a symbol of aggression; perhaps, indeed, both. How did you react to the spear in your dream? Was it ineffective, badly aimed, too heavy for you to carry? If someone else was throwing a spear at you, who was it and how did you react (see *gun*)? There may be a reference to a longstanding problem. This will certainly be the case if other dreams present other phallic symbols in similar contexts.

spectacles Loss or damage to spectacles is often a dream comment on loss of self-esteem or image; but there may be a comment on just how clearly, or otherwise, you are seeing your waking life and its problems.

speech-making You probably have something you badly want to speak out about, in waking life; but if your audience was restive, continually interrupting you, maybe the opposite is true – you have been going on about something for far too long, and it's time you sat down and shut up!

speed A comment on the pace of your life, or on the undue speed with which you are getting through a particular task? Slow down. But maybe you were moving too slowly in your dream, and should speed it a little. If you were particularly conscious of the state of the road and its characteristics, see LANDSCAPE (p. 68), ENVIRONMENT (p. 92).

spell You may be under someone's spell; if so, perhaps the dream is suggesting that you are under some illusion about him or her. But perhaps you have a desire to cast a spell over someone, and the dream was trying to point out other, less devious ways of enticement?

spelling Being unable to spell might suggest that you are not being terribly successful in coping with certain complexities in your waking life. Or you may have to spell out something in great detail to someone, and are afraid of getting it wrong. If you were in school, see other relevant symbols – *school, teacher*.

spending *Money*, presumably – and remember the relationship between money and love; so in waking emotional life you may be overspending – or being a miser. Was it "money down the drain" – emotion spent on someone who turned out not to be worth it? If you were reluctant to spend, in your dream, perhaps you should carefully consider your attitude to your partner. The term "spending" has been for centuries a common euphemism for emission during the male orgasm; maybe a reference to follow up.

sphere See *mandala* (p. 26 and Glossary). But the dream may be commenting on your psychological wholeness; if the sphere was whole and perfect, the dream is a reassuring one, suggesting perhaps that you are in harmony with the spheres. It may also refer to the male testicles.

spices These add colour and flavour to food; perhaps your life needs a few more exotic elements. But did the spices burn your mouth or upset your stomach? If so, a warning is indicated.

spider A common dream "*monster*", if you are repelled by them in waking life. Attack the image and face up to it. But perhaps you were the spider, out to catch a particular fly – laying some kind of trap in waking life. See *insects*.

spine Consider whether your spine needs exercising, whether your posture is bad. But the dream may suggest that you are acting spinelessly, and need to stand up more for yourself.

spinning Spinning what? – a web (see *spider*), or a yarn? A comment, perhaps, on some plan you are constructing at present. Don't forget to consider yourself as the yarn or the wheel; maybe there is a hint that your life is monotonous and needs speeding up.

spiral You may need to see FLYING (p. 84). Your dream may be referring to the Milky Way galaxy, a spiral form (you may know this unconsciously, even if you fail to remember learning it), and hint that you yearn to be at one with it, in the same manner as a dream of a perfect *sphere* can. Being part of a downward spiral can be another form of "falling asleep" (see p. 51).

spirit The dream may have been of a *ghost*, but the fact that you have looked up the dream under the word "spirit" seems to indicate that your unconscious recognizes the dream as being about spiritual belief or conduct, in the religious sense. On the other hand there may be a reference to spirited behaviour, or lack or spirit. If you were drinking spirits there could be the same punning reference.

spit A hint that you perhaps need to "spit it out", whatever "it" may be. If the dream was of a *kitchen* spit, there may be a reference to cooking up a scheme, or to roasting someone in the heat of your contempt. If the juices from the roast spit into your eye, you have a double pun!

splinter Someone may have upset or hurt you recently. Alternatively, the dream may have a sexual reference (see *prick*).

split See *tear*.

sponge Perhaps you should absorb more of what is going on around you in waking life, or of the subject you are studying. If WATER (p. 80) was involved you could react more sensitively to someone's feelings. Or is this a dream suggestion that someone is sponging on you (or you on someone else)? Remember that a sponge is a very simple, basic form of life, so it may represent some very simple and straightforward person.

sport Are you "a sport", or should you be more of one? Do you "play the game"? Perhaps the dream was suggesting that you need to participate rather than just watching. See *game, team*.

spring See WATER (p. 80), *stream, fountain*, perhaps *seasons*. If the spring was of metal, you may be feeling tense at present in your waking life – "all wound up" about some aspect of your life; perhaps you need to resolve problems or face your worries. But you may also simply be ready to spring into action, and in this context are getting support and encouragement from your dreams. A spring is, of course, also a *spiral*; but this reference is so complex that you will need to ask your future dreams for explanation (see p. 47).

spy A hint that you should reconsider your motivation and actions; you may need to "spy out the land" before acting. There may be a reference to someone who wants to influence you unduly.

square See *mandala* (p. 26 and Glossary). Stability seems to be indicated. This symbol is of particular significance to freemasons. There could be a suggestion that you are being rather too square at present, that perhaps you should reassess your outlook and opinions. If the square was a piazza, see ENVIRONMENT (p. 92).

squash See *balls*, *game*. Or you may be feeling squashed because someone has put you in your place in waking life – the game, like the action of squashing or crushing, is aggressive, so you may at present be fighting against bad conditions in waking life, some obstacle to progress.

stabbing A knife is, according to Freud, a phallic symbol, and an act of stabbing may be a metaphor for having sex. So who you were stabbing is obviously important. Were you stabbing them in the back, for instance? Could the dream be suggesting that you are planning to turn a platonic relationship into a sexual one.

stable A pun on your mental or emotional stability? But if there were horses in your stable there could be a statement about how you control your sexual energy. But perhaps you have closed the stable door after letting the horses out? See *horse*.

stage If you were on stage and playing a part, your dream may be suggesting that you are doing so in waking life – masquerading in some way. But there may be a hint that you are too introverted, and should not be afraid to make your presence felt. See *actor*, *cinema*.

stain It seems most likely that a dream of a stain may imply a feeling of guilt. The kind of garment that was stained may be significant. If you were attempting to remove it, were you successful?

stairs Freud claimed unequivocally that "walking up and down steps, ladders or staircases are representations of the Sexual act". Who else was

around at the time? Your personal feelings must obviously be taken into consideration. Apart from this suggestion, there could be a comment on your material and career progress. Ambition and achievement may also be under examination. If you found climbing the stairs a strain, you should perhaps take the hint that you are trying to achieve too much. See ENVIRONMENT (p. 92), if necessary, PURSUIT (p. 66).

stamp Perhaps a pun: do you need to stamp your foot at someone? Or perhaps a *message* is involved; the country or ruler illustrated on the stamp, or perhaps some other reference, may be significant.

stampede A reference to an over-hasty action, perhaps; if you were surrounded by stampeding animals, see *crowd*, but associate it also with

---

Dream Analysis

staircase

Melinda dreamed: *"I was at the bottom of a high cliff, preparing a meal for Alistair. But there and at the top of the cliff, where he was waiting, there were a great many busy people, getting in my way and sometimes pushing me. To get the food to Alistair, I had to climb a very ricketty staircase, for which I was responsible. I was afraid that it would give way, and I would spill the food. I was passed by other people ascending and descending, some of them well known in my profession. I eventually reached the top safely; the grass was marvellously green, and the weather beautifully fine."*

Alistair and Melinda, who is rather older than he, share the same profession. At the time of the dream she was about to start work again after an illness which had been holding her back. The ricketty staircase seemed a symbol for the difficult climb back to her former eminence. The food she was preparing for her lover seemed an allusion to the fact that she would like to bear him a child, but because she was older she had certain apprehensions about possibly spilling it. The dream was reassuring because of its positive climax – success in climbing the staircase, despite the crowding in of rivals, and reaching the top in fine weather and with the meal intact.

abandon, perhaps panic. A reference to wild behaviour or unrestrained passion seems possible so it could be a warning.

stand If you found yourself in a grandstand, what were you watching? Standing implies immobility, waiting. Perhaps (especially if you were alone, detached from the crowd) excitement and involvement seem to pass you by in waking life?

standing A dream of simply standing idly by suggests that you are detached in your waking life, and that perhaps you should seek more involvement; but you may simply be standing waiting your turn, or the right opportunity for action. No doubt your dreams will signal the time for movement!

star Perhaps you were the star you saw shining brightly and clearly; or perhaps the dream suggested that you should emulate it – that you are not so far making the most of your talents. A dream of a film or pop star may be wish-fulfilment; but consider what the figure means to you personally.

starvation Your own starvation in a dream is not likely to be physical: more likely it is being suggested that you are starving yourself of something you badly need, denying yourself the satisfactory expression of your personality or sexuality. A dream of, say, a starving child – with all the emotional trauma with which that image is connected – will be an extremely powerful symbol. If you cannot get to grips with it, ask your dreams (see p. 47) for further help. If you are on a diet consider warning: don't overdo it.

station First, think of yourself as the station, with the bustle of trains and passengers coming and going: is this a symbol of your life at present? If so, how well run was the station, how punctual the trains? If all was chaos, look to the organization of your working hours. If you dream of missing, or just catching a train, perhaps there is a reference to an opportunity you may be about to lose for lack of positive action.

statistics The dream may relate to the pros and cons of some situation you are weighing up in waking life. Because "statistics can prove anything", your unconscious may be expressing doubts about an action you are considering.

statue Of some god, or of someone you admire? There could be an emphasis on change or transformation in your waking life. A statue often honours the subject: what aspect of your life seems so deserving of a good reception from humanity at large? But if the statue is of yourself, consider whether you are "stone cold", perhaps in your emotional life, or towards someone who is fond of you.

steam You may need to increase your energy level – to "get steam up" for some coming prospect which you can then promote powerfully and swiftly. But don't get steamed up about nothing. Perhaps see *train*.

steel A comment perhaps on your determination, your inner strength and willpower. But steel has to be well-tempered, and the dream may be suggesting that you should be flexible as well as sharp (see *sword*). Don't be "cold as steel" in your emotional life: a *duel* with *swords*, or your attacking someone with one, would seem to be saying that. Could there be a pun on stealing? – someone's affections, maybe?

steps See *stairs*; but a punning attribution may suggest you should take a step forward in some way – or indeed should step down from some untenable situation.

stew A stew has many nourishing and tasty ingredients, which may be saying something about your present life. You may be "getting in a stew" unnecessarily. Look at your problems again; they may be presenting opportunities as well as being irritating.

stick Very probably a phallic symbol, and perhaps a comment on virility. Did the stick support you, or break, or was it too heavy to carry? Were you beating some one with it? Similarly, it could represent your feelings towards male sexuality, if you are a woman. But perhaps you have been "taking a lot of stick" from someone recently. Or the dream may even be saying you should stick to what you said, or the plans you made.

stigmata Because the crucifixion is such a major symbol in western culture, people in the West dream of the stigmata, even if they are not practising Christians. Such a dream almost always seems to signal unusual stress, the dreamer being metaphorically crucified. Consider your waking life very carefully, and decide what/who is hurting you so terribly. Your suffering need by no means be positive, though the Jesus myth suggests that it should be. Do not be too Christ-like, too intent on quietly accepting suffering (for whatever reason). And don't feel too sorry for yourself.

sting A reference to sudden, unexpected hurt. Try to get the waking sting out of your life; did you succeed in your dream? See also *prick*.

stitch Do you need to patch up some disagreement? See *sewing*.

stock exchange You may well be attempting to swing some deal in waking life. Is anything notably at risk? Were you reluctant to play your part and, if so, are you inhibited about managing your own financial affairs?

stocking This may be a sexual symbol; or it could be a statement of loss of prestige and self-esteem if you are a woman and had torn your stockings, or they were wrinkled, or fell down. Expectation seems in order if your dream was of a Christmas stocking full of good things.

stomach Apart from a pain (which, as with all dreams of specific ailments, suggests you should check with your doctor) you may be having to "stomach" something unpalatable at present. See *body*.

stone Stone is weighty; so, perhaps, may be your burdens and responsibilities. Should you shed some of them? But perhaps it was the coldness of stone which was most memorable, in which case see *ice*. But remember that while ice can melt, stone has to be positively warmed. On the other hand, one doesn't find precious stones within ice. Were you carving something: if so, what and how did it turn out? There may have been a suggestion that you wish to make something very permanent.

stool Falling between two stools? Or trouble with your bowels?

store See *shop*. But in this case, perhaps a pun on what is in store if you take a certain line of action. You may be storing up experiences, thereby developing psychologically. Perhaps you should ask yourself if you are being covetous.

storm See *sea*, WATER (p. 80), *boat*, WEATHER (p. 74). But perhaps yours is a reassuring storm in a tea cup?

stove See FIRE, (p. 78), *hearth*. On the face of it, a pleasantly warming and reassuring dream – provided the stove was working properly. If it kept going out, is the dream commenting on a current relationship? If you are having to work at clearing out the stove, it may be a comment on the drudgery of your daily round. See also *oven*.

stowaway See *boat*; but the stowaway, perhaps yourself, is there illicitly, so while bewaring attempts to keep you in your place, beware illicit action too.

stranger The chances are that the dream stranger represents aspects of your own personality with which you are not familiar, or which you deny. Did you identify with the actions of the dream stranger, find him pleasant or frightening? Consider whether repressive elements are inhibiting your self-expression. If the dream was of a romantic stranger, consider wish-fulfilment.

strangulation Repressive elements are probably at work somewhere in your waking life, preventing you from full self-expression. Take a critical look at your lifestyle and try to get rid of what is strangling your potential. You may come to the conclusion that you are on a self-destructive course which you should try to arrest. If you were particularly conscious that no one was coming to your aid, you may in some way need help in your waking life.

stray Have you, in the old phrase, "gone astray", feeling out of touch with society? Or were you the stray dog or cat, and are you conscious of having lost your way, in some respect, in waking life?

stream Probably a comment on the flow of your emotions. Think carefully; all may be more than well with your emotional life at present, but is it "running away" in some way, draining you? Perhaps you are expressing yourself over-enthusiastically to your lover. See WATER (p. 80).

street The whole aspect of the street is important (see ENVIRONMENT p. 92). Are you "streets ahead" of rivals, or they of you? Maybe your dream street was one known to you in childhood, and there is some reflection of, or on, your upbringing. However, it may be that what was going on in the street was more important than the place itself.

strength A dream of relative strength or weakness probably referred to your present position in waking life, apropos one particular situation which is concerning you. If you were showing off great strength, the dream will be reassuring. Should the display of strength come from a rival, a warning is probably inferred.

stretching What? Possibly yourself? Money, time, affections? Or were you simply enjoying a good stretch when you awoke and found yourself doing it?

S

stride We usually stride out when we are feeling independent, confident, assertive; so it seems that you are getting considerable support from your dreams at present.

strike Perhaps your dream was protesting at something you have to do in waking life, and suggesting that you should simply stop doing it, whatever the cost. You may feel the need forcefully to attract the attention of others to something of which you disapprove. If someone else was leading the strike, was it someone who, on reflection, you are forcing to do repetitive or boring work without reasonable reward (a wife, maybe)? There may be a pun: you may need to strike a light and shine it into a dark corner – or strike a light in someone else, attracting their emotional attention.

string A dream of untangling string could be a straightforward allusion to the need to untangle some aspect of your waking life. Maybe you need to pull strings to get what you want; you could be a *puppet* on a string, manipulated by someone else. See, perhaps, *rope*.

struggle It is most likely that a dream struggle is a metaphor for a struggle of some sort in your waking life – maybe within yourself (see *duel*). Your progress was probably summed up in some way in your dream, but you may need to ask (see p. 47) for additional help before you can interpret that aspect of it.

study Maybe a simple hint that you should study more, whether you are a student or just someone who feels deprived of some aspects of education, or of self-knowledge. Take that hint.

stumble A dream trip or stumble may have suddenly awakened you near the beginning of sleep, in which case it is probably of the same nature as a dream of *falling* (see p. 51). However, if it occurs in the context of a full night's sleep, it possibly mirrors an error you have made, or are about to make, in waking life.

stunt A hint that you are trying too hard to attract attention, using tricks or stunts rather than solid accomplishment. Could you be showing off or being untrue to yourself?

submarine An interesting symbol which may suggest that you are ready to plumb the depths of your personality, discovering more about your reactions and motivations. Or perhaps you want to discover more about some relationship or waking problem. If your submarine sank or sprang a leak, this could be a warning that you need help. Try to be objective about yourself, and you'll learn a good deal.

subsidence A symbol rather similar to *earthquake*. Your dream could have been focusing on your security and self-confidence, which may not be at its best at present. Perhaps in your dream the ground gave way under your feet; you may then need to go in for some readjustment in your waking life; the ENVIRONMENT (see p. 92) of the dream might offer a clue. Try to establish a more permanent basis to your relationship, your job, or whatever area you are feeling in doubt about.

success Having a success in a dream is in its way almost as rewarding as one in real life! Perhaps your dream was showing you what you are capable of – but at the very least it will have been encouraging. This would seem to be a very positive, confidence-boosting symbol.

succubus See *nightmare* (p. 51). But in some circumstances the dream of a female demon having intercourse could just be wish-fulfilment or possibly, if a woman dreamt it, something arising out of jealousy. Your reaction in your dream is highly significant.

sucking The only action we instinctively perform from the moment of our birth. Perhaps your dream was hinting that you are in need of love and affection, simple closeness to a partner. Comfort, security, warmth are all suggested; the object you are sucking may of course be significant. But have you been "a sucker" in some waking situation?

suffering Compare your dream suffering with any waking situation which is causing you difficulty: the dream may actually be making quite a constructive and helpful comment.

sugar Sweetness, yes; but bad for you – the classic comfort food. So if you are being "sweetness itself" to someone (or they to you) the dream may be making a statement about your real motives. A sugar cane may be a sexual symbol (see *sucking*).

suicide Although suggesting a self-destructive tendency, the dream is not necessarily about killing yourself. It may well be pointing out that some present action is "suicidal"; and you may be ready to make important changes in your life. See BIRTH, DEATH AND CHANGE (p. 76).

suit A suit is a reasonably formal form of dress for either sex, so there may be an allusion to your need to impress someone. Possibly a pun: should you 'follow suit" in some way? – a reference perhaps to recent actions coming under self-scrutiny. Have you acted against your conscience or beliefs recently?

summer A time of fulfilment, happiness, pleasure – unless you find hot weather disturbing. But see *seasons*.

summit If you were standing on a summit, or looking up at one, perhaps a dream comment on your attitude to your own ambitions and current progress. If you were looking down from above on a summit, you have probably outsoared your former ambitions and are ready for new peaks to conquer (see FLYING, p. 84). Perhaps the dream is confirming your ambition.

sun We would not exist without it, so the dream is alluding to something vital to your wellbeing. Were you blinded or scorched by it, or warmed and pleasantly tanned? The heat of your own personality may be under scrutiny, and the dream may be commenting on your psychological development. The symbol of the sun (a circle with a dot within it) is one of the oldest known to man, and is in itself an important *mandala* referring to rewarding intensity.

superiors Your inner parent, boss, or other authority figure is emerging within such a dream. How do you relate to such a person in waking life? You have either made good progress lately or may have to make a greater effort, according to the superior's dream reaction to you (and yours to him or her).

surgery A less frightening symbol than might seem. If your dream focused on a specific *body* area or organ, look it up, and (as we have suggested elsewhere) possibly check up on its actual health. But the dream may merely be suggesting that you need to get something out of your system.

surprise Your dream may be telling you that you can actually do something which you have been telling yourself is beyond you. The dream seems to be focusing on potential; what the surprise was, will of course be significant.

survival You are obviously the survivor, especially if at present you are coping with heavy problems and difficulties in waking life.

suspicion Were you under suspicion in your dream? If so, maybe you should question and re-question your motives for some current action.

swamp Your swamp could be an emotional quagmire. But if you were swamping a courtyard with WATER (see p. 80), the suggestion may be that you are in need of a reassessment, a "clean-up" in some respect, of the way in which you express your love and emotion.

swan The chances are that you were the swan in your dream, seeing yourself as beautiful, elegant, calm and placid, but capable of aggression when roused. Fine, but don't be too self-congratulatory. Were you a black swan – which might mean being out of step with your colleagues?

swimming Against the tide? Or just keeping your head above WATER (see p. 80)? In a race?

swinging Swinging to and fro may suggest enjoyment but also to some extent insecurity – Freud saw this as a sexual symbol. Was someone pushing you? Similar in some ways to *seesaw*. Is there perhaps a reference to swings and roundabouts, or a comment on your attitude to some decision you have had to make?

switch Switched on or off? A hint about your current sex life?

sword Probably a phallic symbol – who was using it, and against whom? Maybe a reference to some oath? Have you made a vow to yourself lately? See, perhaps, *spear*, *steel*.

syrup Sickly sweet and cloying – perhaps describing someone's attitude to you? Or even yours to someone else? See *sugar*, perhaps *honey*.

t

table Depending on where the table was, possibly a hint that you should be more open with other people or a particular person – put your cards on the table. If the table was ricketty and wobbly, perhaps a comment on your sense of security. A round-table meeting will relate to the other people there – a group in which each person may have represented one of your personality-traits? Were they all talking at once?

tail If you grew one in your dream, perhaps a reference to some "devilish" waking action? Perhaps a phallic symbol, or a male sexual allusion – "a piece of tail".

talk Should you speak up, or shut up? See *speech*.

tank If a water-tank, this may be a reference to carefully controlled emotions. If an army tank, then it is more likely a reference to your need to win, to crush all opposition, and a warning if you were the one being run down. But remember, you could be both tank and victim, a hint that your present rough tactics could harm you.

tap A suggestion that your emotions are freely on tap, should anyone want sympathy or help – unless, of course, you turned the tap and no water came out of it. There may be the suggestion that you should husband your emotional resources more carefully, and use them sparingly. If you couldn't stop the tap from dripping, perhaps someone or something is draining you of emotional energy at present.

tape Rather like *string*; but if recording tape, then this may be a *message* dream.

tape recorder See above; but look on yourself as the recorder of your dreams – are you absorbing what they are telling you, recording them accurately? How was the recording?

tar Heavy, sticky, black, and melts in the sun. But tar was an ancient healing agent. Does this remind you of someone who may be rather too clinging, and none too attractive? They may turn out to be a good (if unsocial) friend.

target In the dream were you on or off target, hit or miss? Your dream is probably commenting on the accuracy or otherwise of your waking judgments.

tart Fruity, sweet and tangy, and perhaps a pun on some woman known to you? What is your reaction to her in waking life? For women, perhaps a warning or unconscious fear that you are looking a bit sluttish at present, or a dream suggestion that you should be less priggish or uptight with men. You may need to look for ways of making your sex life more fun or widening your social circle.

taste A comment perhaps on some waking action: whether the taste was sweet, bitter, unpleasant … Perhaps you are tasting a variety of experiences at present. Your dream may be summing up your reaction.

tattoo It is relatively easy, if painful, to acquire a tattoo, but extremely difficult to remove it. Could there be a comment on some habit you are trying to kick? Or a warning about a decision which you have to take, and which may have more lasting effects than you suppose? Pomp, ceremony, showing off seems to be reflected by a dream of military tattoo: were you impressed, intimidated or bored by it? Perhaps you have to measure up to the achievements and abilities of others at present – unless you were the Drum Major!

Dream Analysis

tattoo

Beverley dreamed: "*I was watching a military tattoo from high up on a balcony, looking down on the parading horses and riders which were making D-shaped patterns around a courtyard, coming down the centre in pairs, then separating at the bottom to make a half circle, then joining to repeat the pattern at the far end of the courtyard.*"

This was the third of the dreams relating to Beverley's relationship with a friend who had behaved badly to her (see pp. 174 and 189) D was the initial of her friend's first name. The disciplined parade seemed a positive hint that she should see her friend's actions objectively (from the height of the balcony) rather than emotionally, and should regard them as a temporary demonstration of irritation rather than an on-going everyday emotion. She decided to be magnanimous. Incidentally, there is a pun on "parting" in Beverley's three dreams.

tax Your dream is probably reminding you that you will eventually have to pay for your present actions. Or are you generally over-taxed in your physical, mental or financial resources?

taxidermy Dead figures given an appearance of life? Perhaps the dream is making a comment, whether addressed to yourself or someone else: "Get stuffed!"

taxi The implication is, perhaps, that you are being taken for a ride – or taking someone else for one! Was the fare exorbitant, or cheap? The meter could be as relevant as the driver, as well as the route followed.

tea Tea is refreshing, and a social occasion; a comment about the state of your social life?

teacher Certainly an authority figure, and perhaps your dreams are focusing on a problem or inhibition which goes back to your childhood. You will have to decide what this figure represents to you. Don't be afraid to speak up for yourself: talk to your dreams (see p. 47) if you feel it might help to clarify the situation. You may be getting considerable reassurance, which is excellent, but if your waking experiences with this particular teacher were not good, it may now be an excellent time at which to get them in proportion, see them in a more logical perspective, and finally come to terms with them.

team It seems you may be "getting it all together" if you were a happy part of a winning team. Inner strength will be confirmed. If you felt impatient, unwilling to join the team spirit, you may have problems with colleagues or even the family which you need to resolve. See *game*.

tease If someone was teasing you, or you were teasing someone else, the dream may be suggesting that you are not taking yourself or your life as seriously as perhaps you should. (Sometimes our dreams tease us indirectly, and this can spur us into action. Dream puns are, in a way, a tease).

teeth Loss of a tooth in a dream may be a hint that we are in some way losing self-respect. Your dream dentist and his attitude and skill will be important, if the dream was in the context of a *surgery*. Freud, in what may be one of his more eccentric judgments, connected dreams of teeth with masturbation.

telegram The archetypal *message* dream, whether you were sending or receiving one, or were with someone who was receiving one.

telephone Yet another *message* dream: but remember that you could be the telephone, or the medium through which the message is delivered. Whose voice was at the other end?

telescope Perhaps your dreams are encouraging you to focus on some specific problem or area of your life, enlarge it, bring it into focus.

television Rather like *cinema*, but in a more intimate setting, and therefore perhaps more personal. Seeing yourself on a TV screen may indicate that you are viewing your life objectively, have it under control, are able to distance yourself from problems. If the picture is out of focus or faulty there may be problems where your self-knowledge is concerned.

temptation A comment perhaps on some tempting offer or situation about which you have to make a decision; but perhaps *sin* is involved, and you are suffering from guilt.

tenant If you were a tenant, there may be a suggestion that with or without approval you have moved in on someone else's property – idea, job, or wife, perhaps? Consider, however, that tenants have to pay rent, even if payment is sometimes late.

tennis In tennis there is a particular to-and-fro aspect which may relate more directly to a *duel* than to a team game. Who was your opponent, and with what do you identify him or her?

tent Perhaps a pun: you may be particularly in*tent* on some waking action. Tents are protective but relatively fragile and impermanent: does that help you to assess the meaning of the symbol? Perhaps your unconscious is comparing some present situation with a youthful memory of camping. See *camp*.

terminus The end of the line. Have you reached this, in some waking sense? Reassurance or warning may be involved, according to what took place in the dream: whether your train arrived on time or was delayed, or even early –

whether you had lost your luggage – or whatever. How glad or sorry were you to have reached the terminus? See, perhaps, *platform, station*.

terror To be terrified in a dream is similar to being fearful or afraid, but terror perhaps implies some kind of shock (see p. 51). Does this relate to a waking life problem or situation? If your dream terror is an ongoing recurring one in dreams, try to resolve what it represents in waking life. It could be a sex-oriented problem, or one which has dogged you since childhood, affecting perhaps your relationship with your parents. Try to fight, and come to terms with it, whatever kind of *monster* inspires it.

test The dream test is probably a reflection of waking life, in which you are putting yourself to the test in some way, or passing through testing conditions. Think too about any waking situation which calls for competitiveness. If you were undergoing medical tests, there may be a hint that you should take one.

texture Awareness of texture in both waking and dream life shows sensitivity and sensuousness; your reaction in the dream is a key – but the symbol is the texture itself: consider this (rough, smooth, hard, soft) as a possible reflection of your own characteristics at present.

thaw Possibly a dream suggestion that you are melting, emotionally, in waking life, coming to terms with your own sexuality, ready to enjoy many areas of your life in a more fulfilling fashion – unless the melting ice was dirty and distressing, or you fell through it, in which case the thaw may be too speedy for your own good! See *ice*, WEATHER (p. 74), perhaps LANDSCAPE (p. 68).

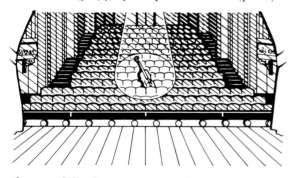

theatre Whether you were performing or watching a performance, there may be a warning here that you are behaving too theatrically, "putting on a show", making a drama – perhaps unnecessarily. Conversely, the dream may be trying to persuade you to take centre stage and express your talents in a more outgoing fashion (this is especially likely if you are basically rather shy). If you were the director or stage manager, there may be a reference to your powers of control over others (are you stage managing some event at present?). Because we usually pay to go to the theatre, and give the stage our full attention, this dream seems likely to be quite important. But don't forget, the stage or theatre itself may represent you yourself. See *cinema, messages*, ENVIRONMENT (p. 92).

theft/thief Does this remind you of some recent loss, or someone who has stolen something from you – your heart, perhaps, or your attention? Or perhaps you feel robbed of some experience because you have had to make a sacrifice. Are you stealing someone's affection and feeling guilty about it? If in your dream you caught a thief in the act, the object he was stealing is an important symbol: if it was money, could this represent affection or love? There could be a comment on the relative emptiness of your life, or a hint not to steal other people's ideas.

thermometer Your temperature may be metaphorically high, especially if you are attracted to someone; but perhaps the presence of a thermometer in a dream reflects a waking preoccupation with fact-finding, or "taking the temperature" of a new project or idea. Don't ignore any physical hints given in your dream; you may literally be a little feverish – a cold coming? Remember too that a thermometer contains mercury, and you could enjoy researching this Roman god's role in mythology, or the planet's astrological influence.

thirst The most important symbol will be what you were thirsting for. If it was water, and the dream was not simply the result of a physical thirst, then your emotional life may be somewhat arid at present; you may be in need of richer experiences, and your dream is making a very direct statement which should not be too difficult to interpret.

threat Your inner authority figure may be threatening you: perhaps you haven't come up to your own expectations recently. Or maybe your dream threat represents an oppressive problem, or a problem person, on the waking scene, undermining your authority.

thrill Hopefully your dream thrill added considerably to your night's entertainment; but maybe you are about to do something thrilling, or is your dream suggesting that you should? Unfortunately such dreams are often wish-fulfilment.

throne Whether you were ascending the throne, sitting on it, or abdicating from it, is obviously crucial; but a throne seems likely to symbolize some achievement at which you are aiming. You may have been making or building a throne, in which case you are perhaps carving out a position of power for yourself. Does the phrase "the power behind the throne" have any relevance? Were there courtiers in view, and what was their attitude?

throw/throwing What were you throwing? If your missile can be clearly associated with a person, your dream may be suggesting that you cast them out of your life. Or it may have been urging you to work off some aggression, to hit out (perhaps verbally) in waking life.

thunder Thunder traditionally expressed the anger of the gods (and was sometimes accompanied by a thunderbolt). Thunder in a dream may express your inner anger, perhaps at one of your own actions. But remember to check that there was not a real thunderstorm while you slept!

ticket If you were buying a ticket, the dream was probably signalling approval for you to go ahead with some new project; consider your general direction in life. If you had lost your ticket, the opposite may be true. A man dreaming of punching a woman's ticket is probably expressing sexual desire. But see, perhaps, *journey*.

tickle Tickling has its sexual connotation, and dreaming of tickling someone possibly expresses the dreamer's desire to give them pleasure or stimulation. Has someone "tickled your fancy".

tie Freud (of course) considered a tie an unequivocal phallic symbol (see the dream quoted on p. 23). But a tie is often, for a man, a way of extending his image and until recently was one of the few means of displaying individuality while wearing formal clothes. So a dream may be underlining this aspect, suggesting that you

time
Margaret dreamed: *"I was standing on the steps of my old college, and everything was just as it had been when I was a student there many years ago; but when I looked at the clock, it had completely changed."*

The dream puzzled Margaret for some time, but she eventually realized that it was simply reminding her that "Times have changed". It was also perhaps hinting, because her old college was the chief symbol, that she should be more ready to listen to other, perhaps younger, people's opinions rather than falling back on those she formed during her own student days.

might give more (or less) attention to one particular personality trait. There may be a reference to vanity, neatness, showiness . . . The tying of knots (lover's knots?) or bows may refer to emotional relationships. Or are you tied to some responsibility?

time A dream in which time is flying, or standing still, may reflect your waking attitude to the process of growing old. A dream of historical time should be interpreted according to the symbols in it: it may be that the setting has been "chosen" in order to emphasize a particular aspect of the dream, or to comment on your attitude to changing times. A preoccupation with time in your dream (too many clocks, too many glances at your watch, a worry about "making it in time") may suggest that you are obsessional about the subject; or there may be a suggestion that you are not sufficiently conscious of the importance of timing. See, if necessary, *clock*, *watch*, BIRTH, DEATH AND CHANGE (p. 76).

timetable A reference to your planning abilities? There may be the suggestion that you should pay more attention to planning in your waking life. If the timetable was all wrong, perhaps a hint that you should not rely too much on evidence which may be faulty.

tin Are you perhaps overvaluing something, or even someone? Such phrases as "tin-pot" or "tin god" are used slightingly, and a tinny noise is thin and unmelodious. A tin can, of course, may contain all sorts of good things; is there a hint that some unpromising situation or person may prove delightful or valuable? Or might you be dealing with "a can of worms"? See also *parcel*.

tiredness An unusual theme, rather like dreaming you are *sleeping*; it may indicate a general state of exhaustion, a desire for more sleep. Sometimes we feign sleep as a means of escape: was there a symbol in the dream suggesting a situation or person to whom that might apply?

toll If you were paying a toll before entering a stretch of motorway, or perhaps crossing a bridge (both important symbols in themselves) the dream may be similar to one of a *ticket* (though without the sexual significance). Hearing a bell tolling may refer to a *funeral*, indicating that you are ready to lay some plan or emotion to rest (see BIRTH, DEATH AND CHANGE (p. 76). If you have lately been thinking about the longterm future, a tolling bell may underline a reference to your destiny.

tombstone There are several records of dreamers reading their own name on a tombstone. There is no need for fear: the focus is probably on some change in outlook or personal development (see BIRTH, DEATH AND CHANGE, p. 76). The same is true of anyone else whose name you may read on a stone: the emphasis will be on changing characteristics, in them or your view of them.

tongue The tongue is closely allied to speech: a sore tongue may suggest you have been speaking cruelly about someone, or telling untruths. Perhaps your tongue has been in your cheek. A dream of speaking in a foreign tongue suggests that you may not have been making yourself sufficiently clear. The tongue plays an important part in our sexual expression; the dream may be referring to that area of your life. Dreams of enjoying a plate of tongue may suggest that you seek better, more extravert verbal expression.

tonic You may be in need of a tonic of some kind, but this will not necessarily be physical.

tool An age-old euphemism for the penis, so your dream could well have a sexual application: how well were you using it? Was it sharp? Did it break in your hand? And so on. Think then of what you were doing with it, and what the results were, and look for other symbols which might refer to waking people or experiences. The tools we use regularly in our everyday lives can be image extenders, and are an important part of us; if there is a non-sexual interpretation, it may be in this area of your life.

tooth See *teeth*; a dream of a single tooth is perhaps more likely to be, as Freud suggested, a phallic symbol – so if it was being pulled, or repaired, what was wrong with it, who was the dentist?

top The dream may be saying that "you're the tops", or referring to your ambitions (if so, see *summit*). But there may be a hint that you're "in a spin", wound up, feeling tense (see *spring*). You may need to relax and rationalize your problems.

torture Probably a suggestion that you are torturing yourself in some way, perhaps unnecessarily; you may need to discontinue a certain line of action, or cut yourself off from some waking situation. A warning dream, in any event. Apply the symbols to yourself, even if you were torturing someone else, but especially if someone was torturing you. Are there sexual implications?

tow Maybe you have someone in tow, or were towing some burden (do you feel like an overworked donkey?) If you were towing a *car* there may be the implication that someone (perhaps you) is not pulling his or her weight in an emotional partnership, or that assistance given to someone else is in question. Is there a pun on "toe"? Check your toes for blisters or corns!

towel Much connected with WATER (see p. 80) in the sense of removing it from yourself by means of drying. So perhaps there is a reference to a need not to be "wet" in emotional matters – you may want or need to see someone or something unemotionally. A towel can be clean and warm, or wet and smelly; might there be a reference to someone you know?

tower Maybe your dream was congratulating you on being a tower of strength to someone else, or – if you were living in one – suggesting that you inhabit an ivory tower, out of touch with reality. Towers are features of many religious buildings: Christian towers with steeples are discreetly described as pointing a finger at the heavens. But a tower is an obvious phallic symbol, strong and potent, and a Hindu tower symbolizes the life force. See *buildings* and ENVIRONMENT (p. 92).

town Possibly the symbol of a lifestyle, or even idea. Familiar or strange? Welcoming or unfriendly? Busy or sleepy? See also *city, buildings* and ENVIRONMENT (p. 92).

toy If you were playing with one, the dream may have been making a statement about your attitude to another person, or warning you about their attitude to you. The words "toy" and "toying" often have sexual connotations: are you toying with someone's affections, less devoted than you pretend? Or could that situation apply to you? Children's dreams of their toys are particularly interesting, and (because the toys are so real to them) often revelatory of how they see their own position in the family, or how they see their parents, brothers, sisters, friends.

traffic *Cars* are very personal symbols, so the first important thing is whether you were driving one. If so, and you were stuck in a traffic jam, the suggestion seems to be that you are frustrated in your (possibly sexual) waking life – though if you suddenly found yourself FLYING (see p. 84) above the traffic, presumably you have nothing to worry about! If you were a pedestrian, intimidated by traffic, that inhibition and fear may be

Dream Analysis

traffic jam
William dreamed: "*I dreamed that I had got out of my car, on a motorway, and was walking along the hard shoulder; the motorway itself was crowded with stationary vehicles, the drivers shouting at each other, sounding their horns to attract attention, while smoke fumes billowed around. I was pleased to be moving forward steadily and clearly making progress while they were stuck in a jam.*"

William was at this time attempting to clear up a multitude of different jobs before going abroad, and wondering which should have preference. The dream suggested that rather than getting bogged down, he should make steady progress where he could with work which could be done, ignoring the other jobs clamouring for his attention, and that he should not be influenced by others against his better judgment.

Cars often refer to personalities rather than abstracts, but in this case individuals were strongly connected with most of the jobs waiting to be done.

t

town *Perspective*, H. Vredeman de Vries

reflected when you are awake. If you were a traffic policeman or warden, you may see yourself as a guardian, guide or authority in other people's lives: remember, such people are not always particularly beloved by the people they serve! If there was a focus on one particular vehicle, try to work out whom, in waking life, you associate with it.

trail What sort of trail? Could it represent a trail of unfinished tasks in waking life? Or is it a reference to some sleuth-like activity you are engaged in at present? Should you be on a trail?

train There are many possible references: among them, the punning ones – are you physically in training, should you train for some job? But the dream seems more likely to be emphasizing setting out or going somewhere. See other relevant symbols: *tunnel, station, platform, railway, engine*. If you were wearing a dress with a train, and someone stood on it, maybe you have been suddenly brought to a standstill in some waking project. How did the situation resolve itself in your dream?

tram A similar symbol to *train*, though mostly connected with the past rather than the present. It is also to some extent freer, though a tram still has to keep to the tracks – so perhaps you need some self-discipline at present – or yearn to break free. You may simply have "gone off the rails".

tramp Think of the tramp in your dream as yourself: do you lack the will to make more of yourself and your abilities, content just to amble about as chance takes you? If you were offering help to a tramp, perhaps your inner self is ready to take you in hand. Could the dream represent some outworn interest to which you should say a firm goodbye? Alternatively, could the lady really be a tramp?

trap Whether you were setting a trap, or were caught in one, the dream is possibly of some waking action or plan. A warning, perhaps, that you are walking into a trap.

trash See *rubbish*.

treason A dream of treason would seem to symbolize some action or attitude which is consciously contrary to the wellbeing of society as a whole, or even an attitude contrary to popular majority feeling. Treason can also be personal – against a lover, perhaps, or even against your own better self. If linked to the traditional harsh punishments, a very strong symbol indeed.

treasure If you found treasure in your dream, you may just have found it in waking life – without necessarily recognizing it as valuable: it may be a new idea, a new attitude, a new person. At all events, life is likely to be the richer for your discovery. Remember the close connection between *money* and love: if you found gold, the allusion may well be to some person to whom you are strongly attracted. But perhaps you found "truth" – a chalice may have been the symbol in that case – as a new way to spiritual development. Any of these – or faith in a new religion – could be represented as treasure. If you lost a treasure, the implication is obvious.

tree The size and condition of the tree will be significant: there may be a comment on your sexual fulfilment, but your spiritual growth could also be in question. Much depends on your attitude towards trees. Sometimes they can be intimidating, especially if they are large, with dark foliage. The desire to fell a tree can be strongly linked to sexual guilt and fear, possibly referring to inhibition. Remember that trees are also a form of protection and shade, and can give sustenance. There could be a reference to your friends, and this may well connect with the type of tree in your dream: a solid oak, an exotic palm, a sensitive willow, etc. See LANDSCAPE (p. 68).

trespass Perhaps a suggestion that you are at present trespassing on someone else's property: being too possessive in a relationship, imposing yourself unnecessarily. Or a warning that this may be about to happen, especially if a notice warns that "Trespassers will be Prosecuted". Of course the opposite might be true: someone may be intruding into your private life.

trial You may yourself be on trial, and you will have to decide what the charge might be in waking life. The judge may represent your innermost self, your conscience. See *court, judge, jury*, if necessary. On the other hand, the dream may simply have made a wry comment on someone who is being a trial to you at present.

tribe A dream of a native, foreign, possibly antagonistic tribe may well refer to a worrying new group of people, or even ideas, which seems to threaten you. If you were a member of the tribe, maybe you are conscious of joining in a movement which you suspect basically of being primitive or uncivilized.

trick It is quite likely that a dream of some trick will refer to something you are planning in your waking life: tricks can backfire. Perhaps the suggestion is that you are being untrue to yourself, or that a higher degree of honesty would be welcome. A dream of a conjuring trick may underline the fact that what appears to be magical or illogical in waking life has a reasoned basis, for which you should search.

triumph If the trimph was your own, it may be that your dreams are echoing some recent success. See also *honour*.

trough A trough usually contains WATER (see p. 80) for animals to drink: what sort of *animal* was drinking? Could this be a reference to your need for succour in your emotional or sex life? Was the water pure or muddy?

truck If you were confidently driving one, the dream may be suggesting that you are confident and in control in waking life. The truck's contents might represent your current waking responsibilities, so will be relevant. But trucks can be cumbersome and unwieldy: are you carrying a heavy load?

truth A dreaming quest for abstract truth probably reflects a waking concern; ask your dreams (p. 47) for further elucidation.

trumpet A rather loud and brassy instrument with exhibitionist attributes ("blowing your own trumpet"). The context should suggest whether your unconscious approves or disapproves of a possibly over-demonstrative attitude. If you are naturally shy, there might be an encouragement to make more of yourself. See *horn*.

tunnel Entering or leaving a tunnel, seeing light at the end of one – these are believed to be very common dream symbols. An impression of a train entering a tunnel is one of the most frequent visual symbols of coitus used in film. Consider this, certainly (and who your fellow-passenger was, if any); but consider too that the tunnel may represent a period of anxiety through which you may be passing in waking life. Are you now emerging into the light? See *underground*.

twin To dream of a twin when one does not in fact exist is perhaps a suggestion that you are objectively facing up to your real self and your problems. There might be an inference that you are in some way repeating yourself, or becoming too predictable (too like yourself) in waking life. You may feel in need of platonic, brotherly or sisterly love.

tyranny Tyranny suggests that in your dream you were forced into conduct against your will or better judgment. Did this mirror a waking situation? Are you being tyrannical, or reacting to the tyranny of others?

u

umbrella An umbrella is a protection against rain or sun, but it may have a tendency to be blown inside out, or lost. In some dreams it has been used as a parachute – not only for descent but also ascent, as one is blown away by the wind, so see FLYING (p. 84). Consider yourself in a protective role, or an escapist one: do you need shelter, or should you offer someone shelter? – and from what. See, perhaps, WEATHER (p. 74), which might suggest the heat of passion or a storm of argument.

umpire An umpire ensures fair play: considering the possible sexual connotations of a *game*, are you perhaps much concerned with the course of your own or someone else's love life? Or is unfairness apparent in some waking situation – someone "not playing the game"? If a dream umpire booked you for bad play, is it an indication of a guilty conscience?

underclothes See CLOTHES AND NUDITY (p. 82). Emphasis is, on the whole, on something private; the extent to which you like pretty, fashionable or plain and utilitarian underclothes may be significant – also whether they were clean or dirty; did you feel ashamed of revealing them?

underground Perhaps you have the unconscious desire to "lie low" or "go underground" because of some waking situation. Examine your motives: you may be about to behave deceitfully for no good reason. Ask your dreams (see p. 47) whether you should not come out into the open. See, perhaps, *transport, train, mine/mining.* If you were burrowing underground, mole-like, there may be the suggestion that you should delve into your unconscious, attempt to get to the root of your psyche (see *archaeology*).

understudy If you felt you could play the part quite as well as the star, this may be an encouraging dream; if you attempted to do so and failed, it may be a warning! Consider who the star represents: are you playing an unnecessarily subservient role in waking life? Or have you a deep-rooted ambition to be as like the star as possible? If the latter, ask your dreams for further details (see p. 47) – such identification may be less desirable than you think. See *theatre.*

undertaker The dream could possibly be making a punning reference to some commitment or undertaking, if you have undertaken a particular task. But see *death, funeral.* Decide whether the undertaker represents an authority figure and, if so, who. Perhaps the passing of time.

unhappiness An overall feeling, a mood, which may well spill over and colour your waking day: so try to understand and thus efface it as soon as you wake. There could have been several mechanical triggers – a physiological condition, perhaps, or something you read yesterday in a newspaper, and which moved you more than you realized at the time. If you can take some positive, assertive action to balance your feeling, that may well exorcize the emotion. If the feeling was rooted elsewhere – in a personal relationship, for instance – your dreams should be asked (see p. 47) for further comment.

uniform Probably a comment on your attitude to conformity: you may have been proud to wear the uniform, and are very happy to conform to the tenets of the society in which you live. Or you may have rebelled against the uniform, and be a social nonconformist. Decide whether in either event you are too extreme in your attitude. A dream of your childhood attitude to school uniform may provide a pertinent comment.

unkindness An unkindness from someone you respect or love can graphically penetrate your dream life (see Beverley's dreams on pp. 174, 189 and 198). You may not immediately get the message, but since you have looked up the dream under this heading, it has presumably displayed itself fairly overtly. Decide whether you are not perhaps being unkind, even cruel, to yourself. If not, then obviously you should try to draw a parallel between the dream incident and your waking life.

unmarried If you are all too married, this may be a wish-fulfilment dream: you simply want to be single again. If the dream accompanies the break-up of a partnership, pay special attention to your future dreams, which may be a help in reassembling your emotional poise after a traumatic period.

upheaval A dream upheaval probably in some way reflects a waking one, though maybe caricaturing, exaggerating or minimizing it – and in that way attempting to correct your waking attitude. There may be hints that you should change your ways, thoughts, opinions.

urine Apart from the possible hint that you should have your urine checked by the doctor in case of kidney disorder, a dream of urine seems most likely to arise from a need to empty your bladder.

V

vacant If you dream of a vacant house or empty rooms, see ENVIRONMENT (p. 92). There may be a suggestion that you are in need of greater space, emotional or environmental; or maybe you are finding it difficult to come to conclusions or reach decisions at present. See *emptiness.*

vacuum A dream of being in a vacuum probably suggests that in some aspect of your waking life you feel isolated and alone, either physically or emotionally. Try to break out of such isolation. A vacuum cleaner, as an image, suggests that you may be sorting out your problems, getting rid of the dust of old, outworn ideas, and spring-cleaning your mind.

vamp Probably, for women, a hint that you should be more forthcoming in your attentions to men, especially when developing new sexual relationships; unless it is a warning that you are being too blatant and obvious, playing perhaps an uncharacteristic role. Your own feelings in the dream may give you the answer. A man who dreams of a vamp must decide who the dream symbol represents (do not rule out the possibility that it is the female side of your personality).

vault See ENVIRONMENT (p. 92). Entire families are usually buried in vaults, into which one descends. Could the dream refer to your laying family problems to rest, or perhaps researching into family history (see *archaeology*)? The research may of course be into your own personality, within the context of your family and upbringing, your inherited personality traits.

vaulting See ENVIRONMENT (p. 92). But the dream could be making a comment perhaps on ambition, or your determination to surmount difficulties (one vaults *over* something). Not only determination but bravery may be in question. The ease or difficulty with which you completed the action must be important, and may indicate the degree of encouragement your dream offers, reflecting perhaps your waking confidence about tasks ahead. If you were engaged in pole-vaulting, there may well be a sexual implication.

vegetables Honest, simple and good for you: there may be a positive hint about living the good life – if they were fresh and properly cooked. Raw or rotten vegetables are another matter. And in any event, the kind of vegetable which appeared in the dream may suggest the real subject: consider, especially, its shape. Hopefully, the hint is not that you are beginning to become "a vegetable". See under separate vegetables: see also FOOD AND DRINK (p. 86).

vehicle In general, perhaps especially for men, the vehicle you own in waking life is an important extension of your image, and often of your sexual personality. See *car*.

veil A heavily veiled woman, in a dream, may well represent an area of your own personality which you tend to conceal (perhaps even from yourself) – for a man, the reference may be to the female (not necessarily homosexual) aspects of his personality. Try to work out the symbolic meaning, to you, of the person or thing behind the veil. Veils are also, historically, attractive and enticing – but also associated with nuns, and the rejection of worldly things.

ventriloquism How were you using this faculty? If through a ventriloquist's dummy, the crucial matter is what it represented – perhaps an aspect of yourself, speaking a message from your unconscious. If the dummy seemed rebellious and unruly, this might be an indication that you are less in control of yourself and your emotions than you think. If you were "sending your voice" through the mouth of someone else, that might reflect a desire to influence that person in waking life. See *puppet*.

verge You could be "on the verge" of some important discovery or action. If you were waiting for help on a roadside verge, there may be a reflection of a hold-up in waking life, or the suggestion that you should be inactive until you receive the support you need. You may be sitting on a verge watching life go by – which may be a good or bad thing: look for other symbols in the dream: how pleasant was the verge – green grass or dusty earth?

vibration Apart from the possibility of a physical vibration triggering your dream, this seems likely to be a hint that you should be more sensible to the vibrations (emotions, feelings) of others. Tune in more carefully to their wavelength. Use your intuition more keenly. There may be a reflection of an interest in the psychic. Or there could be a simple, basic sexual reference not difficult to recognize.

victim The fact that you have referred to this entry rather than to whatever made you a victim (for example, *violence* or *theft*) seems to suggest

veil *The veil*, Georges Seurat

that in waking life you feel victimized, either by someone or as the result of an ongoing situation. Ask your dreams (see p. 47) for more information and advice.

victory An encouraging dream, it would seem – unless the price paid was too great. Did you feel triumph, satisfaction, or guilt for the plight of the vanquished?

view See LANDSCAPE (p. 68). Perhaps a suggestion that you should look objectively at your life plans, or ENVIRONMENT (see p. 92).

village See ENVIRONMENT (p. 92).

villain Decide first who or what your dream villain represented (by no means necessarily obvious). Think about every aspect of your own personality, and consider whether the villain in your dream may not symbolize one of them – or perhaps some silly and dangerous obsessive personal habit (smoking, perhaps, or alcohol, or indulgence in some other drug). The force of the word "villain" suggests that the dream may be an important and significant one.

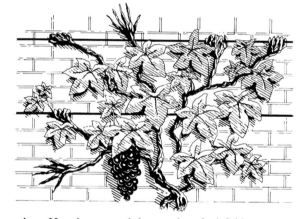

vine Handsome and decorative, fruitful but very clinging plants, vines have much that is sensual about them and, considering the *grapes* they bear, it is not difficult to associate them with full-blooded sexual experience and the free expression of emotion. The clinging aspect may suggest perhaps a degree of claustrophobia: were you pruning the vine, or pulling it away from the wall? There could be the suggestion that you need a certain amount of freedom, despite the vine's richness and health. If the vine was in poor health, bearing no grapes (or small, sour ones) the conclusion to be drawn is obvious. If the vine was in some way trapping you, it may be that you are too involved in your emotional and sensual life, to the detriment perhaps of your freedom of thought.

violin Its music can be beautiful and romantic, or demonic: so this could be a warning dream. But there are comfortable possibilities: is it a question of many a good tune coming from an old fiddle? Old violins can be immensely valuable: could that fit into your dream? Are you playing second fiddle to anyone in waking life, when you should be leading the orchestra? Are you engaged in some kind of "fiddle"?

violence The fact that you have referred to this entry indicates that the theme of your dream seemed more important than the incidents in it. Uncharacteristically violent behaviour in a dream can be a release mechanism: you may have been (or have had to be) too restrained for your own good, in waking life. Even dreams in which you are violently attacking members of your family should not cause undue worry: better batter your baby in a dream than in reality – and the irritation quotient of small babies is too immense to be always ignored by our unconscious. If such dreams recur too often for comfort, it may be, however, that you have a problem which will only be resolved through therapy.

virgin Your dream will either be of yourself as a virgin, or of a virgin figure – perhaps someone you know, perhaps an abstract (possibly religious or spiritual) figure. Remember that the real reference may not be merely to physical virginity, but to intellectual, spiritual or emotional innocence. If you are a woman, you may be bored with your own virginity, or regret having lost it. There may be a general nostalgia, in which case it will probably be important that in waking life you should be more forward-looking. If you are a man, your dream may be commenting on your general attitude to women. There may be a warning involved if you dream of your lover as a virgin: a common masculine problem involves the "worship" of a loved one in an increasingly asexual way, so that physical love becomes as difficult as it would be with a chill statue on a pedestal. The man begins to fear that he insults the woman by displaying his sexual feelings towards her, and a situation can then arise in which he can only express his sexuality towards women he despises. Dreams, "visions", of the Virgin Mary herself may occur in people of a more or less extremely religious disposition. Try to retain a sense of proportion, whatever your attitude to religion.

virility If your virility gave you cause for concern in your dream, there may be a reflection of waking worries (often not founded on fact, but on irrational fears). Remember that worry about potency is self-perpetuating: the more you worry, the more you may have to worry about. If your dream virility seems unduly rampant, there may be the suggestion that you should cool it a little in waking life.

visiting Visiting friends or relations is either a pleasure or a bore, and your dream may be commenting either way. There may be a hint that you should look up someone you have been neglecting – or the suggestion that they could be helpful in some waking predicament. Dreams of visiting places or countries you do not know suggest you are in need of fresh experiences and challenges. But see LANDSCAPE (p. 68), *travel*.

voice Perhaps a *message* dream – unless the voice turned out to be a real one, waking you up. Perhaps a simple memory of a voice, perhaps the nostalgic voice of someone lost to you. Should you be voicing your own opinions more clearly? The type of voice (old, wise, effeminate, childish) may be significant.

void A suggestion that your life is in some way empty? Perhaps a reference to bereavement, or the end of a relationship or friendship. See *space*, *emptiness*, *vacuum*.

volcano Could you be sitting on one, right now? You may feel very much better if you blow your top, let off steam, hurl a few rocks about, or pour lava on some unprepossessing LANDSCAPE (see p. 68). Holding back could be doing more harm than good. Unless, of course, you are under the volcano: in which case, decide what waking form it takes. See, perhaps, DISASTERS (p. 72), FIRE (p. 78).

volunteer Your dream is possibly suggesting that you should become involved in waking situations rather than sitting about waiting to be asked. Be forthcoming. In other words, volunteer.

vomit Unless the result of physical nausea, in which case let us hope you awoke in time, the suggestion seems to be that you should get rid of some unpleasant emotion which you have been nursing to yourself. You are better without it.

vote You are either giving, or seeking, approval. This seems on the whole likely to be an encouraging dream, especially of course if your vote ensured election. Perhaps your dream is inviting you to support someone or some plan which is on your waking mind.

vow Perhaps you have made, or are about to make, an important commitment in waking life; there may be a hint of future progress and your present level of self-confidence. Was your dream of a marriage vow? Wish-fulfilment, perhaps?

voyeur There may be a suggestion that, while much sexuality stems from the mind, you need to act out a few more of your fantasies rather than merely keeping them to yourself. Seek greater involvement. See SEX (p. 90).

vulgarity If you tend to be a rather refined person, there may be a suggestion that you should be less inhibited in an area of your life (possibly sexual) in which you are perhaps somewhat tense. On the other hand, there may be a warning that you are too free in expressing your own uninhibited emotions. The context of the dream should make it clear which attitude is being condemned or approved.

W

W

waffle The appearance or texture of food may suggest someone you know: in which case your enjoyment or dislike of it will have something to say about your relationship. In this case, perhaps you were dreaming of someone sweet and succulent and at their best at breakfast! Or have you been "waffling on" about something lately?

wage Keep in mind the similitude between *money* and love. Wages properly earned – or the wages of sin (perhaps just as hard-earned). Are you receiving enough love and devotion in return for your own expenditure of emotion in a partnership? Or were you being encouraged to wage war in some way?

wagon The symbol may be practical (if you are engaged in farming, for instance) or nostalgic (c.f. the Wild West). Alternatively, are you, or should you be, "on the wagon"?

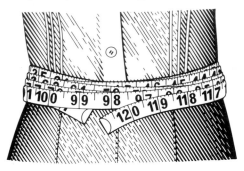

waist Tiny and neat, or spreading and in need of diet or exercise? A double pun? – are you physically wasting away? In certain circumstances this could be a warning against anorexia.

waiter A dream waiter could represent a helpful and supportive friend, ready to offer material assistance (what was he bringing on his tray?) A careless waiter might represent a disruptive influence, or some lack of care on your part. If you were the waiter, there might be a suggestion that you could be doing more with your life than merely obeying the instructions or whims of others. Perhaps you should be more assertive and independent, and less submissive.

waiting Were you patient, or bored and resentful? Look for a parallel in your waking life. The poet Milton noted that "they also serve who only stand and wait" – and patience is a virtue. If you remained calm while everyone else in the dream was frenetic and panicky, this could be a reassuring image.

wake Rather similar to dreaming that you are dreaming, or that you sleep, a dream involving awakening is a complex double image: you may need to "wake up" in real life – except that, in your dream, you wake to a state of dreaming! Ask your dreams (see p. 47) for elucidation. Alternatively, if you were at a wake, there may be simple encouragement to celebrate the attributes of someone lost to you (through death or absence) – or to celebrate the fact that you have recently come through a period of change. See, perhaps, BIRTH, DEATH and CHANGE (p. 76).

walk Walking in general seems to suggest slow, confident, steady progress. What you were walking into will have been significant: see ENVIRONMENT (p. 92), *rooms*, LANDSCAPE (p. 68). There may be a comment on coming commitments, developments or occasions. Difficulties in walking or general lack of progress seems an obvious image of delay.

wall Similar to *fence* or *hedge*, but perhaps more of an obstacle. Possibly you were building one: if so, do you or your family need some kind of extra protection at present? If you were demolishing one, perhaps you yearn for more freedom, for escape from a claustrophobic ENVIRONMENT (p. 92). Have you "come up against a brick wall" in some waking situation?

wallet See also *purse*. The loss of a wallet may infer the losing of your heart – your emotional balance; has someone stolen it? There may be a loss of identity, perhaps, especially if cheque or credit cards were involved. This could be a practical warning against carelessness, or a "worry" dream (see p. 52).

wandering You are probably suffering from a loss of direction in one area of waking life or another. The LANDSCAPE (see p. 68) through which you were wandering will be significant. You may need to search for new interests and involvement for your time and energy. See also TRAVEL (p. 70).

war The war may be within yourself, irrespective of your feelings about conflict in the dream. There may be suggestion that you should do *battle* or put up a *fight*, in some respect, in waking life. See, perhaps, *duel*, and any particular weapons used in your dream.

warehouse This probably represents the store of knowledge and experience gathered during your life; whether you are enlarging it, looking for something in it, or finding new areas of it, will be significant (see Julia Parker's dreams, p. 56).

warmth You may be in need of more emotional warmth and affection in waking life; or perhaps long to give it to others. Consult the context of your dream, and see, perhaps, FIRE (p. 78) and ENVIRONMENT (p. 92).

washing Were you, like Lady Macbeth, seeking to wash your hands of something? What waking deed could have called up such an image? Or were you doing the family wash – which may refer to your desire that they should be clean in other ways than merely physical. Washing yourself, or your own clothes, may indicate a desire to start afresh: a dream of washing money may indicate a wish to offer love and affection as if for the first time. Do you want to wash away some

injury, or wash some man or woman right out of your hair? Do not throw the baby out with the bathwater. See WATER (p. 80).

waste What was being wasted? See FOOD AND DRINK (p. 86) if necessary: you could feel that love and affection is being thrown away on someone, and wasted *money* may have the same reference. Maybe you are being invited to recycle your affections. See *waist* for a punning reference.

watch If you were on watch, or had been told to watch someone, this may be a hint that you should "watch it", in some way; in other words, a warning dream. Be on the alert. This could be true even if you dreamed about your watch; but see, of course, *time, clocks*.

water Often, in dreams, a symbol of our emotions. See p. 80.

waterfall Expressive of freedom, liberty, extraversion. See WATER (p. 80).

waves See WATER (p. 80), *sea*; depth, and a far-reaching, open and expressive emotion seems to be symbolized. Having your hair waved, or dreaming of wavy hair, could be a sexual image.

way A search for the way, or signposts indicating the way or even announcing "no way" or "give way" may well refer to some decision you have

made or are about to make. Take the hint. Consider too the possibility of a pun: how much do you weigh? Or should you weigh up the situation more profoundly? – another warning. And see LANDSCAPE (p. 68).

weapons Many are listed here, so see *gun, spear, knife, sword*, or whatever. A good many of them have sexual implications, and dreaming of using weapons may also suggest that you are in some respect in an antagonistic mood. The way you were using the weapon, against whom, and to what effect, will all be significant details.

weather A major theme (see p. 74) and potentially an important background factor. But remember the possible pun: whether you should do this, or that.

weaving One of the most ancient of all domestic crafts; but an intermediate stage between spinning and making up a garment, so are you in the middle of some task yet to be completed? Or at a middle stage of development of a personal relationship? Are you weaving a spell on someone (or vice versa)?

web Laying a trap for someone? See *spider, net*.

wedding Possibly a wish-fulfilment dream; but perhaps the marriage of two formerly conflicting areas of your personality, so that you are now "one flesh" or one spirit, psychologically whole. If your dream wedding was disrupted, you may have more to achieve, more conflicts to resolve, in this area. Study carefully the authority figures in your dream – the clergyman, your father? These may have a particular part to play, as important as your bride or groom.

weeds A weed is a plant which is out of place. Were your weeds simply unsightly, were they strangling the healthy growth of more valuable plants, were they positively harmful – stinging nettles or thistles, for instance? Could they represent intrusive or obstructive prickly friends or colleagues, perhaps making stinging remarks? Or could they be personality traits of your own, getting in the way of real progress? See, perhaps, *gardens*, LANDSCAPE (p. 68).

weeping See *sorrow*; to wake weeping is an indication that, if we do not exorcize it, our dream is likely to haunt the rest of our day, so try to consider it objectively. Your tears may have been an attempt literally to wash away something negative that has been irritating your unconscious self for some time – in which case you may feel some relief. Tears of joy, alas less frequent, underline a probably important, hopeful and sometimes elating dream.

weighing/weights Concern with your own weight apart, the dream suggests the weighing up of a situation, perhaps as to whether it is really serious (heavy) or insignificant (light).

welcome Whether you are welcoming someone, or yourself being welcomed, the inference is that you are enthusiastically ready to greet new ideas, suggestions, perhaps a different lifestyle, not to mention friends and lovers. If the notice "welcome" is displayed on a mat or a sign, see *messages*; but remember, you may be the door-mat, and that it is not specially positive to welcome the fact that people walk all over you!

welfare A dream of being "on welfare" may have connotations of shame, of an appeal made (perhaps to a friend) in spite of yourself, though "for your own good". There may be a reference to unnecessary, even silly, pride.

well Deep, dark, containing water, this seems likely to be a very potent symbol of your unconscious, your deepest emotions. If you drew water from the well, it seems that you are in waking life drawing on your deepest emotional resources. But at least you reached the water: if your bucket came up empty, or you could not reach the water, then there may be a reference to some aridity which may need careful restoration. See WATER (p. 80), *underground*.

whale The largest mammal, perhaps symbolic of some enormous project or responsibility in waking life, probably concerning other people. Remember the whale that swallowed Jonah: does the project threaten to consume you? See FISH, FLESH AND FOWL (p. 88).

wheel A *mandala* (see Glossary), the wheel is often a symbol of eternity, and your dream may be saying something about your view of yourself as part of the general scheme of things. It could however work on a more mundane level, representing the even tenor of life – or an obstruction to progress (if the wheel was broken). Was the wheel in need of oil, and is there a parallel in waking life? Were you a small but important cog in your dream wheel? Was the wheel out of control (a disconnected steering-wheel, perhaps)? A dream of being securely at the wheel of a car may be very supportive in a crisis. This may be a symbol which future dreams will place in a firmer and clearer context.

whip If you were wielding a whip, you may be in a particularly powerful position, and exploiting it. Perhaps however you need to whip up your own energy, emotion or anger at present. A whip can be an overtly sexual symbol, but may simply suggest that your sexual life needs extra invigoration. Do not let the symbol shock you. If you were receiving "a good whipping", some waking guilt may be in question.

whistle The signal for action? If you were blowing the whistle, you may be ready to give your approval to some waking project. But a whistle can also warn, or be used to attract attention, even call for help.

widow/widower Without being predictive, a dream of being a widow or widower can signal a feeling of being deprived, neglected, deserted, bereft of sufficient love and support from a partner. But perhaps you need to "go it alone" in some way, to be more independent.

wife A dream of being someone's wife, or of having a wife other than your own, may of course be wish-fulfilment. On the other hand, it could be a warning, if the experience seems claustrophobic. There might however be the suggestion that you could give your support to the person you see as your wife or husband: indeed, he or she could represent a project which is dear to you, or even a part of your own personality of which you are not sufficiently aware – perhaps the masculine or feminine side of your psyche. More often than not, our spouses are merely present in our dreams, without being the crux; so the presence of a husband or wife as the main symbol seems likely to be important. A case for asking future dreams (see p. 47) for elaboration and explanation. See also *husband*.

wig For a man, baldness is often allied with fears of impotence; a wig, then, may infer a desire to disguise feelings of insufficiency, or perhaps to disguise some other facet of your personality of which you are ashamed. For a woman, a wig may infer a desire for a change of personality, even a new one. There may be the suggestion that you are behaving uncharacteristically (as well as modifying our looks, we often feel different when wearing a wig).

wilderness See LANDSCAPE (p. 68), ENVIRONMENT (p. 92). There may be a suggestion that life is arid, shapeless, without direction at present. Were you wandering aimlessly, or making your way purposefully forward? Consult other symbols, which may give hints as to waking action.

will A possible pun on your determination, but also perhaps a comment on some "final" decision you have recently reached. There could be a suggestion, if a Will was being read, that past efforts are now about to pay off.

wind Was it blowing hot or cold? – a comment on your present emotions, actions or state of mind, perhaps with regard to a particular circumstance. And see WEATHER (p. 74).

window A dream of looking through a window is likely to be a comment on your view of someone else or their actions – or of course of your own. Whether you were looking into or out of a *room*, whether the *glass* was clean or dirty, whether or not there were *curtains*, whether the window was preventing you from communicating with others, or you were placing a light in it – there were probably many other symbols to be considered, and the interpretation of each should be fairly obvious (you may only have a partial, or distorted, view). The dream will be worth serious thought, for it was obviously showing you something, and probably making an important point.

wine To dream of drinking wine (usually rich, tasty, colourful) would seem to suggest that you are gaining experience at present, especially where your emotional life is concerned. Your relative enjoyment of the wine will obviously be significant; and the person with whom you were sharing it. Bottles of wine may represent people whom you consider more mature than you. A dream of drinking communion wine will have an equivalent reference to your spiritual life.

winning Whatever you were winning in your dream, the symbol is obviously one of success, and the dream an encouraging and reassuring one. But if you were pipped at the post, there may be a warning against complacency. A dream of winning a *game* may have a sexual reference.

winter See *seasons*.

wire If you dreamed of a live wire, perhaps this was a description of yourself. But beware of high tension, especially if electricity was concerned. The state of the wire – rusty, barbed – may be significant, and indicate danger or frustration. See, if necessary, *fence*, or *telegram*.

wish To dream of making a particular wish seems to indicate that you wish it could come true: this may be an interestingly oblique wish-fulfilment dream, especially if it *was* fulfilled. It may relate to a waking achievement which is about to announce itself.

witch An important image in myth and fairytale, the witch is a part of the Jungian collective unconscious. It is also part of the paraphernalia of childhood which sometimes spills over into the adult dream world, together with *giants, monsters,* and others. It may still be a rather frightening symbol, perhaps associated (as often in childhood) with some unlikeable acquaintance, but perhaps more likely to be associated, now, with some aspect of your own character of which your unconscious censor disapproves. If this seems possible, the witch must be faced and un-magicked! A white witch could represent something mysterious and relatively unknown, but possibly beneficial (unconventional medicine, for instance) which you might explore. Moderate scepticism seems in order, however. Remember the traditional association of witchcraft and sexuality: watch that broomstick. If the warning seems apposite, remember that any spell you cast could misfire.

witness We are often witnesses or mere observers in our dreams, so that their function of "showing" us something is underlined, and they seem to be encouraging us to be objective about what may be going on in our waking lives. It may be that this kind of non-participatory dream is more common with people who tend to be somewhat detached and unemotional. If you were a witness giving evidence in a dream *trial*, however, the critical factor may be whether you were telling the truth or lying. If the latter, it may well be that you are deceiving yourself about some crucial matter in waking life. The identity of the plaintiff and defendant will be crucial clues about the dream's waking reference. Think, too, about the reaction of the *judge*.

wolf Were you a wolf in sheep's clothing? Who was your Red Riding Hood (such a dream may have overt sexual connotations)? Or was the dream wolf a threatening *monster*, preying on you or your loved ones? The creature could represent waking problems, more or less severe, and not necessarily financial – though the phrase about "keeping the wolf from the door" may have its significance. Wolves seem to have insatiable appetites: was there a reference to your animal nature, to greed of one kind or another?

womb A dream of returning to the womb (and psychiatrists have suggested we all have a folk memory of this) may represent a deep need for security, the ultimate in protective love, away from the harsh reality of waking life. A dream of being in almost any warm, comfortable enclosed space may echo this, especially if there is an association with WATER (see p. 80). See also, perhaps, *pregnancy*, BIRTH, DEATH AND CHANGE (p. 76).

wood Basic, natural, often beautiful, wood can inspire our creative instincts, and this may be the case if you dream of carving it; there may be the suggestion, however, that you are (at last?) shaping your own life. A dream of rotten wood may suggest something that is "rotting you away" in waking life – jealousy, for instance. Consider too the pun on what you "would" like to do, if . . . See, perhaps, *tree*.

wool Wool is natural, warm and comforting, though it can irritate the skin; the context of your dream may suggest an interpretation. If you were putting on a sweater, who is pulling the wool over your eyes? Yourself, perhaps? Woollen garments can stretch or shrink: could this relate to your lifestyle?

words A dream of words in the abstract may suggest that you mistrust, or should mistrust, someone who seems to be using them too prodigally at present. Random words may reflect a certain confusion in your own mind, especially if you are engaged in heavy study at present. See, perhaps, *messages*.

work Who else was involved in the work, what was its nature, and what were the other symbols? There may be a reference to a need to work more or less hard in waking life, or of course a wish-fulfilment dream if you are seeking work. Remember that it is possible that a dream may suggest areas of potential which you have not yet exploited.

workmen See *work*, above. Dream workmen can however represent areas of your own personality, sometimes as yet unexploited; did they do their tasks efficiently? Or were they lazy and inefficient?

workshop See ENVIRONMENT (p. 92) and *warehouse*. The dream could refer to stored practical experience and knowledge. Get in there, get busy, put it to good use! If you felt apprehensive about using the tools in your dream workshop, this may be because of a certain lack of confidence; if some necessary ones were absent, then perhaps this is a hint that you should seek more experience in the field in which you are working in waking life.

worms Very like *snakes* (see FISH, FLESH AND FOWL, p. 88), but forbidding in a different way – "dirty" (connected with the soil), perhaps more elusive. As phallic symbols, less frightening, perhaps even rather comic. But after all worms are useful creatures, aerating the soil, feeding the birds . . . There may be a reference to your past sexual history, your infant sexuality, perhaps (often stupidly condemned by parents as "dirty") now reaching fruition (or possibly obstructing healthy sexual expression). Destructive worms (woodworm, for instance) may suggest some destructive area of your own personality, or some emotionally destructive force (see *wood*). The connection between worms and *death* could be a comment on your feelings about immortality or the continuing life force.

wound Potentially an important and valuable dream. The kind of wound, its state, its position, whether it was healing or not, is obviously highly significant; the *weapon* which caused it may be an important pointer to interpretation, too. There is often an allusion to a psychological, perhaps sexual or emotional, wound, inflicted perhaps by older people, sometimes of one's own family. Religion can also be an association (see *stigmata*). If the wound was festering, it is very important to discover what it may symbolize in your waking life. Your dreams may suggest a cure: you may have to swallow an unpalatable pill or take some unwelcome action to heal yourself.

W

wrapping See *parcel*, for it is what is inside the wrapping that is important. There may be a reference to your protective instincts, or perhaps to a desire to disguise the truth. Alternatively, have you been "rapped" over the knuckles for a misdemeanour, or been "rapping" argumentatively or provocatively? Or wrapping up some project?

wreath An expression of emotion, usually sympathy, a dream wreath may be a hint that you are feeling too sorry for yourself at the moment, or that you are mourning the end of a relationship or commitment. See BIRTH, DEATH AND CHANGE (p. 76). A laurel wreath is obviously a matter for congratulation.

wreck There may be a suggestion that you look a wreck at present; but there may be a more serious allusion to the wreck of a project, or of your dearest wishes. Since the *sea* is likely to be an associated symbol, your emotions may be involved.

wrestling Possibly simply a cheerful sexual dream; but perhaps an allusion to your wrestling with problems, perhaps internal ones (who your opponent was is obviously important). Whether you were hero or villain, the reaction of the crowd and referee may be a strong hint as to the probity of waking actions.

wrinkles Wrinkles are caused as much by laughter as by frowns; is there a hint there? Or a suggestion that you should take more care of your skin?

writing Perhaps a *message* dream, but if you were writing letters to friends remember that they may be signals from your unconscious to your conscious self concerning your emotions or potential. Perhaps a pun: are you really right, after all? Or politically right – to the extent of falling off the edge of the paper?

y

yard Your own back-yard, the protection of your family, suggesting a certain claustrophobia? If you were measuring something, a reference perhaps to husbanding your resources. Buying fabric by the yard could refer to plans for new projects. See, perhaps, ENVIRONMENT (p. 92).

yellow See COLOUR (p. 94). But are you jaundiced in your waking life?

yoga Physically restorative, spiritually enriching, so perhaps a plea for one or both?

youth Wish-fulfilment, perhaps, if you dreamed of your own youth; possibly a sexual wish-fulfilment, too, if your dream was of an attractive youth. Are you behaving immaturely?

z

zero The figure itself is a *circle* or *mandala*, but the notion that it represents nothing – a *vacuum* – is destructive and negative, so this may be a rather depressing dream. It may reflect the fact that recent schemes have come to naught. But ask (see p. 47) for a more positive and assertive suggestion as to future attitudes.

zipper/zip-fastener If a zip-fastener gives way, a suggestion of insecurity or embarrassment. An obvious possible sexual connotation. See CLOTHES (p. 82), *image*.

Zodiac, the A dream suggesting perhaps that you are part of a universal scheme; but if you are into astrology, the dream may be concerned in complex ways with the characteristics of individual zodiacal signs, and you will need to use your technique to disentangle the symbolic meaning.

zoo Were you a captive animal, or a keeper? See, perhaps, *prison, fence*. Whether you felt secure or constricted will be important; perhaps you longed to break out, which suggests the equivalent feeling in your waking circumstances. Did the animals perhaps represent your own personal characteristics; to be released or caged?

Z

Glossary

Entries which appear in *italics* indicate that the word italicized is defined elsewhere in the glossary.

analysis In the psychological sense, the examination of all the separate aspects of an experience or a mental process. Sigmund Freud developed psychoanalysis itself, as a means of treating emotional disorders, with a special emphasis on the *unconscious* (see below), which it is believed reveals itself particularly in dreams. *Analysts* of various schools of psychology have evolved different methods of approaching analysis since the early original work of Breuer and Freud at the end of the nineteenth century. Jung's method was based largely on free association – when the person concerned is asked to say the first word that comes to mind on hearing a special keyword. Other analysts give the keyword, and ask the subject to follow the train of thought which it suggests. But these are only two of many. It is not necessary to have a psychological problem or neurosis to go into analysis; in the past 30 years or so, indeed, it has become something of a fashion. It is, however, expensive, and is mostly used by those who have personal psychological problems.

anima and animus Jung's terms for the personification of the feminine nature of a man's unconscious and the masculine nature of a woman's. Bisexuality of this sort is reflected in the balance of male and female genes. Anima and animus generally appear in dreams as people: "dream-girl" or "dream-lover", perhaps. Jung also used anima as a term for the soul, the inmost core of the personality.

archetype Jung's term for the content of the *collective unconscious*.

association In dream interpretation, *free association* means spontaneously allowing ideas to occur to you while thinking about the content of your dream – ideas which at first may not necessarily seem to be connected with the dream, but can often help to reveal its meaning. This was Jung's idea; Freud preferred *directed* or *controlled association*, in which the associated ideas are always, hopefully, directly related to the dream situation.

collective unconscious See *unconscious*.

counsellor There are various sorts of counsellors available – to give advice on all sorts of problems, from housing and social security to marriage and sexual difficulties. Such counsellors, if employed by a reputable agency, have usually had training in personal relationships, but it is always as well to discover just what degree of practical experience they have had. They are often an excellent halfway-house for those people who are unable to afford, or do not wish, to consult an analyst.

displacement dream See *dream*.

dream Jung called dreams "a little hidden door in the innermost and most secret recesses of the psyche." By it, we mean the visual images, symbols, impressions which pass through the mind during sleep. Many are not remembered on waking; others are recalled, and can be noted down. Dreams have always been regarded as in some way important, and from earliest recorded history have been noted down and their meaning speculated upon. In a *lucid dream* the dreamer recognizes that he is asleep, can in part direct the course of the dream, and can even sometimes communicate with a waking colleague while still himself apparently completely asleep. A *hypnagogic* dream is one which occurs at the very onset of sleep, is often tied to our last conscious waking thought and tends to be of a fragmentary nature. In a *displacement* dream, visual images are "displaced" so that their references are upset: a house can appear on a mountain-top instead of in a suburban street; large doughnuts may appear on your car wheels instead of tyres. Or images are distorted so that they appear oddly: upside down, or sideways. Basically, *displacement* is to do with the disguises assumed by the dream.

extraversion Jung's term for the type of personality in which one's interests are directed outwards to nature and society rather than inwards to one's own thoughts and feelings.

hypnagogic dream See *dream*.

image Something seen in the mind's eye: it can represent a whole group of similar objects, as a single lion may represent the whole genus: the *archetypal* lion. But also, the general impression made by an individual through his personal appearance and behaviour.

introversion Jung's term for the type of personality in which the direction of interest is inwards into one's own personality rather than outwards to the external world of men and affairs.

libido Sexual desire, but also sometimes the life force or vital energy.

lucid dream See *dream*.

mandala Fundamentally, a mystic circle. Jung took this to be the symbol of the *self* as a whole – the representation of the whole process of self-realization, symbolically represented by the circle or by a *square* or quaternity. In Tantric yoga the mandala is the yantra, or instrument of contemplation, the seat and birthplace of the gods. As Jung pointed out, it is found throughout the east but also (since the Middle Ages) the Christian west, the pattern often showing Christ at the centre, with the four evangelists or their symbols surrounding him. This assembly seems to recall the much more ancient Egyptian representation of Horus at the centre, surrounded by his four sons. "Mandalas", wrote Jung, "usually appear [in dreams] in situations of psychic confusion and disorientation, [as] yantras, instruments with whose help the order is brought into being."

metaphor Likening something to something else, but not in a literal sense, in order to present an idea more vividly: e.g. "he lost his head over her".

neurosis The same as psychoneurosis: a *psychogenic* disorder of the nervous system probably focusing on an urgent basic urge which has been thwarted.

psyche A term which originally meant the principle of life, but which is now often used loosely to mean one's mentality, in a context in which a religious person might use the word soul.

persona Jung coined the word to describe that part of the personality which determines an individual's reaction to any situation, person or thing.

personality In general, by personality one means the general impression given by a human being (or even an animal) in everyday social life, as shown in their physical appearance, moral sense, emotional attitude and intelligence, and built up as a result of environmental and genetic factors, life experience, natural and acquired instincts and beliefs, personal relationships and a host of other ingredients.

phallic The phallus is a *image* of the penis or male generative organ, and in various forms (often carved from stone) was worshipped in many religions as a symbolic representation of the natural life force.

physiology A branch of biology which examines the behaviour of the various parts of a living organism.

psychiatrist A person who practises *psychiatry*; a specialist in mental disorders.

psychiatry A branch of medicine specializing in the treatment of mental and nervous illnesses, rather than in the more general study of the subject implied by the word *psychology*.

psychogenic A disorder which is related to a mental condition, rather than to anything physically wrong.

psychologist A person with a general or specialist training in *psychology*.

psychology Various *psychologists* would describe their discipline in various ways, but the general understanding is that the practice is the study of the life, behaviour and *personality* of men and women in the context of the whole of that life, overt and implied: how it grew and developed, by what it was affected and influenced, and how all its factors interrelate. Though psychology can be employed simply as a means to self-knowledge, for the interest of the subject or for the education of the practitioner, it is more often used in order to cure *neuroses* or personality deficiencies, or to help the subject to recover from some trauma.

psychotherapy The treatment of disorders by means of psychology.

quaternity See *square*.

REM sleep The phase of sleep during which the eyes are seen to move rapidly beneath the closed eye-lids (hence Rapid Eye Movement).

shadow The inferior part of the personality, which (according to Jung in *The Archetypes and the Collective Unconscious*) "personifies everything that the subject refuses to acknowledge about himself, and yet is always thrusting itself upon him directly or indirectly – for instance, inferior traits of character and other incompatible tendencies."

soul A religious term, meaning that part of a human being which is intangible but vital, an immaterial entity, unconnected to the body and unapproachable by science. The word psyche is usually used by nonbelievers. Jung used the term *anima*.

square Or quaternity. Pointing out the universality of the square as an image of order (four elements, four primal qualities, four primal colours, four castes, four ways of spiritual development, and so on) Jung suggested in *Psychology and Religion: West and East* that in order to orient ourselves we must know that something is there (sensation), have the ability to decide what it is (thinking), know whether or not it suits us (feeling), and have the ability to know where it came from and to what it is progressing (intuition).

surrealism The name was coined in 1917 by the writer Guillaume Apollinaire, and the idea developed by André Breton in his review *Littérature*; the artists de Chirico, Arp, Ernst, Duchamp and Dali later promoted it. It was in essence derived from the association principles used in *psychoanalysis*, illustrated visually or in poems or prose.

symbol An object or activity which actually represents something else: in the way that a book might represent knowledge, or a camera lens the human eye. In *psychoanalysis*, symbols are often very remotely connected to the things they represent, and the connection is made by the unconscious.

therapy The word used to describe the practical treatment given to someone suffering from a *neurosis* or other form of emotional sickness in order to enable him or her to recognize the cause of the problem, and resolve it.

trauma The word (derived from the German for a wound) used to describe a severe shock, often having long-lasting effects on the psyche. The shock can be physical and/or emotional.

unconscious, the We are all aware of some of the elements which make up our personality: we know that we perhaps tend to be mean, have a high sex-drive, prefer the town to the country. But many elements of our personality, Freud believed (and subsequent analysts assert) remain seated in our "unconscious" – that is, we do not consciously realize that they exist, let alone know how they came about. These elements or thoughts can only be brought to the surface, if at all, by *psychotherapy* or *psychoanalysis*. As Jung put it (in *Aion*) though theoretically there is no limit to the field of consciousness, "it always finds its limit when it comes up against the *unknown*. This consists of everything we do not know, which, therefore, is not related to the ego as the centre of the field of consciousness. The unknown falls into two groups of objects: The first group comprises the unknown in the outer world; the second the unknown in the inner world. We call this latter territory the *unconscious*." He also asserted that all the past experience of the human species has been built into the inherited brain structure and is seen when one examines the *archetypes* which recur in dreams, and argued that an individual's actions and reactions are a product of an amalgam of this *collective unconscious* as well as of the unconscious recognized by Freud – the personal one.

wish-fulfilment Most obviously, a dream in which something occurs which the dreamer strongly wishes for when awake. But Freud pointed out that dreams often represent wishes of which we are unconscious and would reject, or even be revolted by in our waking lives; and these are also wish-fulfilment dreams.

Bibliography

Artemidorus, *The Oneirocritica*, tr. Robert J. White (Noyes Press, New Jersey, 1975)

Aynsley, H. Murray, *Symbolism of East and West* (1900)

Bailey, H., *The Lost Language of Symbolism* (1912)

Balogh, Penelope, *Freud: a biographical introduction* (Studio Vista, 1971)

Blofeld, John (tr.) *The Book of Change* (Allen & Unwin, 1965)

Bonime, Walter, *The Clinical Use of Dreams* (Basic Books Inc., N.Y.)

Boss, Medard, *The Analysis of Dreams* (Rider, 1957)

Bro, Harmon H., *Edgar Cayce on Dreams* (Paperback Library, N.Y., 1968)

Brook, Stephen, *The Oxford Book of Dreams* (Oxford University Press, 1983)

Colquhoun, W.P. (ed.), *Biological Rhythms and Human Performance* (Academic Press, N.Y., 1971)

Cooper, J.C., *An Illustrated Encyclopaedia of Traditional Symbols* (Thames & Hudson, 1978)

Coxhead, David, and Susan Hiller, *Dreams: Visions of the Night* (Thames & Hudson, 1976)

Crisp, Tony, *Do You Dream?* (Neville Spearman, 1971)

De Becker, Raymond, *The Understanding of Dreams, or Machinations of the Night* (Allen & Unwin, 1968)

Dement, W., and N. Klietman, "The relation of eye-movements during sleep to dream activity, an objective method for the study of dreaming," *Journal of Experimental Psychology, Vol. 53.*; "The relation of eye movements, body motility and external stimuli to dream content," *Journal of Experimental Psychology, Vol. 55.*; "The effect of dream deprivation," *Science, Vol. 131.*

Diamond, E., *The Science of Dreams* (Doubleday, 1962)

Ehrenwald, Jean, *New Dimensions of Deep Analysis* (London, 1954)

Ellis, Havelock, *The World of Dreams* (London, 1911)

Emmons, W.H., and C.W. Simon, "The non-recall of material presented during sleep," *American Journal of Psychology, Vol. 69.*

Faraday, Ann, *The Dream Game* (Temple Smith, 1973); *Dream Power* (Hodder & Stoughton, 1972; Pan, 1974)

Fisher, Charles, Joseph Gross and Joseph Zuck, "A cycle of penile erection synchronous with dreaming sleep," *Archives of General Psychiatry, Vol. 51.*

Fordham, Frieda, *An Introduction to Jung's Psychology* (Penguin, 1959)

Foulkes, D., "Dream reports from different stages of sleep", *Journal of Abnormal and Social Psychology, Vol. 65.*

Freud, Sigmund, *The Interpretation of Dreams* (Vol. IV of the Standard Edition of the *Complete Psychological Works*, Hogarth Press, 1953–74)

French, Thomas M., and Erika Fromm, *Dream Interpretation* (Basic Books, N.Y., 1964)

Fromm, Erich, *The Forgotten Language* (1951)

Giles, Luray, *Sleep* (Bobbs-Merrill, N.Y., 1938)

Grant, Michael, *Myths of the Greeks and Romans* (Mentor Books, 1962)

Graves, Robert, *The Greek Myths* (Penguin, 2 vol., 1955)

Grunebaum, G.E. von, and Roger Caillois, ed. *The Dream and Human Societies* (1966)

Gutheil, Emil A., *The Language of the Dream* (Macmillan, N.Y., 1939)

Hadfield, J.A., *Dreams and Nightmares* (London, 1954)

Hall, Calvin S., *The Meaning of Dreams* (McGraw-Hill, N.Y., 1966); "A cognitive theory of dream symbols," *Journal of General Psychology, Vol. 48.*

Hall, Calvin S., and Vernon Nordby, *The Individual and his Dreams* (Signet Books, N.Y., 1972)

Hill, B., *Such Stuff as Dreams* (Rupert Hart-Davis, 1967)

Jones, Ernest, "*Freud's Theory of Dreams*" (in *Papers on Psychoanalysis*, Baillière, London, 1948)

Jones, Richard M., *The New Psychology of Dreaming* (Grune & Stratton, N.Y., 1970); *On the Nightmare* (Hogarth Press, 1949)

Jung, C.G., *Dreams* (1974); *The Structure and Dynamics of the Psyche* (1960); *The Practice of Psychotherapy* (1954); *Freud and Psychoanalysis* (1961); *Modern Man in Search of a Soul* (Routledge, 1933); *Man and his Symbols* (Aldus, 1964); *Memories, Dreams, Reflections* (Fontana, 1963).

Karacan, I., D.R. Goodenough, A. Shapiro and S. Starker, "Erection cycle during sleep in relation to dream anxiety," *Archives of General Psychiatry, Vol. 15.*

Kerenyi, Carl, *The Gods of the Greeks* (Thames & Hudson, 1951)

Kleitman, N., *Sleep and Wakefulness* (University of Chicago Press, 1963)

Koch, Rudolf, *The Book of Signs*, (London, 1960)

Kramer, M., R. Hlasny, G. Jacobs and T. Roth, "Do dreams have meaning? An empirical enquiry", *American Journal of Psychiatry, Vol. 133.*

Lincoln, J.S., *The Dream in Primitive Cultures* (Cresset, 1935)

Lowy, Samuel, *Foundations of Dream Interpretation* (Kegan Paul, Trench, Trubner, N.Y., 1942)

Luce, Gay Gaer, and Julius Segal, *Sleep* (Heinemann, 1967; republished as *Sleep and Dreams*, Panther, 1969)

Mackenzie, Norman, *Dreams and Dreaming* (Aldus Books, 1965)

Masters, Brian, *Dreams about H.M. the Queen (and other members of the Royal Family)*, (Blond & Briggs, 1972)

McKellar, Peter, *Imagination and Thinking* (University of Chicago, 1963)

Murray, E., *Sleep, Dreams and Arousal* (Appleton-Century-Crofts, N.Y., 1965)

New Larousse Encyclopaedia of Mythology (Hamlyn, 1974)

Oswald, I., *Sleeping and Waking* (Elsevier, Amsterdam, 1962); *Sleep* (Penguin, 1966)

Parker, Derek and Julia, *The Immortals* (Barrie & Jenkins, 1976)

Perls, Frederick S., *Gestalt Therapy Verbatim* (Real People Press, Utah, 1969)

Rosenteur, Phyllis, *Sleep* (Funk & Wagnalls, N.Y., 1938)

Ryecroft, Charles, *The Innocence of Dreams* (1979); *Anxiety and Neurosis* (Allen Lane, 1968)

Sanford, John A., *Dreams: God's Forgotten Language* (Lippincott, N.Y., 1968)

Sechrist, Elsie, *Dreams, Your Magic Mirror* (Dell, N.Y., 1969)

Sharpe, Ella F., *Dream Analysis* (Hogarth Press, 1937)

Stekel, Wilhelm, *The Interpretation of Dreams* (1943)

Ullman, Montague, and Nan Zimmerman, *Working with Dreams* (1979) and Stanley Krippner, with Alan Vaughan, *Dream Telepathy* (Macmillan, N.Y., 1973)

Wolstenholme, G.E.W., and M. O'Connor, ed. *The Nature of Sleep* (J. & A. Churchill, 1960)

Woods, Ralph L., and Herbert B. Greenhouse, ed., *The New World of Dreams* (Macmillan, N.Y., 1974)

Index

Page numbers in *italic* refer to the illustrations

Acknowledgments

Theme illustrations by:
Nick Bantock 68–69, 75, 84–85, 89
Catherine Denvir 66–67, 82–83
Nigel Hills 93
Bush Hollyhead 96
Diana Leadbetter 76–77, 86–87
James Marsh 72, 80, 94
Francesca Pelizolli 70–71, 90–91
Peter Prout 78–79

Other illustrations by:
Karen Cochrane
John Hutchinson
Sue Sharples
John Storey
John Woodcock
Stephen Wright

Photographic retoucher:
Nick Oxtoby

Picture Credits
cover: Susan Griggs/Photofile
6, 7: Hodder & Stoughton/The Mary
    Evans Picture Library; *Russian Tale
    of the Firebird* by Edmund Dulac;
9: ZEFA;
10,11 *l*: Ancient Art and Architecture
    Collection;
11 *r*: BPCC/Aldus Archive;
12: Archbishop of Canterbury and
    The Trustees of Lambeth Palace;
13 *l*: BPCC/Aldus Archive;
13 *r*: Ancient Art and Architecture
    Collection;
14 *t*: Photothéque André Held/Ziolo;
14 *cl*: Claus Hansmann;
14 *cr*: The Mansell Collection;
14 *b*: Scala;
15: BPCC/Aldus Archive;
16 *tl*: Pinacoteca Ferrara/C.N.B. & C.
    Bologna;
16 *tr*: Ancient Art and Architecture
    Collection;
17: British Library;
18 *t*: Axel Poignant;
18 *bl*: National Museum of Denmark,
    Department of Ethnography/Photo:
    Lennart Larsen;

18 *cr*: Tony Morrison/South
    American Pictures;
18 *br*: Claire Leimbach;
19: BPCC/Aldus Archive;
20 *t*: The Mary Evans Picture
    Library;
20 *b*, 21: Jean-Loup Charmet;
22: © A. D. A. G. P. Paris, 1985/
    Courtesy of The Art Institute of
    Chicago;
23: Bettmann Archive/The Radio
    Times Hulton Picture Library;
24 *tl*: Ancient Art and Architecture
    Collection;
24 *tr*: British Library;
24 *bl*: Michael Holford;
24 *br*: MacQuitty International
    Collection;
25: The Mary Evans Picture Library;
26 *tl*: BPCC/Aldus Archive;
26 *tr*: Vautier-de Nanxe;
37 *t*: Archiv Gerstenberg;
44: National Portrait Gallery,
    London;
45: Jean-Loup Charmet;
46: Archiv Gerstenberg;
47: Laura Perls;
49, 50 *l*: Jean-Loup Charmet;

50 *r*: Popperfoto;
51: Bildarchiv Foto Marburg;
52: Gift of Mr. and Mrs. Bert L.
    Smokler and Mr. and Mrs.
    Lawrence A. Fleischman (55.55)/
    Courtesy of the Detroit Institute of
    Arts;
53: Claus Hansmann;
54: ©DACS, 1985/Courtesy of The
    Art Institute of Chicago;
55: Dr. Keith Hearne;
56/7: British Museum;
59: Jean-Loup Charmet;
99: Dover Publications;
103: Archiv Gerstenberg;
119 and 121: Dover Publications;
130: BPCC/Aldus Archive;
137, 140: Dover Publications;
147: © Cosmopress and A. D. A.
    G. P. Paris, 1985/British Museum;
155: © DACS, 1985/British Museum;
179: Jean-Loup Charmet;
190: Mary Evans Picture Library;
203, 207: Dover Publications